7/24/06
B.C.

HOW TO BE
CREATIVE
WITH WORDS

POETIC DISCOURSE IN PAINTING

predominantly intuitive, imaginative, synthetic

The frontispiece reproduction of the fifteenth-century masterpiece by Van Eyck is a remarkable organic fusion, similar to the Gothic cathedrals of the Middle Ages and to the *"summum"* of Dante's *Divine Comedy*. Note the *motif* of the dove (symbolic of divine love), commemorated in Milton's Paradise Lost, I, 19-22:

> . . . *thou from the first*
> *Wast present, and, with mighty wings outspread,*
> *Dove-like sat'st brooding on the vast Abyss,*
> *And mad'st it pregnant* . . .

Note, also, the symbolism of the fountain, indicating the waters of life, natural and divine. These symbols reinforce the central intuition of the Paschal Lamb.

HOW TO BE CREATIVE
WITH WORDS

BY

WILLIAM J. GRACE
Fordham University

FORDHAM UNIVERSITY PRESS

The Declan X. McMullen Company, Inc.

Distributors

NEW YORK

Copyright, 1952
FORDHAM UNIVERSITY PRESS

Printed in the United States of America
By the Cornwall Press, Inc., Cornwall, N. Y.

ACKNOWLEDGMENTS

To Brandt & Brandt, for permission to reprint Stephen Vincent Benét's "The Bishop's Beggar," copyright 1942, by Curtis Publishing Company, and "By the Waters of Babylon," from *Selected Works* of Stephen Vincent Benét (Rinehart & Company, Inc.), copyright 1937, by Stephen Vincent Benét.

To Cannon Mills, Incorporated, for permission to reproduce a section of one of its advertisements.

To Mr. Padraic Colum, for permission to reprint "Tiger Lilies."

To Rev. John J. Coyne, S.J., for permission to quote from *The Nature of Art or the Shield of Pallas,* by Arthur Little, S.J.

To Dodd, Mead & Company, for permission to quote from *In Search of Ireland,* by H. V. Morton, copyright 1931 by H. V. Morton; and to reprint Stephen Leacock's "Buggam Grange," from *Laugh with Leacock,* copyright 1930 by Dodd, Mead & Company.

To E. P. Dutton & Co., Inc., for permission to reprint a selection from "The Willows" from *The Tales of Algernon Blackwood.*

To General Cable Corporation, for permission to reproduce one of its advertisements.

To Harcourt, Brace and Company, Inc., for permission to reprint selections from "The Waste Land" from *Collected Poems, 1909-1935,* by T. S. Eliot, copyright 1936, by Harcourt, Brace and Company, Inc., and from *Main Street,* by Sinclair Lewis, copyright 1920, by Harcourt, Brace and Company, Inc.

To Harper & Brothers, for permission to quote from *Vulgarity in Literature,* by Aldous Huxley, copyright 1930, by Aldous Huxley.

To Houghton Mifflin Company, for permission to quote a passage from *Convention and Revolt in Poetry,* by John Livingston Lowes.

To Alfred A. Knopf and the Executors of the Estate of Willa Cather, for permission to quote a passage from *Willa Cather on Writing,* copyright, 1949.

To Life, Time Inc., for permission to reproduce Van Eyck's "Adoration of the Lamb."

To Louisiana State University Press, for permission to quote from *This Great Stage,* by Robert B. Heilman, and from *Education for Freedom,* by Robert M. Hutchins.

To Harold Matson, for permission to reprint "Luke Baldwin's Vow," by Morley Callaghan, copyright 1947 by Curtis Publishing Company; reprinted by permission of Harold Matson.

vii

INTRODUCTION

The principle assumed in this book is that creative activity is essential to all men, because creativity is an aspect of being truly human. We can learn by the act of making something—a garden, a chair, a poem, a story—just as we can learn from theory and definition. The mind thinks with images as well as with concepts. Creative knowledge, and imagistic knowledge, are basic to a complete education and vitally relevant to "intellectual" knowledge as well. Experiments undertaken in this volume will make the point increasingly clear. At the moment we have only to remind ourselves that "abstract" or "conceptual" thinking is only one mode of understanding. The capacity to "imagine" is no less important. We believe that the imagination can be trained, and should be trained; that it is one of the dominant aims of education to do this. The laws of the imagination are discoverable, capable of being translated into understandable practice, and are available to all. It is one of the objectives of *How To Be Creative with Words* to show what the imagination is, how it works, and to observe its operative laws in action.

The imagination is not confined to isolated individuals or special groups. It may be true that in any field only a few excel. But it is wrong to assume the inference that other practitioners do not matter. We know that during the highest Athenian culture a play of Aeschylus could draw as many spectators as a baseball game does in the twentieth century. The answer to our present cultural situation does not consist in saying, "Well, the Athenians were an educated people, and we are not." The real answer lies in the fact that our people have actually played baseball, they have had a "creative" education in baseball, they understand it and are intelligent spectators. They have not had a creative training in literature to any such degree, they have not commonly used their powers in creative expression, and are frequently alien to it. If the artists have lost their audiences, it is partly because an appreciative audience consists of those who have sufficient practice in an art to understand it, even if they do not excel in it.

In this volume, under the term *creative writing*, are included all kinds of writing that are distinct from *functional* prose—we exclude exposition and argumentation, as serving functional rather than aesthetic purposes. Functional writing serves some other end outside itself—to explain or to prove—and its competency must be judged in terms of fulfilling such an end. Creative writing is written for its own sake, *to be* rather than serve an end outside itself.

In regard to creative writing, distinction is made between two types: creative writing that is predominantly intuitive, imagistic, and synthetic; creative writing that is predominantly logical, constructive, analytical. The first type is classified as "poetry"; the second as "creative prose"—still distinct from "functional" or "scientific" prose. The distinction is not one of surface form, but of essential form based on psychological factors.

With reference to this distinction, emphasis is placed on the methods of mental association, of connotation, as important sources from which material is gathered for creative writing. The use of mental association according to the method set down in this book has produced important work from numerous classes. Mental association is not haphazard, but the result, as modern psychological studies have shown, of the subject's previous experience. Mental association, if properly used and directed, can give to writing the unique flavor of never-to-be-repeated personal experience. It is the basis of the *image* and of the *synthesis* in creative writing— the synthesis being the unique blend of word and image which constitutes the kernel, the very heart of poetry. Although the empirical application of these ideas has special features here, the ideas themselves are as traditional as Horace's *Ars Poetica,* as contemporary as Herbert Read.

In the following of this method, the student learns that creative work is as natural and as instinctive as more ordinary forms of communication. Such methodology enriches the writing of creative prose as well, for creative prose has some of the qualities of poetry, but in subordination to its own proper and specific qualities. This methodology is invaluable not only to the poet, but to the short story writer, to the novelist, and to the orator.

It is most important for the beginning writer to learn to associate form with freedom. Quite early, a student should be able to make intelligent distinctions between surface form, often the result of historical and social accidents, and the essential form necessary to any creation. He should be able to see what he himself contributes to essential form. Art is not a heightened imitation of previous works of art, but a heightened imitation of life or experience. Useful knowledge of techniques can be greatly increased by examining models, but the imitation of such models should be on the basis of essential form and not of surface form.

The models employed in succeeding pages are for the purpose of emphasizing essential forms; they are not advocated as final prototypes. Because of the differences in methodology established between poetry and creative prose, students will come to understand the difference between the more associative procedures characteristic of poetic processes (predominantly imaginative and synthetic) and the more logical procedures necessary in creative prose (predominantly logical and analytical).

A number of tested techniques are presented which are carefully illustrated and easy to carry out. This book is designed to train the intelligence and taste of its readers and to elicit genuine creative activity. It is designed to "educate" in the sense of "to lead out"—and, in this sense, it prevents what is the chief bane of many creative-composition courses, the borrowing of magazine techniques, the rehashing or plagiarizing of somewhat trite commercial material that may excite the instructor's suspicions of plagiarism without offering explicit evidence of corruption. The methods of elaboration suggested for the short story prevent anything but original work. The exercises in poetry, criticism, and examination of the beautiful are similarly proof.

It is hoped that these pages will help to restore the balance necessary between imaginative and conceptual processes. Imaginative training is no less essential to education than the conceptual. In fact, the conceptual is enriched and deepened by its relationship to the imaginative. We are equally concerned with sound processes for training the imagination as with the concrete production of fresh and original work.

It is pleasant to acknowledge the authors of such original classroom achievement as has been used for the purpose of illustrative material. Past and present students at Fordham University and at Notre Dame College of Staten Island whose creative efforts are so used are: Mary Bakaisa, James Canfield, Sister Josephine Carini, Joan Conway, Beatrice Duross, Peter Glickert, Frances Gomez, Barbara Ellen Graves, Kenneth Gredler, Sallie H. Honan, Seymour James, Sister Mary Kieran, Jean Knisel, Mrs. Alfrida Montana, Hugh J. Mooney, Hazel O'Rourke, C. W. E. Phillips, Steffi Rachmann, James Shaw, and Marion Zarczema.

Finally, I wish especially to express my gratitude to my sister, Miss Joan Grace, for valuable suggestions and encouragement and for the preparation of the index.

WILLIAM J. GRACE

CONTENTS

ILLUSTRATIONS

HOW TO BE
CREATIVE
WITH WORDS

Chapter 1

THE CREATIVE WAY

WHAT A CREATIVE WORK IS: THE PURPOSE IT SERVES

A creative work is, first of all, an object that an artist makes. It is not merely an idea, a theory, a system of thought, although ideas, theories, and systems of thought enter into it.

Certain causes lead to the making of an object. Traditionally, there are four causes for an object made by human hands.

There is the *efficient* cause. The efficient cause of a table, for example, is the carpenter exercising his particular skills.

There is the *material* cause. The material cause of a table is the actual material out of which it is made. Wood, for example.

There is the *formal* cause. The formal cause gives the table its distinctive and unique principle of differentiation. The formal cause makes it *this* table, not just *any* table.

There is the *final* cause. The table was made for some *purpose,* such as to be beautiful, to dine upon, to be sold.

A *literary* work of art is primarily something that is made and that is dependent upon these four causes. Since the literary art is complex and intellectual, its final causes are more abstract and intricate than those of a table.

Creative writing has two main purposes, or final causes. First, by expressing beauty, it satisfies the human need for contemplation (the meaning of the beautiful will be discussed later). Second, it serves as a medium for communicating ideas of intellectual and social significance. In this sense, creative writing not only indicates what the artist

1

thought, but also, through its germinative power, it is the source of new ideas for others in the future.

The human artist differs from the Divine Artist, in that the Creator creates out of nothing, but the human artist (the creative writer) has to create out of something. The something out of which the human artist or creative writer creates is experience of life. That is why Aristotle defines art as *mimesis,* or a heightened imitation of experience. Because the artist heightens and selects his experience in the making of his art, he brings judgment and a system of values to bear on his experience. In this sense, creative writing is also a *criticism* of life.

The very process of selection that goes into your making of an object implies an emphasis—a stress on certain aspects of your experience. This stress comes from the way in which you evaluate experience, both consciously and unconsciously. The object that you, as an artist, make has its own selfhood or being, though the making of it has been based on your experience. The resulting object is more than experience. You have created something—you have brought something into being that is valid in itself. Your experience has been transformed into an external, valid object by your act of creation.

WHY WRITE CREATIVELY?

You may have felt skeptical about the need for you yourself to write creatively. Actually, it is an important experience for you, even if the results of your creative activity do not extend farther than your immediate college surroundings, yourself, and your circle of friends.

It is not the primary object of creative composition to turn a man into a journalist, a scenario writer, or a novelist. Aristotle stressed the importance of art as purgative agent or catharsis. By *catharsis* Aristotle implied a purification of the soul through the fruitful release of the emotions in art. Freud, in his concept of "sublimation," or the transference

into art of certain instinctive urges, offers an idea parallel
to that of Aristotle in some ways. To the natural dimensions
of the thinking of these two men, a religious believer will
add a third dimension—a supernatural one—whereby the creation and appreciation of art leads to the habit of contemplation on the natural level and makes contemplation on
the supernatural level more possible.

Art is meant to be beautiful, and beauty is meant to be
contemplated. The enjoyment of the beautiful is a contemplative experience. Self-exploration in the fruitful release
of tension (Aristotle's cathartic effect of art), practice in the
expression of true ideas, the opening of new avenues to intellectual enjoyment and contemplation—these objectives
should come first in our creative activity.

Man, made to the image of the Divine should imitate the
Divine in his creative powers; in the measure that our creative powers are atrophied, we cease in that measure to be
human. For our own psychological and spiritual health we
require creative activity. This importance of creative activity is so great that the question of whether you are an
amateur or a professional artist does not matter. As Dr.
Lawrence Conrad has pointed out—"through the creative
aspect of his work he [the student] learns to control and
direct his feeling, to organize his thought, and to guide his
fancy in ways that can improve his total situation in life.
Thus writing may become for many a ready tool in the exploration of experience." [1]

Just as the love of truth and of beauty for their own sakes
frequently has to be restated and rediscovered, so the satisfaction in the making of a thing—which is art—for its own
validity, needs to be stressed. It is important for you to
create something for your own mental and spiritual health,
even if you follow the custom of some medieval monks who
destroyed their handicraft with the coming of sundown.

[1] Lawrence Conrad, *Teaching Creative Writing*, New York, Progressive
Educational Association, 1937, p. 9.

Even if your work does not excel, it remains important in your own life and enables you to enter into the creative activity of others, because you have yourself experienced its problems and meanings.

A single paragraph from an essay by Eric Gill is particularly pertinent here:

"The value of the creative faculty" derives from the fact that that faculty is the primary mark of man. To deprive man of its exercise is to reduce him to subhumanity. It is not at all out of kindness to animals, the thing we call "humanitarianism," it is not at all from motives of benevolence that we demand scope for man's creative faculty. . . . The value of the creative faculty is that its use enables man to save his soul—for without that faculty he has no soul to save. You cannot save the soul of an automaton; for an automaton has no saveable soul.[2]

Of recent years Mr. Winston Churchill has dramatized the value of being creative, in an amateur just as well as in a professional capacity, by the analogous art of painting. As Eric Newton has pointed out:

The purpose of Churchill's essay is summed up in his title "Painting as a Pastime." Painting, for him, is a means of restoring "psychic equilibrium," it is not an end but a means. "Painting," he says, "came to my rescue in a most trying time." His reason for finding it a relief from the worries or strains of life is that, unlike the solace of reading, it involves the practitioner in a healthy struggle with a medium, and yet, unlike the crafts, joinery, for example, or bricklaying, it provides unlimited outlet for the creative imagination.[3]

Dr. Irwin Edman, a well-known philosopher who has written extensively on the arts, emphasizes in the following news report the value of creative activity for a full and intelligent life, and even for mental health itself.

[2] Eric Gill, "The Value of the Creative Faculty in Man," *American Review*, November, 1935.

[3] Eric Newton, "Churchill the Artist—an Evaluation," New York *Times*, January 2, 1949.

The study of art can become one of the most powerful means of educating responsible imaginative citizens in today's world of public regimentation and private chaos, Dr. Irwin Edman, Professor of Philosophy at Columbia University, declared yesterday. The philosopher addressed 500 teachers from various parts of the country at the eighth annual conference of the Committee on Art Education, a gathering sponsored by the Museum of Modern Art.

"Art or the arts, adequately taught, are perhaps in our day the most central and important means of education," Dr. Edman said. "Far too long in American civilization the arts have been regarded as by-products, luxuries, isolations and escapes."

"Far too long, in the Western world in general, education has been identified with the processes of the discursive, argumentative, measuring and mathematical mind," the speaker declared. "As a result, in America the arts have been regarded as pretty playthings, playful exercises, like lace making or embroidery, or, in the minds of robust Philistines, like cutting out paper dolls."

Dr. Edman attributed the common practice of separating education from art to the fact that modern science had bred "an almost superstitious exaltation of the laboratory method." Only recently, he asserted, has the role of imagination in education been as adequately recognized as that of reason.

"In an age of abstract formality and abstract statistical relations, even the least statistical minded come to think of themselves as neutral units in a society of neutral units," the professor declared. "Between formulas on the one hand and gadgets on the other, existence becomes dull and deadened."

"The arts are the education of our emotions. It is not that emotion has vanished from modern life. The shocking statistics of the prevalence of mental and nervous diseases show how much turbulence of feeling there is in present-day hearts. The arts are a kind of therapy and, at one and the same time, a kind of fulfillment." [4]

Entering into creative experience is important both for the artist who creates the object and the spectator who contemplates it. As Mortimer Adler has ably explained in *Art*

[4] New York *Times*, March 26, 1950.

and Prudence, art is the natural instrument for training the emotions, for encouraging psychological health. Man is not exclusively a spiritual being, or exclusively an animal. For these reasons, the training of the imagination cannot be overlooked any more than can the training of the intellect. Human intuition, though not a material principle, must depend upon contact with the world of matter for its operation. The imagination brings together and fuses the intellect and sense perception, so that the intellect gains in accuracy through its contact with matter, and the images drawn from the material world serve as instruments, as symbols, of intellectual vision. It would be a sad thing if education or society encouraged the production of men who are masters of information and logical process but remain emotional barbarians because their imaginative training has been ignored. As Eric Gill said: "The creative faculty is that one which is the mark of man—it is the one which makes him like God. God created man 'in His own image.' And the dynamic centre or core of the faculty of creation is the imagination."

THE UNIQUENESS OF A CREATIVE WORK

A work of art differs from other objects in that it carries within it certain internal or "immanent" influences and powers which can never be exactly duplicated. A work of art is imbedded, not in the general idea or theory, but in the concrete experience caught uniquely by a freely chosen image and by mental association. A work of art is utterly dependent upon the unique form which its creator gives it. The ideas in a work of art cannot be abstracted and re-phrased in other terms. The concreteness and uniqueness of a poem, for example, are non-transferable. This unique and concrete "form" is also characteristic of the short story, the novel, and the drama in varying degrees, and only disappears when information or logical demonstration becomes a more primary aim in the writing than aesthetic contemplation. The important thing in an argument is that you be logical, that you carry on a logical activity, not that you create a *unique* object. In exposition, the important thing is to give the information according to the proper order. The uniqueness of your form is not an important consideration. You can see the gulf between the two activities if you think of the difference in operation between answering an examination paper and writing a short story. Both poetry and prose fall within the province of imagination in so far as the object of the writer is to serve the purpose of aesthetic contemplation rather than to inform or convince. While prose makes freer use of logic and analysis than poetry does, these characteristics can also serve primarily the aim of contemplation instead of exposition or argumentation. *Creative writing, then, is unique writing serving the end of contemplation rather than that of information or proof.*

By *contemplation* in this context we mean the act of seeing something in itself, and for its own sake. When we contemplate, we see the mysterious aspect of reality—which has no fixed limits. When we see something in terms of its usability, we see it in one light only—the function that it will serve in fulfilling some end that we have in mind. If a lover is talking with his beloved, he sees her in terms of her being, her personality. He *contemplates*. If he were a personnel manager engaging a switchboard operator, he would not contemplate her, but would consider her purely in the light of her qualifications for the job. If you were to take a photograph in order to capture and retain the memory of a scene that has deeply appealed to you, you would function as an artist. You are concerned with the *being* of the thing. If you were to take a photograph for the purpose of identification in a legal trial, you would work as a scientist, not as an artist.

Being is a key word in understanding artistic process. It implies both a certain kind of reality and a certain way of looking at things. Above change, beyond flux, is a permanent reality that we sometimes ignore because we become too preoccupied with function, with activity. We have occasionally to pause in order really to see. It is possible to get so lost in the woods that we fail to see the tree. This truth is neatly summarized by a contemporary poet, Louis MacNeice:

> . . . the end of the news
> Which is the beginning of wisdom. No captions
>   and no jargon,
> No diminution, distortion or sterilization of entity,
> But calling a tree a tree. For this wisdom
> Is not an abstraction, a wordiness, but being silence
> Is love of the chanting world.

Science is concerned with fact, with verified information, with knowledge. Art is concerned with being. An artist is one who makes something—music, painting, novel, short story—that is derived from experience. The artist, by his act of creation, also brings something into being.

Plato, in the *Symposium*, states that "all creation or passage of non-being into being is poetry or making, and the processes of all art are creative; and the masters of arts are all poets or makers." Similarly, Aristotle in his *Poetics* distinguishes poetry as creative art. It is distinct from "history" or what today we would call science.

The distinction between historian and poet is not in the one writing prose and the other verse. You might put the work of Herodotus into verse and it would still be a species of history; it really consists in this: that the one describes the thing that has been, and the other a kind of thing that might be.[5]

This is practically the same distinction that Wordsworth makes in the Preface to the second edition of *Lyrical Ballads,* where he distinguishes "poetry" from "science" or "matter

[5] Richard McKeon, *The Basic Works of Aristotle,* New York, Random House, 1941.

of fact." We are not underestimating the greatness of science, but we must keep in mind that art focuses our attention on being—being, rather than activity. Through art we begin to see the wonder, the complexity, and the opaqueness of reality. We begin to ask ourselves—not what shall we *do* with this—but *what* is this. We see something to love and to enjoy, not to process.

A scientist gives us an organized body of knowledge in a specific field; an artist brings something into *being* that was not there before. This being, as we have said, is meant to be beautiful; it is meant to be contemplated.[6]

The beautiful is not necessarily useful in the narrow industrial or mercantile context. It *can* be useful in this sense, but not *necessarily* so. The lilies "labor not, neither do they spin . . . not even Solomon in all his glory was clothed like one of these" (*Luke* 12:25). The lilies may not be of any immediate practical use. But if one extended the concept of the useful to all that is necessary to the fulfilment of the transcendent spiritual nature of man, nothing could be more useful than the beautiful. Man, it has often been argued, is made for contemplation, and beauty is as necessary to the spirit as is food to the body. As the philosopher Jacques Maritain says: "Art prepares the human race for contemplation . . . the spiritual joy of which surpasses every other joy and seems to be the end of all human activities." [7]

Functional prose, as distinct from creative writing, serves a *function*—to give information, to prove a point. Once its function is performed, its purpose is served. Creative art (poetry and creative prose) is being, rather than function. Its main purpose is to be enjoyed, to be contemplated, not to be used for some immediate end.

Creative work, then, possesses being, and its purpose is

---

[6] But are not some works of art ugly? it may be objected. The fact that a work of art may embrace, and transcend elements considered ugly is discussed in the section on beauty.

[7] Jacques Maritain, *Art and Scholasticism,* New York, p. 62.

contemplation. Creative work is unique. De Quincey stressed this point in "The Literature of Knowledge and the Literature of Power" with these words:

Human works of immortal beauty and works of nature in one respect stand on the same footing; they never absolutely repeat each other, never approach so near as not to differ; and they differ not as better and worse, or simply by more and less; they differ by undecipherable and incommunicable differences, that cannot be caught by mimicries, that cannot be reflected in the mirror of copies, that cannot become ponderable in the scales of vulgar comparison.

He points out that "a good steam engine is properly superseded by a better. But one lovely pastoral valley is not superseded by another, nor a statue of Praxiteles by a statue of Michelangelo."

In the following pages we are primarily concerned with one aspect of creativity—creativity in words. You should keep in mind, however, that the principles that govern art in the broad sense of the term and those governing written expression are the same. Arts differ in the media they employ for the purpose of heightened imitation, but they all share in the universal nature of art.

The plates in the present volume illustrate the similarity in techniques and in aims between the art of painting and the art of writing. The frontispiece, Van Eyck's "The Adoration of the Lamb," is analogous in its images and symbolism to the art of poetry. Dürer's "The Knight, Death, and the Devil" illustrates the universal method of allegory and the type of beauty that arises out of an art of conflict (described in a later section of the book). "Two Masterpieces of Description" illustrate techniques that are similar in creative writing and in painting.

We must remember that art is heightened imitation of experience. It is not experience itself. Habituated as we are to the conventions of art, through education and the common heritage of civilization, we sometimes overlook the fact that art effects its purpose by means of illusion.

All art depends on an intial "let's pretend." We "pretend" that Othello or King Lear, Odysseus or Aeneas, are real people doing real things. To this degree we "identify" ourselves with them. We share in the mood, in the action, of the piece. The appreciation of art depends on this *empathy*—the ability to put oneself in place of another, to "identify" oneself with another. In literature, of course, the aesthetic empathy is with an imaginary, a "make-believe," character. Here, again, the distinction between art, the imitation of experience, and direct experience itself must be maintained. We must not shout out at the melodrama and warn the heroine that the villain is approaching her. If we do so, we confuse two levels of reality—art and life. On viewing the illustration on page 159—"Which Contains Greater Elements of Beauty? Why?"—a student was prompted to ask the instructor with which lady—the Cannon sheet girl or Rembrandt's "Old Woman"—would he prefer to live on a desert island. The question confuses art and reality. The instructor could live with neither lady. The illustration merely gives us artistic forms, "representations." We are merely judging one form in relation to another, not one lady in relation to another.

In looking at a conventional painting which is in fact two-dimensional, we are able to supply, without the slightest sense of strain, depth or a third dimension. On the other hand, we may look at an example of abstract art, the conventions of which are less familiar to us, and we may feel at a loss. Both works are in one sense equally "abstract." Both depend on "conventions"; both represent experience through symbols.

In literary art, however, we seldom seriously have to "suspend disbelief." We can readily transfer ourselves to an experience which, though basically illusory, we can accept as real. But it is not merely the surface statement that satisfies the purpose of communication in art. Communication also consists in what has to be "read between the lines," in what has been implied but not stated, in what has been hinted at or broken off. It is the skillful command of what is "overheard rather than heard" that frequently characterizes the highest creative art.

These points will be explained later, in their proper places. At the moment, it is sufficient to regard a work of art—whether a novel, a poem, a painting—as having an objective self aside from the observer. This "self," however, communicates to us through conventions. It is a convention that this portrait—with only two dimensions, without weight or odor or flesh or a bloodstream—should *re-present* a man. But I am habituated to these conventions and I have no difficulty in recognizing this picture as that of "old so and so." My perception of this picture is an act of my intelligence as much as my perceiving a sum in arithmetic. A dog, untrained to the conventions of art, would not recognize a portrait of its master at all. It would not even recognize a photograph. *Mimesis* in art means the heightened imitation of experience in terms of conventions understood by man's intelligence and embodied in an external and valid object of some sort—wood, canvas, words.

G. K. Chesterton once said that the objective of the artist was to discover the "submerged sunrise of wonder" which is at the heart of being. Dr. Oppenheimer, head of the Institute for Advanced Studies at Princeton, has said that "the problem of doing justice to the implicit, the imponderable, and the unknown is always with us in science, it is with us in the most trivial affairs, and it is one of the great problems of all forms of art." Being as seen by the artist-creator may well be inexhaustible. The particular object he contemplates acts as a prism catching the light of endless transcendent forces—in Wordsworth's words, "truths that wake, to perish never."

One of the great functions of art is to give our intuitions

concrete forms, living expressions. It is always possible for the educated man to return to these expressions, these words of power, to refresh and strengthen himself in the hour when his energies are depleted, when he may have become the victim of detail, of triviality.

Review Questions

(1) What causes enter into the making of a work of art?

(2) What are the two main purposes of literature?

(3) In what sense is literature a criticism of life?

(4) In what sense is art "real"?

(5) Why does art depend upon conventions of some sort?

(6) Why is creative activity important for the individual person?

(7) What is meant by contemplation in relation to the arts?

(8) What is the difference between an art and a science?

(9) What is the broad sense of the word, *poetry?*

(10) Why must a creative work be unique?

Poetry (Creative Writing)	Functional Prose (Science)
According to Plato and Aristotle, creative art, in the universal sense, is poetry.	Functional prose is the equivalent of Aristotle's "history" or Wordsworth's "science."
Aim is contemplation.	It adheres to "facts," to "particulars."
	Aim is utility.

1. *Poetry in a technical sense*

   a. intuition

   b. imagination

   c. synthesis

2. *Creative prose*

   a. logic

   b. construction

   c. analysis

    1. exposition

    2. argumentation

Chapter 2

THE SHAPING SPIRIT OF IMAGINATION

POETRY, CREATIVE PROSE, SCIENTIFIC PROSE

There is no reason why you cannot write poetry in our sense of the word—a discourse which, as we shall show, is distinguished from prose by the predominance of certain qualities.

Poetry is as normal and as instinctive a form of expression as prose.

But do not confuse poetry with external form. You may have been accustomed from childhood to assume that meter and rhyme make poetry. This is not strictly true. Meter and rhyme frequently are accidental, decorative effects in poetry, which may or may not be used. They are not *essential* to every poem.

You may have been discouraged from writing poetry because you were expected to write in some difficult form such as the sonnet. It would be as reasonable to ask you as a modern person to come to class clad in a coat of medieval armor or to dance the minuet at a college prom. Sonnets—and good sonnets—can, of course, still be written. The question of the suitability of the form for a beginning writer is not the antiquity of the form, but rather of its contemporary appeal and the training in freedom it provides.

You should not distinguish poetry from creative prose by surface form, such as meter, rhyme, alliteration, and other technical devices. You should distinguish it by essential and internal form. Rhyme, for example, was not present in Anglo-Saxon poetry. Rhyme is sometimes an impediment to normal expression in English, because the English language

15

has a very limited number of rhymes. If you were to write a line ending in the word *God,* you would probably have to rhyme the next line with such words as *rod* or *sod.* The necessity for having such a rhyme may easily force you to alter your thought and even to say what you have no original intention of saying.

Poetry does not employ material distinct from that of prose, but makes use of a different method of imitating experience. Faculties of the human mind somewhat different from those used in prose are active when you write poetry. The word *prose* is etymologically derived from the Latin *prosus,* meaning "a direct going ahead." Poetry etymologically means a "making." Both are valid arts in their respective media. Comparisons between their places in the world of thought are unnecessary.

In this book the terms poetry and creative prose are used to indicate work that is primarily meant to be a "making" intended for artistic enjoyment. Poetry and creative prose are alike in the essential purpose that they are meant to be aesthetic rather than utilitarian. The distinction between them is determined by the prevalence of certain qualities in them that are specified below. They differ from "scientific prose" which is meant primarily to be functional and utilitarian (exposition, argumentation).

According to Herbert Read,[1] poetry is predominantly intuitive, imaginative, and synthetic. Prose is predominantly logical, constructive, and analytic. He deliberately chose the word *predominantly* because he believes that those qualities present in prose are also present in poetry, but subordinated to poetry's special function. Creative prose, likewise, assimilates the qualities of poetry in a subordinate relationship to its own special function. Poetry attains its end by *synthesis* —that is, by "fusion"; creative prose by *analysis.*

In following Herbert Read's distinction, we shall show how it is possible for the methods of poetry to enrich creative

[1] *English Prose Style,* New York, Henry Holt, 1928.

prose. Prose primarily utilitarian in function is not, strictly speaking, creative and as "scientific" or "functional" prose will not be considered here.

Herbert Read's distinction is not entirely new. Critics like the Renaissance Sir Philip Sidney and the romanticist Shelley made poetry synonymous with creative writing. They tended to identify the technical or scientific writer with the prose writer. Wordsworth opposed poetry to science, or what he termed "matter of fact." A distinction such as we have made between prose used creatively and prose serving for utility avoids Wordsworth's "blanket" classification of prose as "science."

The distinction between creative prose and poetry is not a distinction of quality, but a distinction of *kind*. And this distinction in kind should be made on the basis of "inner" form rather than of "surface" form. Too many attempted definitions of poetry have emphasized irrelevant material such as meter and rhyme as a basis of distinction between poetry and creative prose. Verse and creative prose may be contrasted with one another on the basis of rhetorical usage, but actually it may be possible to have poetry in prose form and prose matter in verse form. Verse is a surface form, and is really *neuter* in determining whether a given piece is poetry or creative prose.

The following passage is written in prose form. Does it seem to be prose or poetry to you?

And the merchants of the earth will weep and mourn over her; for no one will buy their merchandise any more: merchandise of gold and silver, and precious stones and pearls, and fine linen and purple, and silk and scarlet, and all thyine wood, and all vessels of ivory, and all vessels of precious stone, and of brass, and of iron, and of marble, and cinnamon and amomum and spices, and ointment and frankincense, and wine and oil, and fine flour and wheat, and beasts of burden and sheep and horses, and chariots and slaves, and souls of men. And the fruit which was the desire of thy soul departed from thee; and all the fat and splendid things perished from thee, and men will find them nevermore. The merchants of these things, who grew rich by her, will stand afar off for fear of her torments, weeping and mourning, and saying, "Woe, woe, that great city, which was clothed in fine linen and purple and scarlet, and gilded in gold, and precious stone, and pearls; For in one hour riches so great were laid waste!" [2]

The following passage is written in verse. Which would you say it is: poetry or prose?

> Peace to all such! but were there One whose fires
> True Genius kindles, and fair Fame inspires,
> Blest with each talent and each art to please,
> And born to write, converse, and live with ease:
> Should such a man, too fond to rule alone,
> Bear, like the Turk, no brother near the throne,
> View him with scornful, yet with jealous eyes,
> And hate for arts that caus'd himself to rise;
> Damn with faint praise, assent with civil leer,
> And without sneering, teach the rest to sneer;
> Willing to wound, and yet afraid to strike,
> Just hint a fault, and hesitate dislike;
> Alike reserv'd to blame or to commend,
> A tim'rous foe, and a suspicious friend;
> Dreading ev'n fools; by flatterers besieged,
> And so obliging that he ne'er obliged;
> Like Cato, give his little Senate laws,
> And sit attentive to his own applause:
> While wits and Templars ev'ry sentence raise,
> And wonder with a foolish face of praise—
> Who but must laugh if such a man there be?
> Who would not weep, if Atticus were he? [3]

In these two contrasting passages could not a good case be presented to show that the extract from the Apocalypse (presented in prose and "free verse" from the view of "surface" form) contains far more of what are generally considered

[2] *Apocalypse* 18:11-17.
[3] Pope, "Epistle to Dr. Arbuthnot."

poetic elements than Pope's heroic couplets? In other words, the first passage, though the mechanics of its form are those of "prose," might well be considered to be poetry. The second passage, though the mechanics of its form might be considered popularly to be poetry or at least verse, might well be considered to be prose, "good" prose, of course—"creative" prose.

Experiment

(1) Contrast the respective prose and poetry uses of the word "time" in the following short extracts.

Note the logical and analytical (we might also add *humorous*—humor is dependent upon analysis) use of "time" in Alice's conversation with the Mad Hatter:

Alice sighed wearily. "I think you might do something better with the time," she said, "than wasting it in asking riddles that have no answers."

"If you knew time as well as I do," said the Hatter, "you wouldn't talk about wasting *it*. It's *him*."

"I don't know what you mean," said Alice.

"Of course, you don't," the Hatter said, tossing his head contemptuously. "I dare say you never even spoke to time!"

"Perhaps not," Alice cautiously replied; "but I know I have to beat time when I learn music."

"Ah! That accounts for it," said the Hatter. "He won't stand beating. Now, if you only kept on good terms with him . . ."

"Time" in the following extract is used symbolically and is representative of (a) the subtle thief of youth; (b) the will of heaven; (c) the personal moral responsibility of Milton to his Creator. These associated concepts for which the symbol "time" stands are indicated in climactic order.

How soon hath Time, the subtle thief of youth,
Stolen on his wing my three and twentieth year!
My hasting days fly on with full career,
But my late spring no bud or blossom shew'th.

Perhaps my semblance might deceive the truth
That I to manhood am arrived so near;
An inward ripeness doth much less appear,
That some more timely-happy spirits endu'th.
Yet be it less or more, or soon or slow,
It shall be still in strictest measure even
To that same lot, however mean or high,
Toward which Time leads me, and the will of Heaven;
All is, if I have grace to use it so,
As ever in my great Task-Master's eye.

(2) Which of the following statements [4] in regard to time appear "predominantly logical, constructive, analytical"; which, "predominantly intuitive, imaginative, synthetic"?

(a) Time is the image of eternity.

(b)   What seest thou else
In the dark backward and abysm of time?

(c) Is't possible that so short a time can alter the condition of a man?

(d) Procrastination is the thief of time.

(e) Not only has philosophy identified time with history, as H. W. Carr and Benedetto Croce have done, but even history itself has accepted time as a motivation of inspiration. This is particularly the case in Oswald Spengler's *Decline of the West.* The new time, of course, is not the time of common sense; but the new *lived, experienced, intuited* flux in which the subject and object in some way become one, like the poet and the flower in the crannied wall.

(f) There would have been a time for such a word.
To-morrow, and to-morrow, and to-morrow
Creeps in this petty pace from day to day
To the last syllable of recorded time . . .

[4] Taken, in order, from the following: (a) Plato; (b) Shakespeare, *The Tempest;* (c) *Coriolanus;* (d) Edward Young, *Night Thoughts;* (e) Fulton J. Sheen, *Philosophy of Religion*, New York, Appleton-Century-Crofts, 1948, p. 80; (f) Shakespeare, *Romeo and Juliet;* (g) Keats, "Ode on a Grecian Urn."

(g) Thou still unravish'd bride of quietness,
Thou foster-child of Silence and slow Time.

(h) The reading time of "Gloria's Promise" is 8 minutes, 45 seconds.

The respective roles of words in functional writing and in creative writing can easily be distinguished by reference to the over-all purpose in a piece of writing. As we have previously stated, creative writing is concerned with being; functional writing, with process (explanation, demonstration, and proof).

A direct practical distinction is the comparative importance that *connotation* (associative meaning) plays in relation to the *denotation* (explicit meaning) of a word. In creative writing, the part played by connotation is considerably larger.

Nevertheless, denotation is important in creative writing as well as in functional writing, because creative writing carries precise intellectual meaning no less than scientific or functional writing. Denotation may not be so emphatic as in functional writing, but this is partly because functional writing is almost exclusively concerned with denotation.

Poetry (creative writing) cannot be readily translated into "prose" (here, obviously, "functional" prose). By such translation only the denotation is captured—the individuating connotative meaning is not transferred.

Matthew Arnold, in his essay "Literature and Science," points out how in an English school the line from *Macbeth* (V, iii, 40), "Can'st thou not minister to a mind diseased?" was paraphrased "Can you not wait upon the lunatic?" Arnold argues that he would prefer to have a student ignorant of a good deal of scientific knowledge than to have him assume that the translated statement is the equivalent of Shakespeare's. The first statement, presenting the disillusioned Macbeth's concern for his ailing wife, is actually much nearer the reality—in this case, the human reality—of the situation than the paraphrase. *Minister* suggests not only "to wait upon" but "to attend" with loving care and devotion such as a religious might give to the rites of his church. *Mind diseased* suggests pathos, the helplessness of a human person, a person still possessed of human inviolability though her mind has failed. The mere denotation *lunatic* in the paraphrase simply indicates a rationalistic and dehumanized category of human beings viewed unsympathetically or merely clinically. Shakespeare's rich human meaning is completely bypassed in the paraphrase and that, of course, is why Matthew Arnold considers it barbarous.

An interesting contrast between the use of words within creative writing, in poetry and creative prose, can be seen in the following extracts, one from T. S. Eliot's *The Waste Land,* the other from *When the Mountain Fell,* by the Swiss novelist, C. F. Ramuz. In both cases, words are being used artistically—not for functional purposes alone.

In Ramuz' account we are given an intensely dramatic description of the desolation caused in the high Alps by a sudden landslide. The imagery is concrete and personal, so that the reader visualizes the scene without difficulty. Practically every touch in the description reinforces emotion, bringing in complicated memories and suggestions culminating in overtones of pathos at the end. Notice how menacing and emotionally devastating the constant iteration of the word "stones" becomes. "Just stones and more stones, and still more stones." The language here, intensely rhythmical and emotional as it is, is nevertheless part of the process of construction, of "analysis" in the sense of carrying on a story. It is also intuitive, "symbolic." But its predominant characteristics make it the language of creative prose, great creative prose.

The path goes on climbing, the slope is steeper. All around are wide pastures sweeping down from one ledge of rock to another like stairs. You climb from one broad shelf to another. Already you are not far from Derborence; not far either from the country of the glaciers. And now at last there is a pass where the mountains close in again, and just here are the pastures and mountain cabins of Anzeindaz, like a little village, not far from where the grass itself can no longer grow. For a long time now there have been no trees.

Derborence is close by. All you have to do is to walk straight in front of you.

And suddenly the ground falls away from beneath your feet.

All at once the line of grass against the sky, which dips slightly in the middle, is outlining its hollow curve over nothingness itself. You have arrived. A chasm opens abruptly below you, like an immense oval basket with precipitous sides over which you have to lean, because although you are yourself six thousand feet up, the bottom is seventeen or eighteen hundred feet below you, straight down.

You bend over, you lean your head forward a little. Or else lie down flat, and look over the edge into the depths.

A breath of cold air blows into your face.

Derborence. It's first of all like a piece of winter blowing against you in full summer, for it is the home of shadows, which cling there even when the sun is highest in the sky. Then you can see that there is nothing there any more. Just stones, and more stones, and still more stones.

All around it the walls fall steeply, irregular in height, now rough, now smooth, while the path wriggles and twists down them far below like a snake. And whether you look straight ahead or on either side, there they are, standing on edge, lying in their sides, propped up or fallen flat, pushing forward in spurs from the mountain side or half-hidden and folded into narrow ravines—everywhere stones, nothing but stones, everywhere the same desolation.

Where the sunlight shines on them, they gleam with variegated color, but only a few of them, for one wall shadows the other, and the southern mountain cuts off most of the sun from that on the north. For a little while you can still see the top of the parapet all golden like a ripe grape, or red like a rose.

But the shadow is spreading already, it climbs higher and higher up the sides; it rises irresistibly and little by little like water in the bowl of a fountain, and as it rises everything fades, all is chill and silent, everything faints and dies; while everywhere the same sad color, the same bluish tint spreads below you like a fine mist through which you can see two lonely little lakes still gleaming a little longer like flat tin roofs in the gathering darkness. Then they, too, disappear.

The valley is still there, but nothing moves in it. You can look as long and as carefully as you will, everything is as still as death. Look: from the towering walls on the south to those on the north, nowhere is there any room for a living thing. There is nothing but the barren rock.

Once the valley was alive, now everything has been blotted out by something that seems at first glance like a cone of sand, with the narrow end still half held in the northern wall; and from there the rocks are scattered helter-skelter all over like dice from a dicebox, and that's exactly what they are like, dice of all sizes, one square block and another just like it, blocks piled up on top of each other, then a succession of blocks, big and little, choking the valley as far as the eye can see.

And yet many people used to come to the valley in the old days. They even say that some years there were as many as fifty.[5]

T. S. Eliot's passage has some similar stylistic devices, including repetition of a key word with an accompanying emotional intensification. Similarly, there are great overtones of pathos, with the emphasis on sterility and the absence of the reinvigorating "water"—symbol of spirit. The language here, in contrast to that of Ramuz, is predominantly intuitive, imaginative. The symbolic meaning has priority over the constructive meaning. All is rock, the symbol of sterility; there is no "water," no spiritual renewal in the Waste Land.

Here is no water but only rock
Rock and no water and the sandy road
The road winding above among the mountains
Which are mountains of rock without water

[5] C. F. Ramuz, *When the Mountain Fell*, New York, Pantheon Press, 1947, pp. 25-28.

If there were water we should stop and drink
Amongst the rocks one cannot stop or think
Sweat is dry and feet are in the sand
If there were only water amongst the rock
Dead mountain mouth of carious teeth that cannot spit
Here one can neither stand nor lie nor sit
There is not even silence in the mountains
But dry sterile thunder without rain
There is not even solitude in the mountains
But red sullen faces sneer and snarl
From doors of mudcaked houses
>   If there were water
>   And no rock
>   If there were rock
>   And also water
>   And water
>   A spring
>   A pool among the rock
>   If there were the sound of water only
>   Not the cicada
>   And dry grass singing
>   But sound of water over a rock
>   Where the hermit-thrush sings in the pine trees
>   Drip drop drip drop drop drop drop
>   But there is no water [6]

As we continue to consider the function of individual
words in creative writing, certain references will become important. Among these are the *individuation* of a word, its
concreteness and intensity in terms of mental association;
its *universality,* its capacity for suggesting and touching
universal meanings and value; its *overtone,* its capacity to
suggest and go beyond its context; its capacity to stir the
emotions through *color;* its capacity to serve as a *motif* or
key word in an artistic pattern.

The creative word is not inadvertent or repetitious. It is

[6] T. S. Eliot, *Collected Poems 1909-1935,* New York, Harcourt Brace, 1936,
pp. 86-87.

not already implicit in another word already used in the context. The creative word observes the principle of economy in the authentic sense—there is no waste in it. It carries its full load in a piece of writing.

In the sections of the book to follow, you will find a good deal of emphasis on the writing of poetry in a basic and essential sense. Poetry, in the broad sense of the term, means creative art; this is the traditional sense of the term in Plato and Aristotle. Poetry will be considered in a narrower sense as a specific form of art distinct from "creative prose." Both poetry and creative prose are art and, therefore, quite distinct from "functional prose," which is scientific. The objective of a creative work is simply *to be;* the objective of a scientific work is utilitarian, to serve some end outside itself. Poetry is emphasized on the principle that its understanding and application are basic to all creative writing, including "creative prose." If you do not intend to be a poet at all but, rather, a good narrative writer or a good journalist, you will profit enormously by the application of the techniques that are presented.

The creative writer must avoid the trite—the phrase that is so overused that an initial doubt exists in the reader's mind about its sincerity. Certain phrases simply express the universal—they indicate a universally recognized fact or act. Their simplicity—presuming a right context, of course—can hardly be improved upon. "Oh what a beautiful day!" or "I love you": such phrases are basic English and permanent English. It is in the intermediate language that danger lies —language that is not universally simple and yet is not possessed of the freshly perceived image. In exposition and argumentation the besetting danger is jargon—the pretentious, fuzzy gobbledygook. In creative writing, the danger is the hackneyed image, the figurative phrase that is inappropriate or stale.

In the following passage the student writer is heavy and trite:

The Squirrel

A soft, small, furry animal, the squirrel scurries busily about in his chief errand—hoarding. Providing for his family seems to be his chief concern, but in relation to the quantity of provisions he stores away an army would be well fed on similar rations. There is a purpose for this, however, for the squirrel is subject to the equivalent of anemia. He actually forgets most of the storing places for food, and so his "hoarding" is a preventive measure for his family's welfare to counterbalance his retentive shortcomings.

This piece is a struggle that never goes behind the tortured conceptual to the visualized imaginative. Contrast with the above example another student's description:

A little arch of grey-furred unity rises, falls; its bright shoe-button eyes check every object. For a moment it straightens itself —mechanically, rigidly, like an electrical toy. Then suddenly and mutely it loops across the asphalt through the sun-deadened light. Suddenly, it streaks through the grass to the nearest tree, spiraling its thick trunk until it hides itself in the top branches.

The imagery in the second example is fresh, and the description is proportionately vital.

You should cultivate a sense of appropriateness between the subject matter—poetry, creative prose—you have selected and the style by which you express it. This appropriateness is ultimately the guiding principle of all cogent writing. The calm and detached philosophical vocabulary which you would employ for making an exposition of an abstract idea would be quite unsuitable for a candid snapshot of real life. Though even the most "natural" dialogue is "art" rather than "science," you still must aim to capture the overtones of real experience. It would be more appropriate to have the man who sells the newspapers ask, "Whadyya read, Mac?" rather than, "What newspaper will you have this evening, sir?"

You may write very well on expository and argumentative levels where your understanding of semantics (the science of the meaning of words) and the orderly procedures of logic are important, and still run into considerable difficulty in creative writing. There is nothing alarming about this possibility. You will sometimes meet a highly competent professional man, a lawyer, perhaps, who has a fine command of style, yet he will say somewhat romantically, "I wish I could write." By this he means he wishes he could write *creatively.* The ability to write excellent English and to express yourself clearly is not the same ability as that of the creative writer. Depending on your field of interest and the ability you are able to develop, you may or may not be a creative writer. But, on the other hand, your actual practice in the techniques of creative writing will enormously increase your powers of appreciating the art of others, besides enriching your over-all intellectual background.

Perhaps the easiest way to point out the difference between functional writing and creative writing is to say that one pertains more to logic, the other more to imagination. Creative writing should not be explanatory, discursive. It must be concrete, emotionalized, dramatic. You do not want to explain a situation or argue its validity, but to *show* it in line, color, form.

If you wished to show the economic state of the nation, you would do research, draw up statistics, and argue your conclusions. Your work would be explanatory, argumentative. But if you wished to dramatize imaginatively the meaning of the nation, you could use the mental images or "associations"—the line, color, and form of the American flag, as in the following lines:

> Where the gull wheels lightly
> Down the wide meadows of the sea,
> Where the lonely eagle of the sky
> Poises his wings over the redwood forest,

Where freedom of space and golden harvest
Are a cornstalk sunflower Currier and Ives Autumnal:
America leaps with bold, carefree grace
Into the youthful valley of the Mind.
In lucid counterpoint of free blue sky
The streaming lines of its living blood
Are spread out in the white sunshine of its banner.

—W. J.

By mental association is meant the habitual way in which ideas and images go together in our mind through our personal experience, which touches more forces in us than the purely logical or deliberate. You cannot create on an exclusively logical basis—though you could write good exposition or argumentation in this way. You must also use the associative and imagistic powers of your mind. You can have a blank sheet of paper and the best reasoning mind in the world, and you will be compelled to leave the paper blank unless you are moved and stirred by your imaginative powers. The imaginative power is closely associated with the process of mental association. That is why in this book we stress mental association so strongly.

By style in writing we mean the form that is appropriate to the subject matter you wish to express. In expository writing, for example, where you are engaged in a work of clarification—that is, of definition and analysis—you would generally avoid symbols and complex images. In creative writing, where you *re-present* rather than *explain,* you would generally have much more cause to use them.

The appropriateness of form to subject matter (called style) does not imply a specialized vocabulary for different forms of writing. Language is universal and can be molded in many new and unexpected ways by the creative artist, as will be explained later.

Experiment

Give your reasons for classifying the following selections [7]
as poetry or creative prose:

(1) Far off in the cold mountains the immaculate snow is lit
by stars as cold. The terraced trees move not, but hoard
their perfume all the night, till with the dawn released,
green flautists, they stir all the air of the valley to a tune.
The cowherd climbing to the Alpine hut stands for an
instant with the green counterpoint entranced. Then, as
cowbells overtake the high, ecstatic trebles of the snow, he
takes his alpenstock and trudges on.

(2) It seemed to Wolf, as they plodded along side by side
through the muddy lane, that the light-green buds of
those aged willow-trunks were framed in a more appropriate setting under the cold forlorn sky than any sunshine could give to them. Later seasons would warm them
and cherish them. November rains would turn them yellow and bring them into mud. But no other sky would
hang above them with the cold floating weight of sadness
as this one did—a weight like a mass of grey seaweed beneath a silent sea. No other sky would be cold enough
and motionless enough to listen to the rising of the green
sea within them, the infinitesimal flowing, flowing, flowing, that for non-human ears must have made strange low
gurglings and susurrations all day long.

(3) Once Paumanok, when the lilac-scent was in the air and
Fifth-month grass was growing, up this seashore, in some
briers, two guests from Alabama—two together, and their
nest, and four light-green eggs, spotted with brown, and
every day the he-bird, to and fro, near at hand, and every
day the she-bird, crouch'd on her nest, silent, with bright

[7] Taken, in order, from the following: (1) Humbert Wolfe, *The Uncelestial City;* (2) John Cowper Powys, *Wolf Solent;* (3) Whitman, "Out of the
Cradle Endlessly Rocking"; (4) Melville, *Moby Dick;* (5) Poe, "The Pit and
the Pendulum."

eyes, and everyday I, a curious boy, never too close, never disturbing them, cautiously peering, absorbing, translating.

(4) Tied up and twisted;
Gnarled and knotted with wrinkles;
His eyes glowing like coals
That still glow in the ashes of ruin;
Untottering Ahab stood forth
In the clearness of the morn;
Lifting his splintered helmet of a brow
To the girl's fair forehead of heaven.
Oh, immortal infancy and innocency
Of the azure!
Invisible winged creatures
That frolic all round us!
Sweet childhood of air and sky!
How obvious were ye
To old Ahab's close-coiled woe!

(5) Unreal!—even while I breathed there came to my nostrils the breath of the vapor of heated iron! A suffocating odor pervaded the prison! A deeper glow settled each moment in the eyes that glared at my agonies! A richer tint of crimson diffused itself over the pictured horrors of blood. I panted! I gasped for breath! There could be no doubt of the design of my tormentors—oh! most unrelenting! oh! most demoniac of men! I shrank from the glowing metal to the centre of the cell. Amid the thought of the fiery destruction that impended, the idea of the coolness of the well came over my soul like balm. I rushed to its deadly brink. I threw my straining vision below. The glare from the enkindled roof illuminated its inmost recesses. Yet, for a wild moment, did my spirit refuse to comprehend the meaning of what I saw. At length it forced—it wrestled its way into my soul—it burned itself in upon my shuddering reason. Oh! for a voice to speak!—oh! horror!—oh! any horror but this! With a shriek, I rushed from the margin, and buried my face in my hands—weeping bitterly.

INTUITION—THE VISION OF BEING

The words used in Herbert Read's distinction between poetry and creative prose—intuition, imagination, synthesis—need explanation.

By intuition in this context we mean a natural power of perception so refined by experience and training that it can discern truth—even complex truth—without going through the formal or labored process of logic, though its conclusions are conformable to those of logic.

Intuition, in the wide sense, implies a sense of certitude, of fitness, of aptness, of justice, in seeing some aspect of being—of experience, of man, of God. It means the ability to share in something that is universal—the ability to see in the most deeply human sense, to see positively, directly, with enthusiastic faith. A lover sees his beloved intuitively—not through her I.Q., her psychological tests, her data sheets, or financial statements. Intuition is the vision of being—it is the capacity to see in a new light, with a new intensity, even quite familiar experience such as the courage and the nobility of "commonplace" people in "commonplace" situations. It is the basis of love, of any great creative or religious experience.

Consequently, when we speak of intuition in creative writing, we speak of those flashes of truth that are so expressed that their intensity wins universal acceptance. It is because of the presence of intuition in this sense that we may say that a creative artist does not have to seek after the unusual, but only to make us *see* what we already *know*.

The word intuition has different technical meanings in various philosophical systems. As applied to creative process, it can best be understood by examples.

In the lines from *The Uncelestial City* by Humbert Wolfe, an image symbolizes the union of the soul with God through the instrumentality of death. The creative artist "intuits" the meaning of divine love through the images of "the dark eyelashes" and "the eyes of God."

> Then you shall enter at last by your own path
> Treading the streets only your footsteps trod,
> Till under the dark eyelashes of death
> You suddenly look into the eyes of God.[8]

In such examples intuition is revealed in its fullest power when symbol and thought perfectly coincide. When the poet's imagery is "apt" or "just," he gives dramatic immediacy to his intuition. A concept like "God's grandeur" has occurred many times in meditations, sermons, but we may not react very strongly because the concept lacks immediacy. We are not brought to an intuitive realization of it. But Gerard Manley Hopkins brings out the meaning of this idea powerfully by the use of such familiar symbols as "shook foil" and "the ooze of oil." We are simultaneously brought into the world of immediate sense experience and of universals. The acceptance of the reality of the one ("shook foil," "ooze of oil") is transferred to the reality of the other ("God's grandeur").

> The world is charged with the grandeur of God.
> It will flame out, like shining from shook foil;
> It gathers to a greatness, like the ooze of oil
> Crushed.

The creative artist handles his intuitions symbolically. His purpose is neither to explain nor to prove, but to *represent*. A symbol is a representation. "Shook foil," "ooze of oil" are images, also symbols.

Intuition in creative writing is expressed through the symbol. By a symbol is meant a sign which represents a larger world of meaning by a kind of index or token rather than by a demonstration or by an argument. A symbol points to a truth but does not attempt to explain it. The "Stars and

[8] Humbert Wolfe, *The Uncelestial City*, New York, Alfred A. Knopf, 1930, p. 5.

Stripes" indicate the United States, but the indication is to a vast and indeterminate field of meaning. The meaning of the national flag is not explicit.

An extensive use of symbolism in a highly organized and "architectonic" form is found in the *allegory*. An interesting example written by a student is to be found in Peter Glickert's "Cosmopolis" (see page 313).

We sometimes overlook the fact that art effects its purpose by means of conventions—*symbols*. Suppose we have a table in front of us. Why do we call it a table? Because it is in itself essentially a table, or because it corresponds in some way to an idea of a table we have in our minds? If we were to read the tenth book of Plato's *Republic,* we would be told that we call this object in front of us *a* table, because it is an imitation in material form of an idea we have in our minds—*the* table. Actually, we might describe the object in front of us as a collection of pieces of wood. If we had a very powerful microscope, we might actually see what the scientists tell us is present: a vast world—perhaps infinite in the sense of being indefinitely divisible—of protons, electrons, and neutrons as vast and as complicated as the mighty stellar system that we can behold above our heads. In this sense it may well be argued that we call the object in front of us *a* table, merely to indicate the function or use to which we put it, rather than to say what it is essentially. It serves a purpose I have in mind—"the table purpose." If I make a drawing of the table, the drawing is even more symbolic, for then I make lines on a flat surface that symbolize a table —a table, which, in fact, is not a flat surface, but three-dimensional (length, breadth, and depth)—and these lines are an abstract matter for the human intelligence in the same way that an equation in algebra is. The drawing is even more "symbolic" than the table. Of course, both the table and the drawing have their own reality or being.

It is important to understand the function of the intelligence in understanding a symbol—a sign that through mutual

DÜRER: *The Knight, Death, and the Devil*

Symbolism—Allegory

Beauty Rising out of an Art of Conflict

agreement or convention stands for a transcendent meaning. I talk to you. What am I really doing? On one level, I am merely making sounds. Scientifically, we could measure the type and variety of the sound waves. After they have hit your nervous system through your sense of hearing, you accept these sounds as symbols of meaning. Your intelligence acts upon these sounds and you see them as *meaning-bearing* sounds. The sounds that I make with my diaphragm and throat are symbols as complicated and as wonderful as anything you will find in the higher calculus. Fortunately, of course, they are more familiar to us.

Symbolism is habitual to us. Even ordinary courtesies—like shaking hands, or removing one's hat—are symbolic actions. The action only has meaning as a sign or symbol of a value that is not explicit or obvious but is understood through convention and experience.

In art, symbols may occasionally offer added difficulty or subtlety, but, basically, they are not unfamiliar to us. Symbols—"images"—are used to convey "overtones" of meaning which are implicit. The shaking of hands is a simple physical act. Its "overtone" of meaning is the universal and abstract idea of friendship. In writing, the artist chooses his word symbols, not merely to express an actual, outward fact, but also an "inner," "transcendent," meaning. Thus, you might walk along the shore and notice the seagulls and you might make a mental note such as "I have heard the seagulls, singing each to each." But T. S. Eliot, in "The Love Song of J. Alfred Prufrock," uses a special word symbol "mermaids" to signify the imaginative vision that has disappeared from the life of Prufrock—an actual bird would not suggest this overtone. "Mermaids" rather than "seagulls" provide better symbols of his meaning. "I have heard the mermaids singing, each to each."

Symbols convey meaning on many levels and frequently on more than one level at one time. Particularly in poetry, a specific and concrete meaning is presented on one level of the discourse; a transcendent and no less important mean-ing, on another level. There is a close connection between the seeing of a material object deeply and intensely and the understanding of transcendent meaning. Depth on the one level of understanding increases comprehension on the other. "Being" is not easily exhausted. It always offers a new aspect to the vision of the sympathetic beholder. Thus, the Spirit of Milton's *Comus* describes, on one level, the effect that music has had upon him.

> . . . I was all ear,
> And took in strains that might create a soul
> Under the ribs of Death.

But the reference to music here has also become a symbol of being, of life. Music and its beauty seem so dominant to the poet-beholder that, as a symbol of life, it is affirmed in the very bones of negation. The effectiveness of these lines results from combining the abstract concept of "soul" with the very visual "ribs." An effect of intensity is brought about by the sudden intrusion of the immensely "imagistic" *ribs.*

In poetry, what is specific, what is "individuated," is com-bined with what is transcendent, what is universal, in expres-sion, covering multi-dimensional levels. We shall consider this point in detail in the section on synthesis.

Overtone and the pathetic fallacy are special techniques through which intuitive thought is presented in art.

Overtone is characteristic of the intuitive method of ex-pression in creative art. By overtone the artist expresses himself intuitively; by overtone he is understood intuitively.

Creative writing, because it is essentially dependent on mental association (p. 83), on connotation, demands more than a "literal" reading. A creative artist has not only to be heard; he has also to be *overheard.* The overtone is the further meaning in creative writing that is implicit rather than explicit. The image functions symbolically and the further extension of the writer's meaning consists in all that area to which the symbol points.

In order to get a creative artist's full meaning one must not only note what he says; one must also note what he refrains from saying. To illustrate on a simple level—one might say that "the countryside is quiet tonight"; the same information is conveyed by overtone in the statement "the train whistle wails through the valley." We hear the train whistle *because* the countryside is quiet. The overtone here suggests the quietude of the valley—the word *wails* suggests how the quietude is broken.

Overtone is symbolic of psychological conditions, implied but not directly stated. For example, Macbeth, in speaking to his wife of the king he has murdered, says: "After life's fitful fever he sleeps well." The overtone of meaning lies in the ironic envy that the murderer feels toward his victim. The victim has not lost the great gift of sleep—but Macbeth has.

Overtones often indicate an unstated intellectual evaluation. When W. H. Auden says in "The Unknown Citizen":

> And had everything necessary to the modern man,
> A phonograph, a radio, a car and a frigidaire . . .

he really condemns the thesis that such things should be "necessary" to man, modern or otherwise. Frequently, overtone is ironic and dramatic. In Hugh Walpole's "The Tarn," there is a "deceptive reassurance" about the Tarn's quiet words that is spine-tingling: "I will stay with you, so that you are not lonely." The literal meaning appears friendly; the overtone is ironic and ominous.

Overtone is of particular importance in the forms of writing that employ humor and irony. These forms will be discussed later.

Willa Cather has said that "whatever is felt upon the page without being specifically named there—that, it seems to me, is created. It is the inexplicable presence of the thing not named, of the overtone divined by the ear but not heard by it, the emotional aura of the fact or the thing or the deed, that gives high quality to the novel or the drama, as well as to poetry itself." [9]

Ruskin coined the phrase *pathetic fallacy*—an unfortunate title for a very real artistic device. "Fallacy" is applied to this type of image merely in the sense that nonhuman objects are assumed to have human characteristics. Ruskin places that artist highest in the natural order who both sees and feels truly. Some artists see more truly than they feel; others feel more truly than they see. Ruskin holds that the highest vision of which man is capable is likely to be confused, because the artist is then penetrating knowledge that is new and mysterious and of which he is not the complete master. The pathetic fallacy for Ruskin means a use of imagery in which there is a violation of objective truth. The heavens do not in fact *weep;* the trees do not *dance;* the sunlight does not *laugh.* On the other hand, all art works through illusion; art is not direct experience, it is experience imaginatively interpreted. Art is responsible to truth in the sense that within the terms of illusion—to quote Coleridge, within the terms of "the willing suspension of disbelief"—there should not be an illusioned view of life. Working in illusion, art should not give us illusioned values. In regard to the pathetic fallacy, it may be said that such a statement often possesses subjective, *imaginative* truth. But Ruskin is correct in warning us that, because there is a loss of objective accuracy, the pathetic fallacy should be used with moderation.

[9] Willa Cather, "The Novel Démeublé," *On Writing,* New York, Alfred A. Knopf, 1949, pp. 41-42.

Experiment

Locate the pathetic fallacy in the following [10] quotations:

(1) Where were ye, Nymphs, when the remorseless deep
    Closed o'er the head of your loved Lycidas?

(2) Arise, fair sun, and kill the envious moon,
    Who is already sick and pale with grief,
    That thou her maid art far more fair than she.

(3) A skylark wounded in the wing
    A Cherubim does cease to sing . . .

(4) Dear God! the very houses seem asleep;
    And all that mighty heart is lying still!

(5) Season of mists and mellow fruitfulness,
    Close bosom-friend of the maturing sun . . .

(6) The mountains and the hills shall break forth before
    you into singing, and all the trees of the field shall clap
    their hands.

(7) Nature in awe to him
    Hath doffed her gaudy trim
        With her great Master so to sympathize . . .

The pathetic fallacy is present in many of our great poems. It basically assumes that nonhuman nature can share human attributes. Effects of irony can often be secured by merely reminding the reader that nonhuman nature cannot really share the nature of man. Nonhuman nature can correlate with man's experience, but man's nature is also radically different from that of his external environment.

[10] Taken, in order, from the following: (1) Milton, "Lycidas"; (2) Shakespeare, *Romeo and Juliet;* (3) Blake, "Auguries of Innocence"; (4) Wordsworth, "Composed upon Westminster Bridge"; (5) Keats, "To Autumn"; (6) *Isaias* 4:12; (7) Milton, "On the Morning of Christ's Nativity."

Experiment

Locate the symbolic image in the following [11] statements, and attempt to reconstruct the intuitive meaning suggested by it:

(1) But felt through all this fleshly dress
Bright shoots of everlastingness.

(2) Blind Mouths! that scare themselves know how to hold
A sheep-hook . . .

(3) Not mine own fears, nor the prophetic soul
Of the wide world, dreaming on things to come
Can yet the lease of my true love control.

(4) By all thy lives and deaths of love;
By thy large draughts of intellectual day,
And by thy thirsts of love more large than they . . .

(5) To the high fantasy here power failed; but already my desire
and will were rolled—even as a wheel that moveth equally—
by the love that moves the sun and the other stars.

(6) He is not here; but far away
The noise of life begins again,
And ghastly through the drizzling rain
On the bald street breaks the blank day.

(7) The world is charged with the grandeur of God,
It will flame out, like shining from shook foil;
It gathers to a greatness, like the ooze of oil
Crushed.

Must the artist's intuitive sense correspond to reality, to *truth?* Yes, in the sense that it corresponds substantially to the valid experience of men. Not every reader will neces-

[11] Taken, in order, from the following: (1) Vaughan, "The Retreat"; (2) Milton, "Lycidas"; (3) Shakespeare, "Sonnet 107"; (4) Crashaw, "The Flaming Heart"; (5) Dante, *Paradiso* 33; (6) Tennyson, *In Memoriam;* (7) Hopkins, "God's Grandeur."

sarily grasp the intuitive meaning, since perception depends on experience and sensitivity to the overtones in art. Art communicates more than the surface statement. For example, Shakespeare places in the mouth of Macbeth the terrifying statement:

> . . . It [life] is a tale
> Told by an idiot, full of sound and fury,
> Signifying nothing.

But the full meaning Shakespeare conveys is more than this explicit statement. We are also to remember that these are the words of a man, disillusioned and despairing because of the course of evil he has undertaken. Shakespeare's poetic "intuition" covers all this—both the *explicit* statement and the overtone, implicitly understood.

Intuition in poetry is frequently connected with the poet's capacity to see the universal and the concrete at one and the same time. The image is the concrete focus which symbolically points to the universal. Note how the images of *leaves* serve as the concrete means by which the universal is symbolized in the following passages.

Great hearted Tydeides, why enquirest thou of my generation? Even as are the generations of leaves such as those likewise of men: the leaves that be the wind scattereth on the earth, and the forest buddeth and putteth forth more again, when the season of spring is at hand; so of the generations of men one putteth forth and another ceaseth.[12]

Thus a Homeric speaker expressed the sadness of men as they abide the recurring experience of death. Glancing over the pages of a Milton or a Homer, you will come across complex images in which the universal and the concrete are fused together to suggest vastness and grandeur. Thus Milton "intuits" with the same image of "leaves":

[12] Homer, *The Iliad,* trans. Lang, Leaf, Myers, New York, Modern Library, 1947, p. 105.

> . . . he stood and called
> His legions, angel forms, who lay entranced
> Thick as autumnal leaves that strew the brooks
> In Vallambrosa, where the Etrurian shades
> High over-arched embower . . .

Ruskin, in his "Of the Pathetic Fallacy," particularly stressed the greatness of the poetry that combined two levels of reality, the transcendent and the individuated, without any loss of the distinctness between them:

When Dante describes the spirits falling from the bank of Acheron "as dead leaves flutter from a bough," he gives the most perfect image possible of their utter lightness, feebleness, passiveness, and scattering agony of despair, without, however, for an instance losing his own clear conception that *these* are souls, and *these* are leaves; he makes no confusion of the one with the other.

IMAGINATION—IMAGE OF THE UNIVERSAL

Do not be misled by common ignorance which tends to set the "imaginative" in opposition to the "real." Imagination is distinct from fantasy (p. 208), and "fantasy" stories are not necessarily "imaginative" stories.

Why be imaginative? Imagination deepens our view of things, of life. We see new beauty, we enrich ourselves, we deepen our power of empathy. The exercise of the imagination makes us more fully human. The imagination also has its practical values, though these are not its most important aspects. The power to vision, to outline in images, to recall with freshness and immediacy, enables us to get the maximum results from experience.

We learn through the senses. We have the ability within ourselves to capture and retain sense impressions on what we may metaphorically call a "mental screen." That is why I can recognize again a person I once met. I see an identification between the person in front of me and the image of him that my memory retained. The capacity of the mind to form and retain images is one of the first characteristics of the imagination. I am connected with reality, first of all, by imagination in this way.

But imagination means more than the mental picture of an object. It means also a mental picture which has become fused with intellectual meaning; it means, therefore, an image which is also a symbol. On a simple level I can image "bread." My image may be different from yours in that I think of wholewheat bread, you of French rolls. But the general meaning of *bread* in the sense of "denotation" is clear for us, though it does not indicate an intellectual value beyond this denotation. But when I speak of the *bread of life,* then *bread* is not only an image, but a symbol of meaning far transcending the purely sensuous image.

Secondly, therefore, the imagination connects me with reality by the use of the intellect as well as by the use of the senses. The intellect is in itself a main guide to defining and evaluating reality.

It is particularly the function of the image to mirror intellectual meaning, to be the symbol of the universal. When we speak of the "creative" imagination, as distinct from mere "imagination," we mean the mind's creation of an image that is fused with intellectual meaning.

Experiment

List ten of your most driving and powerful convictions about life, people, experience. State each one in a clear-cut prose sentence, making your denotation as accurate as possible. Then make another list of imaginative expressions, attempting to symbolize each of these convictions by a fresh and vigorous image. The images do not necessarily have to form complete sentences.

By *imagination,* then, is generally meant the image-making power of the human mind. We can shut our eyes, for example, and recall the shapes, colors, and outlines of a given scene. We not only have a visual screen, but a mental screen by which we can retain experiences, scenes, emotions in the storehouse of the memory. This image-making power is closely associated with mental association and connotation. By "mental association" we mean, as we have already stated, the habit of the human mind of associating one image or idea with other images or ideas for psychological causes based on experience rather than for strict logical causality.

By imagination is also meant the capacity of the creative artist to use images as "symbols" of larger areas of meaning that he explicitly states. Such images are not purely sensory or purely intellectual, but are both these things at the same time.

Images help to create intellectual ideas, and intellectual ideas in creative writing naturally seek imagistic expression. Let us look at this quotation from Humbert Wolfe's *Uncelestial City:*

> . . . for one lost life that finds in death
> the village lights of Nazareth . . .

"Village lights"—symbol of friendship and tranquillity—is an image brought about by its mental association with Nazareth, birthplace of the Savior. The identification of "village lights" with "death," however, is the result of an intellectual process which, in turn, was encouraged by the images. The beauty of Wolfe's phrase results from the union of transcendent meaning with the concrete and individual image. The reader awakens at once to the visualization of the picture, then proceeds to understand the meaning of death viewed in spiritual terms.

Now let us look at these lines more closely to see how the laws of imagination work. Nazareth is a geographical and historical *name.* But does Humbert Wolfe think of it here as merely a geographical or historical concept? He does not. He thinks of Nazareth imagistically. Nazareth by mental association is for him *village lights*. But is Nazareth merely *village lights?* No. The symbolism of *village lights* is more important than the literal meaning. *Village lights* in terms of mental association connote peace, friendliness, security. But does the overtone of meaning stop here? No. Peace, friendliness, security are viewed, not merely on the secular level, but on the spiritual level. Nazareth is also the birthplace of the Savior. Consequently, by the "village lights of Nazareth" the poet symbolizes the peace, friendliness, security to be found in the personal relationship of man with the Savior.

Now, the idea-equivalent of the "village lights of Nazareth" given in these lines is *death*. *Death* here is not placed in a purely logical context. Its meaning derives from the poetic discourse, the interrelated system of mental associations. *Death* is the "village lights of Nazareth" with all the associated and correlated meaning that this phrase has gathered. Death means all this to "one lost life." The *lost* in "one lost life" refers to the Gospel paradox that he who loses his life shall find it, and he who saves his life shall lose it (*Matthew* 16:25). This paradox, incorporated in the poetic discourse here, implies a rejection of purely materialistic values.

It may be noted that the poetic discourse is a concentrated discourse in which much of the depth of the meaning is *symbolized* rather than directly stated.

In an actual experiment, members of an audience were asked to put down what came into their minds imagistically on hearing "village lights." One man thought of the lights of the village gradually appearing to a beholder descending from a mountain into a valley at dusk, perhaps to a hiker seeking the comfort and refreshment of the village inn. The lights are then symbols of friendship and security. Another thought of the "lights" as the means of sight, therefore of knowledge, therefore of the understanding of man with man. The "village lights" for him, therefore, were symbols of intellectual *light.*

In order to understand art it is necessary to make such extensions from the immediate image to the transcendent meaning which it represents. Imagination is allied to reality. As a mental screen which stores sense impressions, it brings us into contact with the external world. The image thus arising from contact with the external world is fused with intellectual meaning. The intellect enables us to understand the external world that our senses reveal to us, so that in an another important way we are in contact with the real. A dollar bill, for example, might literally be considered to be a picture of George Washington. But a dollar bill is also a symbol—a symbol of exchange value. We would certainly miss its meaning if we simply accepted the immediate sense impression of the dollar bill without fusing that image with its appropriate intellectual meaning.

Symbols *coordinate* in poetic discourse. "Village lights" mean not only the literal village lights but the intellectual values associated with them—peace, security, friendship. "The village lights" of *Nazareth* are all that we have stated, plus the imagistic and intellectual values symbolized in "Nazareth." Nazareth is not just any village. It is the village of Christ. Consequently, "the village lights of Nazareth" denote the peace, security, and friendship of *Christ's* village. Death, then, is the peace, security, and friendship of Christ's village, plus all the immediate mental associations this image stimulates in us.

It is important to keep constantly in mind the fact that an artist is not merely presenting the external world. He is also presenting his interior emotional and intellectual response to it. Imagination, for example, will often exaggerate outward circumstances in order to register the true impact of inward emotion. The metaphors of action used in Wolfe's later lines, while not objectively accurate, are subjectively very apt. They are creative in the imaginative sense:

> But suddenly the mists were ript asunder
> By two great hands, and in the space laid bare—
> No mountain, but a clap of lovely thunder,
> Jungfrau all gold in twilight took the air.

Experiment

Show in detail how the imagination is operative in the following [13] passages. Show how the images symbolize intellectual meaning and how they *coordinate* together.

(1) Till death like sleep might steal on me,
    And I might feel in the warm air
    My cheek grow cold, and hear the sea
    Breathe o'er my dying brain its last monotony.

(2) We listened and looked sideways up!
    Fear at my heart, as at a cup,
    My life-blood seemed to sip!
    The stars were dim, and thick the night,
    The steersman's face by his lamp gleamed white . . .

(3)   Fair daffodils, we weep to see
            You haste away so soon;
        As yet the early-rising sun
            Has not attained his noon.
                Stay, stay
            Until the hasting day
                Has run
            But to the evensong:
        And having prayed together, we
            Will go with you along.
        We have short time to stay, as you
            We have as short a spring . . .

[13] Taken, in order, from the following: (1) Shelley, "Stanzas Written in Dejection Near Naples"; (2) Coleridge, "The Rime of the Ancient Mariner"; (3) Herrick, "To Daffodils"; (4) Hopkins, "Heaven—Haven"; (5) Henley, "I. M. Margaritae Sorori."

(4) I have desired to go
　　Where the springs not fail,
　　To fields where flies no sharp and sided hail
　　And a few lilies blow.
　　And I have asked to be
　　Where no storms come,
　　Where the green swell is in the havens dumb,
　　And out of the swing of the sea.

(5) A late lark twitters from the quiet skies;
　　And from the west,
　　Where the sun, his day's work ended,
　　Lingers as in content,
　　There falls on the old, gray city
　　An influence luminous and serene,
　　A shining peace.

SYNTHESIS—THE FUSION OF WORDS

Synthesis means a union, a cohesion—a state by which elements are integrated into new substances.

The synthetic power of poetry is its pivotal characteristic. Synthesis basically implies a "uniting or bringing together." In chemistry we synthesize separate elements so that they form a new substance, a compound, which is radically different from the elements that enter into it. In poetry, for example, image-bearing words can be fused together to form a unique and untranslatable expression which carries so individuated a meaning that no other equivalent can be found for it. The synthesis is inevitable in poetry because an outstanding characteristic of this art is "bringing together"— fusion, the seeing into many levels of reality at once.

An outstanding characteristic of the synthesis is the uniting of the abstract idea and the concrete setting or circumstance. This characteristic derives in part from the fact that the creative mind works on two levels. On one level it perceives the external world as it is. On another level it perceives the *internal* world of the mind *as it also is, possessed of emotional and intellectual values,* in the *act* of *reaction* to the external world. The creative artist unites in his work "the difference between reality as the eye sees it and the world of action as the mind perceives it."

Note the effect of uniting the concrete "green" with "thought" and with "shade," in the following extract from Marvell's "The Garden":

> Meanwhile the mind, from pleasure less,
> Withdraws into its happiness:
> The mind, that ocean where each kind
> Does straight its own resemblance find;
> Yet it creates, transcending these,
> Far other worlds, and other seas;
> Annihilating all that's made
> To a green thought in a green shade.

Notice the successful impact of the abstract "death" with the concrete "village lights" in Humbert Wolfe's lines noted previously:

> . . . for one lost life that finds in death
> The village lights of Nazareth . . .

The meaningful symbol—the unique picture—is more vital in poetry than the actual denotation of words. Horace, in his *Ars Poetica,* spoke of the *callida junctura* (the warm junction or fortunate blending of words). The *callida junctura* is the indissoluble union between the word and the image, brought about by mental association. It is this combination of words and image that is the basis of all poetry.

Herbert Read uses the word *synthesis* for this type of combination. A synthesis consists in a type of expression at once powerful and unique. In the synthesis the individual words are lost in the combination of which they are a part. Not one word can be altered or taken away without destroying the synthesis. The point in any given verse where the poetry is most distilled constitutes the synthesis—the artistic union of one word, image, and sound with one or more words, images, and sounds.

Consider the use of language in Francis Thompson's "Hound of Heaven." A metaphor featuring a horse—symbol of speed—has been used throughout the poem ("clung to the whistling mane of every wind") to signify the soul's mad, unavailing flight from the pursuer. Eventually, with an intensifying power of suggestion created by the interrelated imagery, a synthesis emerges—

> I knew how the clouds arise
> Spumèd of the wild sea-snortings.

The expression *sea-snortings* is an excellent synthesis, because in it you can see the crystallization of the poem's whole artistic development, in the sense that the image of the speeding horse is now symbolically infused throughout the language, carrying its overtone of the relentlessly pursuing God.

It sometimes happens that a line or two will express the entire poignancy of a poem. Such lines are Milton's description of Adam in *Paradise Lost* (IX, 892-893) when he has learned of Eve's sin:

> From his slack hand the garland wreathed for Eve
> Down dropped, and all the faded roses shed.

The roses here faded with the conscious knowledge of sin. The poet achieves a clever use of the pathetic fallacy (the assumption that nonhuman nature is capable of sharing the moods and thoughts of man).

The greatest syntheses in poetry result from the wedding of universal meaning with the immediately graspable image, so that from sensory impression we can leap to the exercise of the intelligence which, in a certain sense, is universal and not bound by specific limitations. Such a synthesis is to be found in *Macbeth* (II, ii, 61-62):

> . . . No, this my hand will rather
> The multitudinous seas incarnadine . . .

Incarnadine has the literal and sensory meaning of "to stain blood-red." In the context of the play, however, it symbolizes the "universal guilt" of Macbeth's deed in killing the King. The enormity of Macbeth's crime is suggested through the mental association of the total synthesis, *the-multitudinous-seas-incarnadine* (it might logically be written in this way as one hyphenated word).

But syntheses are not all on a level in regard to their depths of meaning, though all are concrete, compressed, symbolic statements. The general discourse or context of the poem, however, will tend to determine their intellectual depth. In Keats' "Isabella," the two brothers who have determined to kill Isabella's lover are thus described:

> So the two brothers and their murder'd man
>   Rode past fair Florence . . .

The use of the word "murder'd" here is distinctly poetic and synthetic, but it is a descriptive compression rather than a penetrating symbol. In the same stanza is to be noticed the effective use of the word *quiet,* which forms a total synthesis with *for the slaughter:*

> . . . They pass'd the water
> Into a forest quiet for the slaughter.

The word *quiet* is uniquely adapted and united to *slaughter.* Keats is not giving us any cosmic meaning, but he is giving us dramatic and ironic overtone. "Murder'd" is a compression of the situation—"whom they intend to murder." It is not a penetrating symbol in the sense of the "hand" in the previous quotation from *Macbeth.*

Syntheses might logically be written as one expression. Poets frequently coin words, without hesitation and without apology to the dictionary. Note Keats's invention of "deep-damask'd" in these lines from "The Eve of St. Agnes":

> Innumerable of stains and splendid dyes,
> As are the tiger-moth's deep-damask'd wings . . .

Damask, a noun, is given the form of a past participle, and is then blended with the adverb, *deep.* Keats uses language very freely here. A beginner should be more discreet. But this tendency toward synthesis, even in word coinage, is natural in poetry.

Experiment

Note the italicized syntheses employing verbal liberties in the following [14] quotations.

(1) The carved angels, ever *eager-eyed,*
     Stared, where upon their heads the cornice rests . . .

(2) Authority forgets a dying king,
     Laid *widow'd* of the power in his eye.

(3) They clanged his chariot 'thwart a heaven,
     Plashy with flying lightnings round the *spurn o' their feet.*

(4) . . . and for lightning see
     Black fire and horror shot with equal rage
     Among his Angels . . .

(5) . . . for thou art
     As glorious to this night, being o'er my head,
     As is a winged messenger of heaven
     Unto the *white-upturned* wondering eyes
     Of mortals that fall back to gaze on him . . .

THE DISCOURSE OF POETRY—A REVIEW

Though you have noted several of the distinctions between poetry and creative prose, you may not yet know clearly what poetry *is.* Poetry is a synthetic creation; it fuses diverse elements into a new whole, so that the newly created unity, in scientific terms, is a compound and not a mixture.

For example, let us take a phrase from Milton: "the in-

[14] Taken, in order, from the following: (1) Keats, "The Eve of St. Agnes"; (2) Tennyson, "The Passing of Arthur"; (3) Thompson, "The Hound of Heaven"; (4) Milton, *Paradise Lost;* (5) Shakespeare, *Romeo and Juliet.*

cense-breathing air." The three words, *incense, breathing,* and *air,* are fused into poetry, and we have a creation which we realize exists but which only Milton has named. Each word is part of the poetry. Not a single word could be subtracted without destroying the whole effect.

Let us take a longer example of what might be called "pure" poetry, which would be recognized as such apart from its context—as distinct from circumstantial or dramatic poetry. The lines are from Shakespeare's Sonnet 73:

> That time of year thou mayst in me behold
> When yellow leaves, or none, or few, do hang
> Upon those boughs which shake against the cold,
> Bare ruined choirs where late the sweet birds sang.

What is Shakespeare giving us in these four lines? He gives us two pictures: (1) the picture of an almost denuded autumn tree about to lose its leaves before the oncoming winds of winter; (2) the picture of a tree abandoned by the birds, like a monastery abandoned by its members (Shakespeare feels the pathos of the destruction of such institutions, an event which occurred in his own time)—so abandoned that not even birds (characteristic of the joyful English countryside) sing there. The branches are compared in their near-winter desolation to the crumbling cloisters.

Is there any logical connection between these two pictures? How does the last line manage to fit in with the first three?

The fact is that these two pictures are images or symbols. They have a poetical connection—a symbolical, but not an expository, bond. The first picture symbolizes the old age of the poet. The second picture symbolizes the loneliness and abandonment of the poet.

In functional prose Shakespeare might have said of himself that he was advanced in years, that he had not long to live, that his hopes had perished, and that he lacked the consolations of friendship. In prose, the significance and connection of the information are paramount. In poetry, it is the meaningful symbol, the unique picture, the particular combination of words that are chiefly important.

Shakespeare conveyed by poetic means a vivid suggestion of sadness and pathos, economically and directly, without any of the slower, step-by-step processes of prose. Poetry is colorful, concrete, symbolic.

Poetry contrives to be direct and convincing, because the poet employs language for its symbolic value. He employs words not just for their obvious meaning, but for their traditional literary associations and musical and pictorial effects.

Connotation, too, plays a more important part in poetry than in creative prose. The connotation of a word is its "mental association." Some mental associations are highly individualistic and unpredictable. But connotations or mental associations do not have any exact limits as far as the individual mind is concerned.

An amusing account of a lecture given by T. S. Eliot at the University of Chicago illustrates the way in which the discourse of poetry, so dependent upon mental association, works. As long as basic intellectual meaning has been communicated, mental association is free, as T. S. Eliot's tolerant attitude shows, to take many diverse forms.

Readers of poetry are different from readers of philosophy: they are more apt to draw conclusions that the poet never intended. "You know," said Eliot in a confidential digression, "in one of my poems I use the words 'the spectre of a Rose.' Now, I intended that to refer to the Wars of the Roses. Then I wanted it to hint of Sir Thomas Browne's famous 'ghost of a Rose' . . . But I was also quite pleased to hear that some people thought it referred to Nijinski (and the ballet associated with him)." Nobody had any trouble following such poet's wordplay, so Eliot continued with more confidences—this time about the young man in *The Love Song of J. Alfred Prufrock* ("I grow old. . . . I grow old. . . . I shall wear the bottoms of my trousers rolled"). "The young man in *Prufrock*," said Eliot, "is meant to signify someone young and sportive and a man conscious of growing old."

Broke in a girl in the seminar: "I have always thought the rolled trousers meant an old man who could not swim and had to wade, kind of."

Said Eliot: "If it suits you that way, then that is all right with me." [15]

Do not be tempted, because of the variation in mental association, to assume that poetry may mean anything to anybody. Poetry has its framework of stability; within that framework there may well be an unpredictability of meaning, something that may have a very personal interpretation for each reader, something that is indefinite, not in the sense of lacking in meaning, but rather in not having fixed and ascertainable limits. There are traditional mental associations, as well as highly personal ones. H. W. Garrod remarks upon the literary associations of words as follows:

No word, but as it beats upon the mind's ear, carries, not merely in meaning, but in the mere sound of it, infinite varieties of association. It comes, not merely with the sound of itself, but with waifs, with errant glories, from all the sound-contexts and all the meaning-contexts with which ever in speech or in song it has been associated.[16]

John Livingston Lowes once remarked that "it is the successful blending of the undefined and definite in words that constitute the triumph of the poet's art."

Poetry is much more than a conglomeration of beautiful sounds or pleasing images. It offers the special kind of knowledge that is characteristic of creative art—knowledge that arises from making something based on experience. Because poetry, in a technical sense, is predominantly characterized by intuition and imagination, it has an imagistic form of knowledge to offer that is no less valuable than the more strictly conceptual and "intellectual" knowledge of creative

[15] Courtesy of *Time*, copyright Time, Inc., 1950.
[16] H. W. Garrod, *The Study of Poetry*, Oxford University Press, 1936, p. 54.

prose. We shall next examine what this special knowledge is. To form some idea of it is useful to you either in writing or appreciating poetry.

POETIC KNOWLEDGE

You can easily see that there is a field of knowledge and experience that does not fall primarily within the conceptual-logical field. It is one thing to say: "It was a beautiful sunset"; it is quite another thing to *transfer* your experience of the sunset so that another person can really share it. Such a statement is purely on a conceptual level; it communicates ideas, but not *experience*. Henley's lines are expressed on a different level—the imagistic:

> . . . the sun,
> Closing his benediction,
> Sinks, and the darkening air
> Thrills with a sense of the triumphant night.

You might perceive intensely the beauty of a flower; you might desire to communicate the experience of that perception. How is this communication to take place? The physical reaction, the peculiar color, the fragrance are, as such, incommunicable. Words cannot transfer the exact experience, yet the poet is determined as a creator and communicator of experience to do this very thing. He has no concepts in the usual sense of the word, if by a concept we mean a clear conception that can be expressed in any of several choices of adequate vocabulary. Now, when a sudden analogy (metaphor, simile) comes to him intuitively, he is able to express his experience of the flower. This analogy is the result of creative act, of making an object (poem). It is imagistic knowledge. It is not the result of choosing to illustrate a concept through a choice of suitable similitudes (rhetoric). Take, for example, these lines from Humbert Wolfe's *The Uncelestial City:*

> . . . snow-drops, nun-like, flawless, crisp,
> Less flowers, than a little gasp
> of white astonishment.

Flawless, crisp are adjectives applied in a subordinate conceptual way, but suddenly the experience is born and transferred into art by a symbolic image:

> Less flowers, than a little gasp
> Of white astonishment.

Paradoxically, in spite of the statement that they are "less flowers," they are, in fact, *more* flowers to us than ever before—when they cease to be snow-drops, and become a "gasp of white astonishment."

We may say that we really know the flower-experience of the poet once we see it as *something else.* That is why mental association becomes so important in creative writing. Mental association provides us with that *something else.* The flower has also become a symbol of the transcendent values that illustrate it—the "nun-like, flawless, crisp," the mystic wonderment of universal innocence.

Poetry is expression; poetic knowledge is "knowledge *expressed.*" But the poet in expressing an experienced knowledge of an object must present it in terms of something else, and, in so doing, by a catalytic [17] agency he touches the world of intuition, the world of universals, so that the transcendent values are expressed in the snow-drop and yet the snow-drop is even more flower-like than before.

Strangely, the transcendent values actually enable us to see the concreteness of the flower. We see its "itness," if you like, when our minds have glimpsed the universals connected with it.

The catalytic agency in poetry is an amazing thing, and it is not easy to explain in rationalistic terms. The thing be-

[17] The *American College Dictionary* defines *catalysis*: "The causing or accelerating of a chemical change by the addition of a substance (*catalyst*) which is not permanently affected by the reaction."

held, the image of the *snow-drops,* remains unchanged, yet it has brought about the great synthesis of meaning that we have described. This is truly the function of a catalyst which, we are told in science, may be recovered intact at the end of a reaction.

A natural consequence of the way in which poetic knowledge works is the type of image found in the *simile* and the *metaphor.* Through simile, one thing, relation, or idea is explicitly compared to something else. A metaphor is more succinct than simile and the comparison is implicit rather than explicit. A simile would state that a ship goes through the water "like a plow through a field." A metaphor would state that the "ship plows the water."

What is important creatively about the simile and metaphor is the use of the mental association whereby the meaning of the original idea is extended imaginatively. The mind is led to think imagistically as well as intellectually. Every figure of speech extends the original meaning of the idea through the concreteness of mental association. Intellectually, one thinks of the ship moving through the water at a certain speed. When we "image" the ship as "plowing through a field," we also see in visual terms the slow stubborn resistance to the plow, and the plow's strength and its inevitability as the furrow is cut. The more compact, "synthetic" in our sense of the word, the greater the impact of the figure of speech. But even a purely decorative simile, sometimes even worked into a complete picture in itself as in the case of the famous "Homeric simile," enriches material by creating mood and atmosphere. The "Homeric simile" extends the imagistic picture beyond the mere point of comparison. *A* might be compared to *B* from the point of view of running. This is the end of the actual comparison, but then the poet goes on to describe *B* in its complete setting—with the dust of the track, the shouts of the onlookers, the colorful costumes, the clouds and the sunlight.

Note how the meaning of Vaughan's line, "I saw eternity

the other night," is both extended and clarified by the subsequent simile:

> Like a great ring of pure and endless light,
>   All calm as it was bright.

The simile here gives something firm for the mind to associate with the difficult and abstract idea of "eternity."

A metaphor of Vaughan's indicates the somewhat more
compressed effect of this type of figure. Poets cannot always
prefer metaphors to similes, because the greater difficulty of
the metaphor may create an obscurity which does not support
the poet's purpose. The metaphor of "jewel" in these lines
is sufficiently difficult to excite interest, without causing confusion.

> Dear, beauteous death! the jewel of the just,
>   Shining nowhere but in the dark . . .

Note the completely successful transference of the personality of the woman merely by means of two images here, one
a metaphor, the other a simile, in the lines of Wordsworth:

> A violet by a mossy stone
> Half-hidden from the eye!
> —Fair as a star, when only one
> Is shining in the sky.

In Byron's "The Destruction of Sennacherib," are similes,
decorative rather than intellectually profound, that serve to
create "mood" and "atmosphere."

> The Assyrian came down like the wolf on the fold,
> And his cohorts were gleaming in purple and gold;
> And the sheen of their spears was like stars on the sea,
> When the blue wave rolls nightly on deep Galilee.

In the Homeric simile, the point of the comparison is elab-
orated into a complete picture which is contemplated and
enjoyed for itself. Both Homer and Virgil are famous for the
complete pictorial images which create "mood" and "atmos-

phere" by imaging for us a complete physical experience. Thus Homer says in Book V of the *Iliad:*

Even as a wind carrieth the chaff about the sacred threshing-floors when men are winnowing, what time golden-haired Demeter in rush of wind maketh division of grain and chaff, and so the chaff-heaps grow white—so now grew the Achaians white with falling dust which in the midst the horses' hooves beat up into brazen heaven, as fight was joined again, and the charioteers wheeled round.

And Virgil, in Book IV of the *Aeneid,* describes the preparations of the warriors of Aeneas for their departure from Carthage:

One might descry them shifting their quarters and pouring out of all the town: even as the ants, mindful of winter plunder a great heap of wheat and store it in their house; a black column advances on the plain as they carry home their spoil on a narrow track through the grass. Some shove and strain with their shoulders at big grains, some marshal the ranks and chastise delay; All the path is aswarm with work.

PRELIMINARIES TO WRITING POETRY

In order to write "poetry" and "creative prose" as well, you must realize, first, that the power of creative writing lies in *inner* form. It is not found in its surface form. You may put aside, for the moment, meter, rhyme, and traditional poetic arrangements. Of course, you must not overlook the real usefulness of these devices. But they are *not essential* to poetry. For the person who is beginning to write poetry, they are frequently definite hindrances. Unless they are handled carefully, they may set up a false taste, a bad rhetoric, and devitalize poetic power. Free verse is the best means in the early stages of creative writing for encouraging freedom of expression and strong, connotative imagery. By *free verse* is meant a type of verse in which the line corresponds, not to a fixed metrical pattern, but to a unit of vocal de-livery, determined at will by the emotional or intellectual emphasis which the writer seeks to impose. If you want to write poetry, you must above all not associate poetry with an obvious kind of bangy rhythm, upon whose measured waves sails a sterile and hackneyed rhetoric.

Second, you must realize the value of the image. The image is so important in poetry that in the late nineteenth century we had a definite school of "imagistic" poets who subordinated all other poetic values to that of the image. In poetry, however, reflection, exposition, even argumenta-tion, may enter in a subordinate way and actually enrich the poem. But the image is to poetry what exposition, connec-tion, argumentation are to prose. It is to be remembered that images fulfill different values, from the merely decora-tive to the deeply compressed and symbolic.

The use of the image in creative prose is to provide con-creteness, definiteness in the style, particularly effective in the short story. It often serves to concentrate emotion, to create an abrupt and powerful shock. But in creative prose the image is subordinated to considerations of expository and logical relationships.

The material of your writing is anything that you can suc-cessfully handle. It is impossible to generalize about the raw material of creative writing. Poets, for example, have touched upon practically everything. Nevertheless, the pre-dominant themes of creative writers have been the main climactic points in human experience: birth, marriage, con-flict, war, death. Creative writers like to deal with the aspect of these subjects that contains "fruitful mystery" and remains still to be explored by the individual experience of men. The basic subject matter of creative writing is not, therefore, primarily what you know through reason. It is that half-glimpsed knowledge which you attempt to penetrate and which is least reducible to exposition.

As preliminaries to your own actual writing of poetry, you

should briefly consider the problems of poetic diction, word-order in poetry, metrical pattern in poetry, the artistic value of formalized patterns, the use of the imagination, the stimulation of your powers of mental association. A discussion of these points follows.

POETIC DICTION

The thesis has often been put forward that poetry has a diction of its own distinct from that of prose. Wordsworth, in reaction to such ideas, took the viewpoint, in his Preface to the *Lyrical Ballads,* that there was a common vocabulary for both poetry and prose:

And it would be an easy task to prove . . . that not only the language of a large portion of every good poem, even of the utmost elevated character, must necessarily, except with reference to the meter, in no respect differ from that of good prose, but likewise that some of the most interesting parts of the best poems will be found to be strictly the language of prose when prose is well written. . . . It may be safely affirmed, that there neither is, nor can be, any essential difference between the language of prose and metrical composition.

Coleridge, in *Biographia Literaria,* revised Wordsworth's theories considerably. He pointed out, for example, that the language of a poet like Milton is not the language of prose or of the merely good speaker of English. It is a specific creation of the poet Milton. It is a "generic and ideal" language constituting an aesthetic creation. But Coleridge's emendation does not support the thesis of a *special* vocabulary for poetry.

There is no distinct vocabulary for poetry. In fact, whenever a special diction has been set up, it has rapidly become dated, as in some of the verse of the eighteenth century. But it may be clearly shown, on the other hand, that poetry uses words in a different way from that of prose, though the *same* words themselves are used. Words in poetry are symbolical and representational; in prose they are logical and analytical. Because of the symbolic value of words in poetry, even the word order is important, just as in the religious ritual the proper placing of the signs is essential to the meaning and the impact of the symbol as a whole.

John Livingston Lowes suggests that

if the imaginative energy is strong enough, almost no word can remain insoluble, and a flat denial of poetic possibilities, in the case of any vocable, is liable to disastrous refutation by a triumphant "poeticizing" of that very word.[18]

He goes on to point out how limited seem the possibilities of the word "intrinsicate." Yet Shakespeare introduced it into magnificent poetry in these dying words of Cleopatra:

> . . . Come, thou mortal wretch,
> With thy sharp teeth this knot intrinsicate
> Of life at once untie.

WORD ORDER IN POETRY

Poetry, in the specific sense, like all art aims at emotional impact. This impact often depends on an orchestration that leads up to the climactic use of a particular word. Take, for example, the line, "Blooms again the broad blue flower of day." The effect of movement, of surprise, of broadening grandeur, depends on the position of *blooms* as first in the line. Placed in another position, the word will fail to win the emotional impact it has here. Note how flat the reverse order would be: "The broad blue flower of day blooms again." The line now suggests boredom rather than dramatic impact.

The following lines afford a relevant illustration of the impact of word order in poetry:

[18] John Livingston Lowes, *Convention and Revolt in Poetry*, Boston, Houghton Mifflin, 1919, p. 189.

Over the breast of the spring, the land, amid cities,
Amid lanes and through old woods, where lately the violets
    peeped
from the ground, spotting the gray debris,
Amid the grass in the fields each side of the lanes,
    passing the endless grass,
Passing the yellow-speared wheat, every grain from its shroud in
    the dark-brown fields uprisen,
Passing the apple-tree blows of white and pink in the orchards,
Carrying a corpse to where it shall rest in the grave,
Night and day journeys a coffin.[19]

This passage is directed toward the emotional climax suggested by the word *coffin*. The whole of the setting, skilfully
vivid, is closely identified ("every grain from its shroud in
the dark-brown fields uprisen") with death by the method
of suggestion and of symbolism. The whole of nature seems
to bear the weight and momentousness of the coffin. The
writer isolates by his symbols the essential fact, the death of
the man for whom all mourn as one. To speak profanely, we
are made to feel that there is only one coffin in the world of
any importance.

Whitman is not primarily appealing to our reason. His
intention is to make us feel the emotional weight of the occasion. He is making a direct appeal to our emotions through
imagery, especially through the symbolism of the word *coffin*.

The word *coffin* is a unique poetic expression in Whitman's poem by reason of its *placement*. It only accidentally
means what is usually meant by a coffin. Rather, here it is a
symbol of the abrupt tragedy that is passing over the surface
of the earth. But the word would not contain this suggestive
power if it were not for the preceding elements fused with it.

To illustrate this point, it is interesting to see what happens when the word coffin is transferred to the first line:

Night and day journeys a coffin
Carrying a corpse to where it shall rest in the grave,

[19] Walt Whitman, "When Lilacs Last in the Dooryard Bloom'd."

Over the breast of the spring, the land, amid cities,
Amid lanes and through old woods . . .

The subsequent expressions here simply give the itinerary of the coffin, and it seems to be somewhat like a commercial bus taking a detour.

METRICAL PATTERN IN POETRY

Following the distinctions made between poetry and creative prose, we should not consider poetry essentially dependent upon meter or "fixed rhythm." All language, in fact, has rhythm. But metrical form consists in a special pattern of repeated rhythms.

For example, in what light are we to consider the great psalms of David? They are obviously poetry, but they do not possess a metrical pattern in the usual sense of the word.

By the rivers of Babylon,
There we sat down, yea, we wept,
When we remembered Zion.
Upon the willows in the midst thereof
We hanged our harps.
For there they that led us captive required of us songs,
And they that wasted us required of us mirth, saying,
Sing us one of the songs of Zion.
How shall we sing Jehovah's song
In a foreign land?
If I forget thee, O Jerusalem,
Let my right hand forget her skill.
Let my tongue cleave to the roof of my mouth,
If I remember thee not;
If I prefer not Jerusalem
Above my chief joy.

For a modern example, we may take Whitman. Consider these few lines, and ask yourself whether it is not possible for the highest lyricism—and by that we mean the highest lyricism from the point of view *of music*—to be obtained without any regular metrical pattern at all.

Soothe! Soothe! Soothe!
Close on its wave soothes the wave behind,
And again another behind embracing and lapping, every one
    close,
But my love soothes not me, not me.

Low hangs the moon, it rose late,
It is lagging—O I think it is heavy with love, with love,

O madly the sea pushes upon the land,
With love, with love.

O night! do I not see my love fluttering out among the breakers?
What is that little black thing I see there in the white?

Loud! Loud! Loud!
Loud I call to you, my love!
High and clear I shout my voice over the waves,
Surely you must know who I am, my love.

Low-hanging moon!
What is that dusky spot in your brown yellow?

It is difficult to appreciate the beauty of Whitman's rhythm in a short extract, because his structure, like that of the psalms, is symphonic. Free rhythms are very suitable for what we might call architectonic poetry. Even a classical writer such as Milton loved the freer forms. Yet, Milton felt that he had to make some defense of his use of blank verse, and his disregard of rhyme:

The measure is English heroic verse without rime, as that of Homer in Greek, and of Virgil in Latin—rime being no necessary adjunct or true ornament of poem or good verse, in longer works especially, but the invention of a barbarous age, to set off wretched matter and lame metre; graced indeed since by the use of famous modern poets, carried away by custom, but much to their own vexation, hindrance, and constraint to express many things otherwise, and for the most part worse, than else they would have expressed them.

He went even further in practice and was on the point of approaching the *free verse* of today in his *Samson Agonistes,* although he still adheres to an "iambic" undercurrent in the rhythm. The following extract indicates the direction that Milton was taking in his latest work.

The Sun to me is dark
And silent as the Moon,
When she deserts the night,
Hid in her vacant interlunar cave.
Since light so necessary is to life,
And almost life itself, if it be true
That light is in the soul.
She all in every part, why was the sight
To such a tender ball as the eye confined,
So obvious and so easy to be quenched,
And not, as feeling, through all parts diffused,
That she might look at will through every pore?
Then had I not been thus exiled from light,
As in the land of darkness, yet in light.
To live a life half dead, a living death,
And buried; but, O yet more miserable!
Myself my sepulchre, a moving grave;
Buried, yet not exempt,
By privilege of death and burial,
From worst of other evils, pains, and wrongs;
But made hereby obnoxious more
To all the miseries of life,
Life in captivity
Among inhuman foes.

In our own day, when so much of our finest poetry is written in free verse, we are forced to depart from the traditional assumption that meter, in the sense of a *regular* metrical pattern, is an essential of poetry. In fact, we realize that free verse is in itself a very adequate form of poetic expression. The following poem, leading economically to its quiet and relentless climax, gains its power from the fact that each part of the structure carries the necessary weight of meaning without being in any way forced by adherence to meter.

> A late lark twitters from the quiet skies;
> And from the west,
> Where the sun, his day's work ended,
> Lingers as in content,
> There falls on the old, gray city
> An influence luminous and serene,
> A shining peace.
>
> The smoke ascends
> In a rosy-and-golden haze. The spires
> Shine and are changed. In the valley
> Shadows rise. The lark sings on. The sun,
> Closing his benediction,
> Sinks, and the darkening air
> Thrills with a sense of the triumphant night—
>
> So be my passing!
> My task accomplished and the long day done,
> My wages taken, and in my heart
> Some late lark singing,
> Let me be gathered to the quiet west,
> The sundown splendid and serene,
> Death.[20]

Free verse, merely because it is *free*, demands particular restraint and judgment to obtain its greatest effects. In other words, the sense of form, of control, does not depend upon any external and fixed pattern. The form must be imposed by the writer himself. In this matter, Coleridge's distinction between "mechanic" and "organic" form is relevant.

The form is mechanic, when on any given material we impress a predetermined form, not necessarily arising out of the properties of the material; as when to a mass of wet clay we give whatever shape we wish it to retain when hardened. The organic form, on

[20] Henley, "I.M. Margaritae Sorori."

the other hand, is innate; it shapes, as it develops, itself from within, and the fullness of its development is one and the same with the perfection of its outward form. Such as the life is, such is the form.

Many of the great passages of the Bible, particularly the psalms, offer important free verse structures, as in the extract quoted earlier. Ideological contrasts, irony, dramatic tension (see Peter Glickert's "Cosmopolis," p. 313) are particularly well conveyed through the medium of free verse. In free verse you have to devise your own sense of emphasis. The emphasis can be at the end of lines, or lines can be run on, with the emphasis coming in the next line or in a single isolated word.

The rhythms of free verse are very close to the rhythms of good natural speech. Each line corresponds to a unit of vocal delivery. Thus, in "Margaritae Sorori," Henley, in his special sense of emphasis, makes the climactic word *death* one line, just as he makes the much longer statement "thrills with a sense of the triumphant night" one line.

Free verse demands modulation, cadence, economy, and climax. Looking at Henley's lines, one sees:

(1) *modulation*—"a transition from one key to another." Note the abrupt and broken effect of the following lines; note how the transitions, through constant interruption, suggest impetuous movement:

> The smoke ascends
> In a rosy-and-golden haze. The spires
> Shine and are changed. In the valley
> Shadows rise. The lark sings on. The sun, . . .

(2) *cadence*—"the fall of the voice as in speaking." Note the change in tempo after *content:*

> . . . the sun, his day's work ended,
> Lingers as in content,
> There falls on the old, gray city

An influence luminous and serene,
A shining peace.

(3) *economy*—in the sense of nothing wasted or extraneous, as in the climactic word *death* at the end of the poem:

The sundown splendid and serene,
Death.

(4) *climax*—the phrase of culminative importance, even if it is as brief as one word, has a line to itself:

There falls on the old, gray city
An influence luminous and serene,
A shining peace.

In writing free verse, it is important to avoid the inversions sometimes necessary in rhymed metrical verse. In free verse there is no necessity to force the order of words to obtain rhymes, and one of the beauties of free verse is destroyed when it echoes technical devices of rhymed verse. Note the inversions below:

To this dealer in the souls of men
who, allured by *power incredible,*
blinded by *concupiscence unbridled,*
snatches at the infinite.

This passage improves by the use of normal word order:

To this dealer in the souls of men
who, allured by incredible power,
blinded by unbridled concupiscence,
snatches at the infinite.

Never introduce rhyme into free verse in an obtrusive way that reminds the reader of formal metrical patterns.

Poor

Have you ever stopped and listened
to the sounds made by winter?

The sounds that walk along with you from the station?
The crunch of the snow and the rattle of the trees?
The music of the icicles snapping in the breeze.

Improvement

Have you ever stopped and listened
to the sounds made by winter?
The sounds that walk along with you from the station?
The sound of crunching snow and rattling tree
The music of an icicle snapped in the wind.

Experiment

A student took the following report from *Time* magazine and recast it into free verse. How adequate do you think the result is? Try a similar experiment of your own.

There are scenes in which its storytelling is brilliant. A Polish railway junction rises up slowly as an opening flower to meet a diving Nazi plane; and across this landscape moves the shadow, slow and angular as a windmill, of the plane's propeller. From the air Warsaw and Rotterdam lie naked and intricate as ripped honeycombs. On the unwounded streets of Brussels, occupation imposes its frostlike patterns of order. A bombed cathedral spire shifts a little at its base, hangs intact a half second and, with the slow gesture of a great dancer, reluctantly stoops almost vertically into its dust. Flames for which hollowed buildings are the flues roar like blowtorches. Day & night, guns deafen or blind the screen, jab and recoil with the wild delicateness of cats' paws or snakes' heads.

A Polish railway junction rises up
slowly as an opening flower
to meet a diving Nazi plane;
and across this landscape
moves the shadow,
slow and angular as a windmill,
of the plane's propeller.

From the air
Warsaw and Rotterdam lie naked and intricate
as ripped honeycombs.

On the unwounded streets of Brussels,
occupation
imposes its frostlike patterns of order.

A bombed cathedral spire
shifts a little at its base,
hangs intact a half second and,
with the slow gesture of a great dancer,
reluctantly stoops
almost vertically into its dust.

Flames
for which hollowed buildings
are the flues
roar like blowtorches.

Day and night
guns deafen or blind the screen,
jab and recoil with the wild delicateness
of cats' paws
or snakes' heads.   ——A. M.

THE ARTISTIC VALUE OF FORMALIZED PATTERNS

Creative activity develops your taste and intelligence. In the process of your development, however, you are frequently obliged to proceed step by step. The principles and exercises in the section of the book dealing with poetry do not stress the formal patterns of traditional verse, because we are thinking of poetry here, not in its most highly refined or technical aspects, but as the key to all creative writing, including creative prose as well. The approach you take to creativity should not be mechanical. Rather, you should think of *form* as the shape of what you say. You should not think of the shape, and then tailor your material to fit the shape. But in rejecting the narrowness of formalized approaches to creativity, we do not wish to overlook the possibility that for a particular writer a traditional form may well be such a matter of second nature to him that it actually helps him toward the conceiving and executing of a work.

First of all, it is a proved fact that an artist, in meeting the demands of a rigid form, is often compelled to take extra pains so that his work has the extra tension, tautness of "difficulty overcome." It is, of course, possible to meet the requirements of a rigid form by dilution—the addition of extra wordage, illustration to fill out meter and rhyme requirements. The first approach indicates the right use of traditional form; the second, the wrong use. Keats, in "The Eve of St. Agnes," first wrote these lines:

> Sudden a thought more rosy than the rose
> Flush'd his young cheek and in his painfle heart
> . . . riot fierce . . .

Keats's second version, an improvement, ran as follows:

> Sudden a rosy thought
> Heated his brow and in his painfle heart
> Made purple riot . . .

Constantly struggling with the form, Keats eventually evolved these great, tense lines:

> Sudden a thought came like a full-blown rose,
> Flushing his brow, and in his pained heart
> Made purple riot . . .

The "full-blown rose" as an image expressing *action* ("came") is a magnificent image, suggesting color in violent and fluid moving, passionate and beautiful. It was not exactly spontaneous, however; it arose from difficulty overcome.

"Difficulty overcome" must not destroy spontaneity; it must merely canalize spontaneity. We are told in Dorothy Wordsworth's *Journal* that "William tired himself seeking an epithet for the cuckoo." It is well to seek, but creativity seldom issues from tiredness, from forcing oneself to meet the required form. On the other hand, it is undoubtedly true that some of the great statements in poetry have been the result of "the happy guidance of a rhyme."

We must not think of traditional forms as static. Great traditional work has a great deal of variety and tension within a settled order. Art, as will be indicated in the section on beauty, often presents a harmony that, as Coleridge would say, is a reconciliation of opposites, or "discordant qualities."

We have said that a fixed metrical pattern is not essential to poetry, but it may be *essential* to a *specific* poem. The poem is a thing that is made—it is what it is. The finished product is a whole and all that enters into its unity is essential to it. But metrical pattern is not essential in the sense that it must be characteristic of *all* poetry. In this sense, Edgar Allan Poe exaggerated when he said that poetry was "musical thought."

Aldous Huxley illustrates the danger of making poetry too "poetical" in the common sense of that term.

It is when Poe tries to make it too poetical that his poetry takes on its peculiar tinge of badness. Protesting too much that he is a gentleman, and opulent into the bargain, he falls into vulgarity. Diamond rings on every finger proclaim the parvenu. Consider, for example, the first two stanzas of "Ulalume."

> The skies they were ashen and sober;
> The leaves they were crisped and sere—
> The leaves they were withering and sere;
> It was night in the lonesome October
> Of my most immemorial year;
> It was hard by the dim lake of Auber,
> In the misty mid region of Weir—

It was down by the dank tarn of Auber
In the ghoul-haunted woodland of Weir.

Here once, through an alley Titanic,
Of cypress, I roamed with my soul,
Of cypress, with Psyche my soul.
These were the days when my soul was volcanic
As the scoriac rivers that roll—
As the lavas that restlessly roll
Their sulphurous currents down Yaanek
In the ultimate climb of the pole—
That groan as they roll down Mount Yaanek
In the realms of the boreal pole.

These lines protest too much (and with what a variety of voices!) that they are poetical, and, protesting, are therefore vulgar. To start with, the walloping dactyllic metre is all too musical. Poetry ought to be musical, but musical with tact, subtly and variously. Metres whose rhythms, as in this case, are strong, insistent and practically invariable offer the poet a kind of short cut to musicality. They provide him (my subject calls for a mixture of metaphors) with a ready-made, reach-me-down music. He does not have to create a music appropriately modulated to his meaning; all he has to do is to shovel the meaning into moving stream of the metre and allow the current to carry it along on waves that, like those of the best hairdressers, are guaranteed permanent.[21]

Huxley recasts the dignified lines of Milton, where music and sense go together appropriately, into the flashy vulgarity of Poe's rhythm:

Milton
Like that fair field
Of Enna, where Proserpine gathering flowers,
Herself a fairer flower, by gloomy Dis
Was gathered, which cost Ceres all that pain
To see her through the world.

[21] Aldous Huxley, *Vulgarity in Literature*, New York, Harper, 1940, pp. 27-31.

Poe

> It was noon in the fair field of Enna,
> Where Proserpina gathering flowers—
> Herself the most fragrant of flowers,
> Was gathered away to Gehenna
>   By the Prince of Plutonian powers;
> Was borne down the windings of Brenner
>   To the gloom of his amorous bowers—
> Down the tortuous highway of Brenner
>   To the god's agapemonous bowers.

It is important in the use of metrical forms that the emphasis in the writing grow *justly* from the expression. Inversions or unassimilated phrases to fill out the meter destroy the efficiency of the discourse. The following student poem achieves dramatic effect by breaking regularity at climactic points, particularly at the word *insane*. The last line brings the discourse to a quiet close, without in any way lessening its tension.

> Through the apple-soaked meadows
> And knee-high grass
> She runs and laughs in strained delight,
> This child with the soft, brown-haloed hair
> Tossed back in the misty meadow-light,
> Pulled back like a sparrow's speckled wings . . .
> How strange she sings!
> Let's watch her pass.
>
> How white and thin and fast she moves
> Who searches for the fevered loves
> Of mountain rivers in the dawn;
> Her mind, a freckled faun, is gone
> Insane . . .
> As wild as rain
> Let loose upon the meadowlands,
> This child of want with star-starved eyes,
> A stormy passion reined too tight,
> Broke loose in thunder-smitten laughter,

Laughter like the rain at night,
Secret, shrill and impotent.

She claws and clutches at her skirt
And scrambles over the broken wall,
Her cotton-stockinged, skinny legs
Wet to the knee from the meadow grass
Are stuck with burrs and scratched by thorn
That bridges the gap in the old stone wall;
The rain, as cold as bitter scorn,
It seems will never cease to fall.

—H. O'R.

There are a number of weaknesses in this composition, but it is good in its free use of rhyme and in its dramatic sense. The following student exercise is conventional in thought, but it gains strength and impact from its formality.

Endymion, did you, too, once lie at night
   Upon a green moss-covered hill
And search among the brightest of the stars
   For your beloved, who was brighter still?
Did you, too, yearn to touch the sky—
   To lift love's golden goblet high
Which Artemis alone could fill?

Did the heart within you ache, Endymion,
   Until it seemed too much to bear?
Did your own mortality oppress you
   And helplessness become a gaping snare?
Tell me the night did this to you
And that you stretched your hands out, too—
   Reaching for moon-dust in the air.

—J. C.

In an appendix to this book English metrical forms are separately outlined. It is wise, however, in the early part of your training to follow the procedures set down here which are primarily designed to release and cultivate the imaginative powers of the mind.

POETRY AND RHETORIC

Since poetry (and, to a lesser degree, creative prose) exercises its peculiar power through the symbolic image, your problem in *writing* a poem, as distinct from *appreciating* a poem, consists in creating the image based on mental association and building up the synthesis that depends on it.

General experience indicates that the greatest poetry results from a fusion of a powerful universal concept, basically intellectual, with an image that is the result of distinct, personal associations and which therefore tends to be unusually concrete and even unique. Notice how in the following passage the piling up of concrete images ultimately reinforces the abstract idea and value (the selling of "the souls of men" —a metaphorical commodity with a symbolic meaning) and how the abstract idea ("souls of men") becomes more universal through its "synthetic" relationship to the specific objects of trade associated with it.

And the merchants of the earth will weep and mourn over her; for no one will buy their merchandise any more; merchandise of gold and silver, and precious stones and pearls, and fine linen and purple, and silk and scarlet, and all thyine wood, and all vessels of ivory, and all vessels of precious stone, and of brass, and of iron, and of marble and cinnamon and amomum and spices, and ointment and frankincense, and wine and oil, and fine flour and wheat, and beasts of burden and sheep and horses, and chariots and slaves, and *souls of men.*

Or, for example, examine these lines from Shelley's "Adonais":

> Life, like a dome of many-coloured glass,
> Stains the white radiance of eternity.

In these lines we have concrete color symbolism, whereby whiteness is considered the union of all colors and, therefore, the "mystical" color in which all diversities are united in the oneness of eternity. The "many-colored" glass stands for the separateness of temporal and earthly life. Here, again, we have the fusion of an abstract idea with unique imagery.

Thinking imaginatively should be a natural and instinctive habit. If it were not for certain self-conscious attitudes—inhibitions sometimes produced by too great an emphasis on rationalistic process in education—we would be able to write poetry and creative prose as easily and as fluently as functional prose.

Thinking imaginatively is natural and instinctive, because of the normal tendency of the mind to work through associations (relationships of image to image). Trains of imaginative thought proliferate through "families" of images. The naturally poetic language to be found frequently in children results from unimpeded association whereby one experience is intimately connected with another through the correspondence of images.

The writing of poetry is intimately connected with the use of image, with the imagination as the image-making power of the human mind. In contrast to the intellectual mode of knowledge in which conceptual thinking takes precedence, imaginative process is concerned with the symbolic meaning of the image and its emotional impact.

The power of poetry (and to a lesser degree, creative prose) resides in the image. The effective image must always be individual and unique, because the image is an individuated object, not a general concept. This fact, however, does not prevent the image from reflecting a universal meaning. The symbolism of poetry is such that an individual, single, or partial thing refers to a whole order of things.

If any distinction need to be made between poetry and rhetoric (the method here does not insist on these distinctions), it can be on the basis that, in poetry, the image fulfills its imagistic purpose—we actually contemplate the image. In rhetorical usage, on the other hand, the image is primarily important for its denotation, rather than for those physical aspects of the image which are actually registered on the mental screen and set the imagination aflash, so that it transcends the image and perceives the universal world to which the image-symbol points. Thus, for example, the phrase, "the swirling ocean of adventure," primarily denotes the *conflicting currents* of adventure (abstract idea), whereas the phrase, "the secret immensity of the ocean," stresses the *imagistic* meaning of *ocean,* which, in its synthesis with the intellectual and abstract "secret immensity," then proceeds to *symbolize* rather than *state* conceptual meaning. "Swirling ocean" in the first example stresses, on the other hand, the *conceptual* meaning of *adventure.*

In rhetorical writing, although it is imagistic and emotion-arousing in the manner of poetry, the chief emphasis is analytical. What does the writer mean by "adventure" in the "swirling ocean of adventure"? "Swirling ocean" illustrates the conceptual meaning—the ebb and flow, the unknown element of *adventure.* In the second phrase, "the secret immensity of the ocean," the reader is encouraged to form his own mental associations with the image of *ocean.* Here the appeal is imagistic rather than analytical. It is not so much a matter of what the writer means (denotation), but a matter of the experiences that the reader is encouraged to recall for himself.

Frequently, among the older writers, imagery was used as an external aid or decoration to previously determined material. Imagery was a kind of pleasant frosting to an essential cake. In poetry rather than rhetoric, however, imagery is essential and organic—part of the thought process itself. It is not something unessential that can be applied externally to material that already has achieved its form.

In imaginative writing, especially in poetry, the image and the intellectual perception that goes with it are born and grow together. The image and the thought are organically one. You do not have thought first, then the image. You do not create the image, then pour thought into it. Poetry is not a literary grace or embellishment that is applied from the outside to previously formulated material. It is something that grows from within.

Review Questions

(1) What are the respectively predominant characteristics of poetry and creative prose?

(2) In what ways do the use of words differ in poetry, creative prose, scientific prose?

(3) What is meant by style?

(4) Explain the use of the word *intuition* as applied to art.

(5) What is a symbol?

(6) What is meant by an overtone?

(7) In what sense does the artist's intuition correspond to reality?

(8) In what ways does the imagination connect one with reality?

(9) How does the use of imagery help to make poetry a "concentrated" discourse?

(10) Why does poetic discourse naturally form "syntheses"?

(11) Explain the "catalytic" function of the poetic image.

(12) Is there a specific "poetic" diction?

(13) Why is word order important in poetry?

(14) What is the value of a formalized artistic pattern?

(15) What is the difference between rhetoric and poetry?

Chapter 3

MENTAL ASSOCIATION AT WORK

HARNESSING YOUR POWER OF MENTAL ASSOCIATION

It is evident that, though you may use exposition and perhaps argumentation in a supplementary way in poetry, your basic artistic tools are connotation, suggestiveness—in a word, *mental association.*

Poets and creative writers generally attain much of their emotional and psychological power through connotation. It is through connotation that a great poem gives us the most pointed image, without ever giving us any generalized, explicit surface meaning.

Consequently, you must accustom yourself to the use of mental association if you wish to write poetry or many forms of creative prose. Mental association does not operate haphazardly. It is based upon experience and emotional factors. Actually, you spend comparatively few of your waking hours in logical and expository thought. Most of your time is spent in reviewing images flashed on the mental screen through association. "Day-dreaming"—mental association—is a normal, legitimate part of our experience, but we should know what it means and how to use it. Educational procedures, it is true, emphasize expository and logical thought. But you should not minimize and, under no conditions, should you despise the associative power of your mind. You should cultivate a discipline whereby you can use mental association for the purposes of concrete imagery and metaphor—the basis of the synthesis of poetry.

Fortunately, there is a technique you may employ to regain

the poetic and imagistic power that you probably possessed as a child. This technique depends on harnessing mental association. Psychology and psychiatry employ analogous practices. There is a crude adaptation of it in the "stream of consciousness" school of writing. Only recently, however, have instructors adopted mental association as a normal method with well-defined objectives in education and creative expression. You must bear in mind, of course, that employing free mental association does not imply a sub-rational approach to art. Such association is to be controlled by reason and submitted to the "line of art," or to the law or *logos* that determines the making of an object for a final cause or purpose.

The "line of art" implies the kind of objective control that exists in the very act of making an object what it is. Thus, for example, if you were to make a table, your operations are limited to the extent that a table has a specific function to perform, and this function limits the range of form in which the table may be expressed. The same principle holds in poetry and in all creative writing.

When a synthesis has been achieved, as, for example, in the collective exercises illustrated elsewhere in this book ("the dangerous perfection of the rose"; "hidden in the solitude of night"; "the hungry river shadowing its way toward the settled sadness of the sun"), we may often have an expression, especially in the case of nature associations, that constitutes a special poem in itself. We have in such work the equivalent of Far Eastern practices in art. It is a common custom in China for a person to decorate his house with paper streamers containing isolated pictures or aphorisms that delight the owner because of their power of suggestion and their ability to open new imaginative vistas. A phrase like "the hungry river shadowing its way toward the settled sadness of the sun" absorbs to itself a large area of undetermined meaning which makes it rich material for contemplation, whereas a definite prose statement such as "the Hudson flows into the Atlantic" is exhausted once its information has been perceived.

One of the tests for poetry or creative writing is the question: Is the meaning of the statement exhausted once the denotation has been understood? Or does the statement have the power to constantly renew itself through association? For example, does such a phrase "the secret immensity of the ocean" lead you to further imagery and evolution of ideas? Or has its meaning been absorbed at once?

In creative writing, full resources of mental association and of connotation should be utilized, because from them spring the richness and emotional texture indicative of great art.

Experiment

(1) Contrast the following statements. Which of them are not exhausted when the denotation has been perceived?

(a) The road lies quiet under the tired music of the sunset.

(b) This road leads to Kingsbridge.

(c) This church cost $100,000 to build.

(d) The deserted church meditates alone.

(e) The hero is rationed in agony of blood.

(f) He died in the Battle of the Bulge.

(g) God's mercy cruises its black waters, its unbounded dimensions, the illimitable roar of its immensity.

(h) The ship fought and won a prolonged conflict with the typhoon.

(i) The light of apple blossoms spreads plenitude over earth and grass.

(j) Apples will cost more this autumn.

(2) We know from the manuscript of Milton's poems preserved in the library of Trinity College, Cambridge, that Milton wrote in the earlier draft of "Lycidas":

> the cowslip wan that hangs the pensive head
> and every bud that sorrows liverie weares

In the finished version, this was amended to:

> With cowslips wan that hang the pensive head
> and every flower that sad embroidery wears

Can you see any reason in terms of mental association why Milton preferred "sad embroidery" to "sorrows liverie"?

Which of these two versions of Milton is, in your opinion, preferable?

(a)   Bring the rathe primrose that unwedded dies.
       Bring the rathe primrose that forsaken dies.

(b)   Under the glimmering eyelids of the morn.
       Under the opening eyelids of the morn.

EXPERIMENTS IN MENTAL ASSOCIATION

A useful classroom or group experiment in mental association has been devised according to the following procedure.

(1) The instructor or group chairman draws up a list of ten (or any multiple) words and their opposites (if a relatively strict opposite is not available, a word sufficiently contrasting in meaning may be selected, for example, day—night, violet—oak tree).

(2) The instructor or group chairman should read each of the words on his list slowly and deliberately, informing the students that they should put down on paper whatever comes into their heads upon hearing the given word. The instructor should allow time enough for the slower students to finish,

pointing out that, if any one wants any extra time, in dealing with any word, all he has to do is to ask for it.

The students should not write in their exercise books more than five key words to the page. There are two reasons for allowing plenty of space: room must be allowed for the student's own personal set of associations and also for the set of collective class-room associations (master list) to be formed subsequently and inserted under the appropriate key words. At the instructor's discretion, the latter can be inserted on fresh sheets of paper. The class syntheses that are to be formed also can be inserted on fresh sheets, with a view to leaving space for the preparation of the class poem.

(3) After going through his list of prepared words, the instructor then calls upon the members of the class, in alphabetical order, to read their list of mental associations. As he hears each list, he chooses certain words to be inserted on the class list—words that have the most suggestive, concrete, or imagistic quality, or indicate the most universal concepts. As he isolates these words, he asks the class to write them down on the class master list of mental associations. The instructor should make clear that he will explain subsequently why he chose certain expressions rather than others. It is not necessary to explain the reasons for selection while in the process of drawing up the list. The students will soon notice the amount of repetitions, translations of ideas, vivid expressions, distinct images, apposite abstractions, and so on, that the recitation in the course of drawing up the list produces.

(4) After drawing up the class list of mental associations, the next step is the formation of syntheses. This will take place about the third meeting of the class (a two-hour session of a class of about twenty members is assumed here). The instructor should point out that he will read the class list of associations aloud and the class will note how certain words

immediately seem to go together, partly because they are already bound by the laws of mental association. The students are invited to go behind the scenes and see how the imagination works. The instructor cannot guarantee that all the expressions will be equally valid or effective. Criticism should come *after* creation; criticism should not inhibit creativity.

Thus, under the key word *dawn*, the following class associations were formed: rose-colored sky, feeling of freshness, hope, milkman, tranquillity, peace, promise, farm, alarm clock, quiet solitude of rainy sky, awakening, rebirth, sun, light, work, untouched city, skyline, tiredness, wonder. From these phrases the two following syntheses were formed: *quiet solitude of dawn reawakening over the untouched city; tranquillity of promise in the wonder of dawn.* The instructor, in forming the syntheses, should confine himself to the class list, although a change in the grammatical form of a word (from noun to verb, for example) or the introduction of a connective is permissible.

After the syntheses are formed, it is easy to place them in a simple poetic structure such as that of generic description (p. 131). Advice may be sought from members of the class as to how to dispose of the syntheses in the best order of climax.

Not all the syntheses that are created will be equally good or effective. The group leader or instructor simply takes the class behind the scenes to show the imagination at work. Spontaneously, in front of the class, he creates what he can. There is time later on when the class poem is under way to weed out the less effective expression from the more competent.

In drawing up the master word list, the instructor should remember that syntheses form most easily from the union of a universal idea with a specific image. Images alone, or ideas alone, will not provide sufficient groundwork for the imaginative expression. Both are required together.

Experiment

Using the class master word list and the class syntheses, write a free verse poem dealing with any idea suggested by the master word list. In this connection, you may use your own mental associations and any syntheses springing from them. You may use any method you please, but a very practical one in the circumstances is the generic description technique using the first person.

An interesting feature of the experiment is that the same key word lends to rather different results in different classes, though there are resemblances as well. It is frequently possible to build a long poem by joining the work of different classes. Note how the work of classes A and B on the subjects of war and peace could easily be fused together.

War

Class A

I am War
the yearning emptiness of desolation
the brutal rationing of bodies in the mud:
the embalmed catastrophe of death
under the empty and sick smell of flowers.
I have famished the love of God
in the barren chaos of bombed cities
in the bitterness of anguished faces.

Class B

I am War
I stretch out my feverish hands of hunger.
I deny the haggard child, begging thinly.
Along the musty rooms of jobless tenements
I inspect the drawn-in faces of a million deaths.

Pillaging God with my crimson tactics
I am War
welcoming
with the cruel *rigor mortis* of inevitability
the dark violence of the morgue
the flagged coffins, confessions of guns.

Peace

Class A

I am Peace
the quiet solitude of the dawn reawakening
over the untouched city:
the tranquillity of promise
in the wonder of morning.
I am the home-returning beauty
of the sunset's glory.
I am the sound of cold church bells
in the flaming horizon.
I am the settled beauty
of the closing day.

Class B

I am Peace
the loving cry of birth, unaware of evil
the beauty of dawn in the calm freshness of the forest
the solitude of beauty, the aftermath of tranquillity.
I am Peace
the close of the sunset quietly returning.

Sometimes, the work of a given class is so highly individualistic that the work is non-transferable.

Negation

I am aloneness
the nothingness in the universal whiteness
the oblivion of sand by the sea:
the street lamp unlit, the stark image of night,
the blizzard book of man's soul:
I am negation, gathering a dead universe.

Mass

Quest ends
in the finality of Mass
in the white death of the Host
in whiteness awake with peace and knowledge.

Both these pieces stemmed from associations with *whiteness*, but they gave birth to more powerful ideas—"Negation," "Mass"—that absorbed the original key word.

It is helpful in selecting the list of words *to have them already associated, either by opposites or similarities.* Thus, the piece on war from Class A grew out of the following key words and syntheses:

hunger: bitterness of anguished faces; love of God famished in the barren chaos of bombed cities; yawning emptiness of desolation.

death: embalmed catastrophe of death; end of quest in finality of the mass; empty and sick smell of flowers.

war: brutal rationing of bodies in the mud.

These words will obviously tend to form associations that will go together. The Class A poem on peace used syntheses formed for the following key words: *dawn, sunset, peace. Dawn* and *sunset* will go with the idea of *peace,* just as *hunger* and *death* go with the idea of *war.*

In the spring term of 1946, in a class of veterans preparing to enter law school at Fordham University, the experiment was carried out as follows.

The members of this class were older, more mature students than is the general rule in colleges in normal years. This fact was, in a sense, to the instructor's advantage. On the other hand, older men with a very practical objective, such as these students had, usually have too often and too exclusively directed their minds into expository and logical channels. They are impatient about being asked to use their dormant powers of mental association. On the other hand, once engaged upon this experiment, the class delighted in its own manifestations of imagistic and colorful expression. The imagination became a vivid and real force to some members of the group for the first time in their educational experience. In this particular case the results were not extraordinary, it is true, but they were good enough to prove the effectiveness of the method.

Here are some typical associations obtained in the classroom that were considered good raw material for poetry. For *death* the class offered: *draped, clinging, creaking stair.*

Imagistic syntheses were formed from these words as fol-lows:

"The draped finality of death."

"The steady bleakness of the skull."

"A soul clings to a creaking stair."

These syntheses have poetic impact, but how they fit into the "intellectual elaboration of art" depends upon other activities of the mind. These syntheses may not connote a religious concept of death, for example. We might not agree with them as they stand. But they may be used as contrasting images to such a concept. Again, they might be put into the mouth of a pagan speaker. In such syntheses, we are far from having poetry in the full sense of the word, but we can more rapidly approach that goal through this method than through any other. After the class understands what a synthesis is, fresh associations very often will be conceived already in the form of syntheses. For example, this particular class offered the following:

"Gazing on the hypocrisy of death."

"The earth's muffled thud on the casket lid."

"Inverted birth."

"Death's black vacuum."

(5) After the instructor, in cooperation with the class, has formed the associations and syntheses, a free-verse structure may be written, incorporating a fair portion of the raw material contained in the master list of images and syntheses.

From this experiment, one student produced this poem on the "Oak Tree" (italicized words are class associations):

The Oak Tree

Brown bastion of ironic beauty
When did you rise, will you ever fall?
The time of the flesh leaves you unscarred.
Impassively you watch our fevered actions
With sentinel silence, like *granite judge.*

You have felt the laughter of starched children.
As they frolicked in your *columned sunlight.*
Lovers have known the warm embrace
Of the *churchlike sanctity* of your world
And in the twilight your puppet shadows
Have toyed with the memories of the old.

Stolid and somber, strong and sturdy
You tower imperial between God and man.
Spidery tentacles tie you to weary land.
As your tawny limbs surge toward the blinding blue.

These lines do not, of course, contain important poetry either emotionally or intellectually, but we are at least getting a beginning along natural and spontaneous lines. The student is drawing on his powers of mental association. He is learning how to use these powers in the manner of the creative artist.

There is no secret about these powers or about their use. Poetry in its full scope is, of course, organically connected to many other powers, including intellect and reason, to other arts such as music and decoration. But the best beginning, because basic, is on the level of mental association.

The emphasis on mental association need not be restricted to poetry. It enters all aspects of creative writing. The following example illustrates a combination of a lesson in mental association (the class associations are again italicized) and a lesson in *thematic contrast*—the basis of a short story without plot. This extract is not a story; it is merely an exercise in thematic contrast (see page 232).

Young Water and Old

Water, young and zestful, vigorous and lithe
The mountain stream leaps eagerly down its circuitous
    route.
Lofty quiet, broken only by the *gurgling turmoil* of
    busy waters.
Water twisting, leaping, bounding and rebounding,
Water slapping angrily at the *obstructing stones*
Chattering and aggressive toward any delay.
Noisy, darting from rock to rock, intent only upon de-
    scending.
Scrambling around staunch logs and tree stumps
Now dashing precipitously over sheer rock—impetuous,
    daring—
Flashing and sparkling back into a pearly spray
A glistening spray that lingers, *minute microscopic mist.*
Then impatient to rush on again—mobile, fluid—
    vibrant, free water.
Alive water.
Young water.

Old water, heavy, serious and somber,
Regal and lordly—testy at times and even vindictive—
Rolls relentlessly the mighty ocean endless in its ex-
    panse.
Of *infinite bleakness,* restless and uneasy in its ceaseless
    bobbing.
Threatening and challenging puny man's invasion,
Lashing violently in a crashing display of power,

A lashing monstrous *blue-green phosphorescence* glow-
ing in the moon's shivering path,
Under the day's heat-filled sky the sullen, irascible mass
relaxes
Into a *shimmering green corduroy,* no longer angry or
ominous,
Smug in the knowledge of its undisputed majesty:
Determined, deliberate, crowding, ponderous, measured,
Mature water,
Old water.

—K.G.

This piece may be criticized legitimately on the ground
that it is too adjectival, too unselective. Yet the student has
developed and initiated his own sense of form, and the writing is alive.

The heart of the matter is that creative power lies in the
emotional impact of association and connotation. The raw
material for this impact, in turn, is born through further association. Remember that mental association is not purely
haphazard. Your particular train of mental association is
dependent upon past experiencce.

In broad terms, what happens in the classroom is that the
teacher or discussion chairman has to make an important
creative contribution in selecting the most pertinent of the
raw material that the class creates. If the class hours permit,
it is advisable to have one or more students act as selectors
of material for the class syntheses.

The final result of the experiments in mental associations
in the classroom is a class poem which is partly a communal
effort and partly the creative contribution of the teacher or
leader. The greatest value to be derived from the experiment
is the actual perception of the imagination at work. Frequently, too, the final poem is of interest in itself.

The class should be asked to suggest titles for the final
product. Three titles were suggested for the following—
"Winter"; "On Guard"; "Armistice." "On Guard" was

thought to be most indicative of the tension in this particular piece.

Roars the mountain from the height of isolated pines
Knocks the cold ribs of the winter night.
Whiteness spears the blank earth in its mask of war.
From the chill cycle of the insecure night
Death telephones its cold freedom.
In fearful beat, the foam of war breasts its mortal beach.

These syntheses were formed from the following class list of mental associations:

Death: sickness, telephone call, night, carrying woe, glory, freedom, peace, beginning of life, cold.

Night: stars and sleep, foreign, valve, wakefulness, fear, insecurity, lights, cycle, twinkle, chill.

Cold: snow, winter night, rock, wall, knock, rib, ice, fire, coat, skating, dark, discomfort.

Mountain: peaks, peaceful, roar, pines, dome, height, isolation, achievement, rarefied atmosphere, goal, deliberation, calmness, power, effort, space, danger.

Whiteness: sheets, tender, spear, light, flash, purity unattainable, blank earth, cool, mask of snow, war.

Ocean: waves, space, breast, torn, bulb, crash, horse, foam, far-off lands, beach, sand, fear, beauty, beat, spray, crest, force, deep, wide.

Naturally, as the syntheses go together, and the theme becomes evident, certain key words serve to assimilate the imagery, as in the example of *war* above.

IMPROVING IMPACT IN ASSOCIATIVE EXPRESSION

The problem of improving impact in expression of the results of the associative process is basically that of all art—

cutting away the superfluous, the unnecessary "fluff," so that what remains contributes strongly and organically to the total work.

In writing, the effective expression cannot merely stand by itself. Placed in juxtaposition with an ineffective expression, the good expression must lose part of its effectiveness. What does not strengthen a piece of writing weakens it.

Examples follow from a classroom assignment in generic description, subsequent to exercises in mental association and syntheses. Common errors in technique consist in adding too much in the way of "soft" words, adjectival expressions, so that tension is lost; in distracting the reader from the force of an idea by going into particularizations that are not imagistic but "scientific" and overanalytical; in making additions to the thought that are already included and imaginatively indicated in a prior statement. These are the more subtle errors; the most common error, of course, is simply the use of the dead expression, the cliché, the phrase that is just too heavy to move and come to life.

One student in describing the ocean wrote the following line: "unfathomable deepness hides my world of mystic, shimmering sands." The idea of *deepness* is obviously already contained in that of *unfathomable*. *Mystic* is a word that, properly used, has a very specific and important meaning. Here all it means is "mysterious" and that idea is already contained in *unfathomable*. The line gains in impact by letting the word "unfathomable" bear its maximum responsibility: "the unfathomable hides my world of shimmering sands." But what about the phrase, *my world?* Is that not already contained in *shimmering sands?* Another word is cut away, and we finally get a stronger expression, more full of imaginative appeal: "the unfathomable hides my shimmering sands." Once the "fluff" goes, the imagination becomes strong and active; the words gain in dramatic intensity.

Another student wrote:

I am night
the cloak of darkness.
Within my dancing shadows lurk
deadly mysterious images
waiting to clutch the weak of heart.

Cloak of darkness as it stands is a cliché. The concluding phrase, *weak of heart,* reduces the universality of the idea, restricting the meaning to those who actually have weak hearts. Rewritten, the phrase develops "impact":

I am night—
within my cloak of shadows
lurks
a dead mysterious image
waiting to clutch.

Sometimes, an added remark or allusion reduces the impact of an idea, because the addition is not on the same level of intellectual meaning or emotional force:

I am the mirror
indispensable to
the cracked vision of humanity
that shocked the lady of Shalott.

The last line adds nothing, and destroys the climax after the word *humanity.*

Phrases should not be presented in obviously logical form, in terms of consequences and inferences, because in this way they tend to impede or destroy imagistic impact. The writer is conveying meaning through the image, not through overt reasoning. Note how the last two lines are ineffective in suggesting a logical consequence in the following piece.

I am the chopping white caps and the sea gull's screech
I am the green fertility of infinitude
I am the daring death of the breakers.
I am the ocean so full of fury and life
that I personify stillness and death.

Actually, the last two lines do not offer a logical consequence but a paradox, and a paradox should be presented in terms of a stark contrast:

> I am the ocean in fury and life
> I am the ocean in stillness and death.

The language of scientific or "functional" prose can intrude unhappily into an otherwise imaginative piece. Note the unsuitability of the italicized words in the following extracts from student experiments:

> I am laughter
> the sunbeam dancing on the ripple
> the enchanting explosion of a pricked balloon
> *the common denominator of youth.*

> I am the Soul of Man
> a fathomless ocean that no line has sounded
> the object of God's *special approbation.*

> I am a skyscraper
> bedecked with jeweled windows
> shrouded in a cope of clouds
> *symbolic of an advancing civilization.*

> I am Hope
> the plasma of renewed life flowing
> *the eternal factor* that helps man.

Phrases such as *common denominator, eternal factor* belong to the special language of mathematics and they are too special to synthesize in creative writing. Phrases such as *special approbation, advancing civilization* just cannot come alive.

Sometimes, the student doesn't know when to stop. The following description of St. Patrick's Cathedral is good in the sense of an over-all mood and evaluation:

> My suppliant spires in majestic immensity mirror
> awful power:

I stand a tribute of eloquence in mute and lifeless
   stone
Vivified by the heat of the great heart within,
A trysting place of faith and timeless love.

But the lines that follow in the experiment distract the
reader from this good effect by a minor consideration of an
analytical and "prosaic" kind:

Hallowed walls tolerate a steady stream of human faces
Window-shopping for the art of ages
Or seeking the silent thrill of peace.

In a class analysis of the poem, one student suggested a con-
cision of these last three lines that would add an ironic sharpness that would contrast with the opening lines:

Hallowed walls tolerate a steady stream of human faces
Window-shopping for the art of peace.

It is possible, of course, to use what seems very heavy language, provided the force of the initial idea is sufficiently
great. The same student thus presented the atom bomb—the
theme suggested by an article stating that the H-Bomb would
assure United States supremacy at low cost, since the elements
were available from nature:

Born from nature in monopolized secrecy
Will it regenerate us with a baptism of uranium?
An incendiary question mark mocks
The fathomless future of our race:
In hoc signo vinces.
The power to destroy
The epiphany of idolatry
Pales all other in its penumbra.
Spurning the impotent Omnipotence
Uncertainty assures the certainty
Of an abysmal darkness.
                                        —M.K.

Improving the impact of imaginative expression implies a transforming of the abstract and the general to the specific and concrete without loss of any transcendent meaning. Individual words in the creative process must have concrete intensity and at the same time the capacity for touching universal meaning and values. They must be able to make suggestions that go beyond their context.

The concrete intensity of a word implies the capacity of a word to carry its full load in a piece of writing. It is not inadvertent or repetitious; it is not already implicit in another word used in the context. As has been said, the creative word observes the principle of economy in the authentic sense—there is no waste in it. The principle of mental association and the synthesis that derives from it reveal the unitive energy of the particular and universal, of the limiting and transcending.

MENTAL ASSOCIATION AND COLOR SYMBOLISM

It is possible to convey the imaginative meaning of a situation almost entirely in terms of color because of the mental associations that color excites.

Herbert Read says, regarding color:

Properly speaking, form cannot be perceived except as color, you cannot separate what you see as form from what you see as color, because color is simply the reaction of the form of an object to the rays of light by which we perceive it. Color is the superficial aspect of form. Nevertheless, color has a very important part to play in art, because it has a very direct effect on our senses. The range of colors, indeed, might be placed in a series to correspond with the range of our emotions; red corresponding with anger, yellow with joy, blue with longing, and so on. There is probably a simple psychological explanation for this correspondence, the pleasure or discomfort being determined by the frequency with which the waves or rays of light strike the retina of the eye. That is the physiological aspect of color, but color has also its psychological aspects. Some people like or dislike colors because they associate them with their general likes or dislikes—they like green because they associate it with springtime, or blue because it reminds them of Italian skies; they dislike red because they associate it with danger, or mad bulls. . . . Such associative values have nothing to do with the aesthetic value of color as such, though they have a great deal to do with any particular individual's reaction to a particular work of art. The aesthetic reaction to color is simply this: that we enter intuitively into the nature of the color, appreciate its depth, or warmth, or tonality—that is to say, its objective qualities—and then proceed to identify those qualities with our emotions.[1]

An interesting essay on the associative value of color is to be found in Herman Melville's *Moby Dick.* On the surface, this book deals with whaling in New England. The characters in the story are hunting Moby Dick, the *white* whale. Whiteness has been a traditional symbol for such abstract concepts as innocence, purity, and mysticism. It is not merely a whale that is being sought in the ocean, but the whale as a symbol of man's own transcendent spiritual quest. In order to bring emphatically to his readers' attention the connotation of *whiteness,* for the purpose of the symbolism of his story, Melville wrote the following passage:

The Whiteness of the Whale

What the White Whale was to Ahab, has been hinted. What, at times, he was to me, as yet remains unsaid.

Aside from those more obvious considerations touching Moby Dick, which could not but occasionally awaken in any man's soul some alarm, there was another thought, or rather vague, nameless horror concerning him, which at times by its intensity completely overpowered all the rest. It was the whiteness of the whale that above all things appalled me.

In many natural objects, whiteness enhances beauty, as if imparting some special virtue of its own, as in marbles, japonicas,

---

[1] Herbert Read, *Education Through Art,* New York, Pantheon Books, Inc., 1940, p. 22.

and pearls. Various nations have in some way recognized a certain royal pre-eminence in this hue. Even the barbaric, grand old kings of Pegu placed the title "Lord of the White Elephants" above all others, and the modern kings of Siam unfurled the same snow-white quadruped in the royal standard. . . . Whiteness has been even made significant of gladness, for among the Romans a white stone marked a joyful day. This same hue is made the emblem of many touching, noble things—the innocence of brides, the benignity of age. In many climes, whiteness typifies the majesty of Justice in the ermine of the judge, and contributes to the daily state of kings and queens drawn by milk-white steeds. . . . In the Vision of St. John, white robes are given to the redeemed, and the four-and-twenty elders stand clothed in white before the great white throne, and the Holy One that sitteth there white like wool. Yet for all these associations, with whatever is sweet and honorable and sublime, there yet lurks an elusive something in the innermost idea of this hue, which strikes panic to the soul.

The thought of whiteness, when divorced from more kindly associations and coupled with any object terrible in itself, heightens that terror to the furthest bounds. Witness the white bear of the poles and the white shark of the tropics. What but their smooth, flaky whiteness makes them the horrors they are?

Most famous in our western annals and Indian traditions is that of the White Steed of the Prairies, a magnificent milk-white charger, large-eyed, small-headed, bluff-chested, and with the dignity of a thousand monarchs in his lofty, over-scorning carriage. He was the elected ruler of vast herds of wild horses, whose pastures in those days were only fenced by the Rocky Mountains and the Alleghenies. At their flaming head he westward trooped it like that chosen star which every evening leads on the hosts of light. The flashing cascade of his mane, the curving comet of his tail, invested him with housings more resplendent than gold and silver. To the eyes of the old trappers and hunters he revived the glories of those primeval times when Adam walked majestic as a god, bluff-browed and fearless as this mighty steed. Always to the bravest Indians he was the object of trembling reverence and awe. It was his spiritual whiteness chiefly, which so clothed him with divineness; and this divineness had that in it which, though commanding worship, at the same time enforced a certain nameless terror.

It cannot well be doubted that the one visible quality in the aspect of the dead which most appalls the gazer is the marble pallor lingering there. And from that pallor of the dead we borrow the expressive hue of the shroud in which we wrap them. Nor even in our superstitions do we fail to throw the same snowy mantle round our phantoms, all ghosts rising in a milk-white fog. Yea, while these terrors seize us, let us add that even the king of terrors, when personified by the evangelist, rides on his pallid horse.

Therefore, in his other moods, symbolize whatever grand or gracious thing he will by whiteness, no man can deny that it calls up a peculiar apparition of the soul.

What is there apart from the traditions of dungeoned warriors and kings that makes the White Tower of London tell so much more strongly on the imagination of an untraveled American than those other storied structures, its neighbors—the Byward Tower, or even the Bloody? And those sublimer towers, the White Mountains of New Hampshire, whence in peculiar moods, comes that gigantic ghostliness over the soul at the bare mention of that name, while the thought of Virginia's Blue Ridge is full of a soft, dewy, distant dreaminess? Or why, in reading the old fairy tales of Central Europe, is the "tall pale man" of the Hartz forest, whose changeless pallor glides through the green of the groves, more terrible than all the whooping imps of the Blocksburg?

The mariner, when drawing nigh the coasts of foreign lands, if by night he hears the roar of breakers, starts to vigilance, and feels just enough of fear to sharpen all his faculties; but under precisely similar circumstances, let him be called from his hammock to view his ship sailing through a midnight sea of milky whiteness, then he feels a silent, superstitious dread. The shrouded phantom of the whitened waters is as horrible to him as a real ghost. In vain the lead assures him he is still off soundings. Heart and helm, they both go down. He never rests till blue water is under him again. Yet where is the mariner who will tell thee, "Sir, it was not so much the fear of striking hidden rocks, as the fear of that hideous whiteness that so stirred me"?

To the native Indian of Peru, the continual sight of the snow-covered Andes conveys naught of dread. The backwoodsman of the West with comparative indifference views an unbounded prairie sheeted with driven snow, no shadow of tree or twig to break the fixed trance of whiteness. Not so the sailor, beholding the scenery of the Antarctic seas, where at times he, shivering and half shipwrecked, instead of rainbows speaking hope and solace to his misery, views what seems a boundless churchyard grinning upon him with its lean ice monuments and splintered crosses.

But thou sayest, methinks this white-lead chapter about whiteness is but a white flag hung out from a craven soul.

Tell me why this strong young colt, foaled in some peaceful valley of Vermont, far removed from all beasts of prey—why is it that upon the sunniest day, if you but shake a fresh buffalo robe behind him, so that he cannot even see it, but only smells its wild animal muskiness—why will he start, snort, and with bursting eyes paw the ground in frenzies of affright? There is no remembrance in him of any gorings of wild creatures in his green northern home. What knows he, this New England colt, of the black bisons of distant Oregon? Yet, though thousands of miles from Oregon, when he smells that savage musk, the rending, goring bison herds are present.

Thus, the muffled rollings of a milky sea, the bleak rustlings of the festooned frosts of mountains, the desolate shiftings of the wind-rowed snows of prairies; all these, to Ishmael, are as the shaking of that buffalo robe to the frightened colt!

But not yet have we solved the mystery of this whiteness, and learned why it appeals with such power to the soul. Is it that it shadows forth the heartless voids of the universe? Or is it that, as whiteness is not so much of a color as the visible absence of color, there is such a dumb blankness, full of meaning, in a wide landscape of snows? Consider that other theory of the natural philosophers, that all other earthly hues—the sweet tinges of sunset skies and woods; yea, and the gilded velvets of butterflies, and the butterfly cheeks of young girls—all are not actually in substance, but only laid on from without. Even light forever remains white or colorless in itself, and if operating without medium upon matter, would touch all objects, even tulips and roses, with its own blank tinge. Pondering all this, we gaze ourselves blind at the monumental white shroud that wraps all the prospect. And of all these things the White Whale was the symbol. Wonder ye then at the fiery hunt?

Experiment

(1) "The Whiteness of the Whale."

(a) What does whiteness mean to Ishmael? How does he explain his reaction to whiteness?

(b) Make a list of the author's mental associations connected with the word "whiteness."

(c) Show how Melville achieved imaginative strength and power in his description merely by harnessing these mental associations.

(d) Has Melville employed his images haphazardly? List any that seem haphazard. Are others disciplined and submitted to the "line of art"? If you feel that they are so disciplined, show by example how he has assembled these images and refined them into a pattern of artistic unity.

(e) Show how the mental associations contained in this selection contribute to the effect of mystery. Show how they suggest a powerful symbolism. What artistic techniques contribute to these effects?

(f) Explain how Melville achieves an accumulatively intensive effect in his description of the "whiteness" of the whale.

(g) Write an essay of 200 words developing one of the following ideas: (1) Why do you think this an effective or ineffective descriptive passage? Submit any criticisms which come to mind. (2) Employ the techniques suggested by Melville in an original description of your own dealing with one of the following: the blackness of night, the green of spring, the redness of fire, the blueness of heaven.

(2) Check your knowledge of the connotation and symbolism of common colors by matching the colors and the mental associations.

violet	fertility
purple	majesty
green	death
blue	rose
vermilion	humility
black	Heaven
white	"the gorgeous East" (Milton)
pearl	mysticism
azure	flowing with milk and honey
golden	blood
velvet	twilight
gray	Orient
ebony	linen
mahogany	tiger-moth
damask	Africa
lavender	hardness
silver	autumn
ruby	fire
diamond	purity
rust	moon

It is possible in the above list to make roughly correct associations with more than one alternative. You have to use your judgment about which alternative is the best. For example, *pearl* has a literary association from Milton's famous line, at the beginning of Book II of *Paradise Lost.*

> High on a throne of royal state, which far
> Outshone the wealth of Ormus and of Ind
> Or where the gorgeous East, with richest hand,
> Showers on her kings Barbaric pearl and gold.

Pearl also has a scriptural association, as in "the pearl of great price," which in the above list might be applied to the concept of purity. Both *ebony* and *mahogany* might be associated with hardness. But which of the two is more closely associated with Africa?

One connotation in the list may cause you difficulty—*damask*, etymologically derived from Damascus, one time fabulous center of the dye and silk trade, applies to rich cloth often dyed a rose color. It has been immortalized in Keats's

> Innumerable of stains and splendid dyes.
> As are the tiger-moth's deep-damask'd wings.

(3) Connotation is the indispensable means of communication. But, whereas denotation has a universal value easily ascertainable in any dictionary, connotation can be indefinitely extended in the mind of any listener or reader. You may have a very rich imaginative life or you may be comparatively sterile. Exercises in word association will help you to determine how you stand. You may live on a purely surface level, more or less following a pattern of vague ideas and emotional clichés. Or your mind may be sharp, observing, and rich. It is possible, in case of imaginative anemia, to make progress, particularly through reading and imaginative training, toward a greater degree of sensitivity and perception. Below are two sets of word associations by two different students. Which, in your opinion, has the more developed ability for creative writing?

Student A

> *hunger:* food
> *food:* meat
> *wealth:* nice home
> *poverty:* unhappiness
> *birth:* baby
> *death:* sorrow for loved one
> *peace:* happiness and prosperity, contentment
> *war:* death and destruction, greed
> *dawn:* sunrise in the country
> *sunset:* sun sinks in the west, beautiful sight
> *night:* stars shine, full moon

blood: red
crimson: rich shade of red
rose: red, pink, or white
cold: shivering, unheated apartment
mountain: tall and stately, covered with snow for skiing
whiteness: cleanliness
spring: summer follows and vacation time
joy: happiness felt over some event
autumn: football games
ocean: trip to Europe
charity: kindliness to neighbor

Student B

hunger: Europe, war, jobless
food: appetite, fragrance, satisfaction
wealth: easy living, Godlessness
poverty: hard work, suffering
birth: family, love, joy, suffering
death: sadness, loss, emotion, blackness
peace: ease, satisfaction, freedom, self-assurance
war: hunger, suffering, injustice
dawn: light, brightness, beautiful, sun, day
sunset: color, restfulness, quietude
night: dark, fear, home, restfulness
blood: suffering, distasteful, obnoxious
crimson: blood, sun, color, blush, material
rose: garden, plant, vase, beauty, fragrance
cold: homeless, poor, suffering, coat
mountain: height, impassable, far-off design
whiteness: pale, fainting, snow, clouds, clean-souled
spring: birds, green, song, light-heartedness
joy: love, emotion, short-lived, happiness, smile
autumn: leaves, trees, brown-and-yellow coloring
ocean: vastness, ship, meditative, contemplation
charity: love of God, kindness, self-happiness

(4) The following is a list of syntheses arrived at by collective participation in three composition classes. Which of

them do you find effective? Which do you consider unsatisfactory?

(a) *Hunger:*
"The hollow-eyed scavenger of the Black Market"
"Pity the gaunt-cheeked animality of hunger"
"The jobless bones of poverty"
"Hunger at home in a shack by the railroad"

(b) *Food:*
"The multitudinous strength of essential bread"

(c) *Wealth:*
"A faded quilt of corpulence"
"The economics of spiritual death"
"Boredom locked in an iron box"

(d) *Poverty:*
"Naked—no tree, no green"
"Alone in cold dirt"

(e) *Birth:*
"A crocus breaks the dark soil into sunlight"
"The stillness of the dawn broken by a cry for recognition"

(f) *Death:*
"The rigid boy in a field of stiffened bodies,
A free emigrant from death"
"A door shutting off the noise from the street"
"A lone track into the forest snows"
"The shock of the immaculate shroud of whiteness"
"The helpless restrospect of black veils"
"The Mass flowering from the finality of stone"

(g) *Peace:*
"To meditate in the high mountains in the time of whiteness"
"The tranquil assurance of yellow wheat fields"

(h) *War:*

"Catastrophe of blood"
"A uniform flash in the night
Lighting the loveless steel rails
Into the vacuum"
"The tension of the heart and the wasted ideology
of war"
"Against the motionless music of eternity
The mandatory cosmology of mud"

(i) *Dawn:*

"The alarm clock cracks the autumn dawn on an
orange cloth"

(j) *Sunset:*

"The hungry river shadows its way under the settling sadness of the sun"

(k) *Night:*

"The snug lamppost was sightless under the windy
moonlight of the trees"
"The black of aloneness"
"The solitude of the hidden night"
"The silhouette of moonlight"
"By the water's edge the cricket's song and the
call of birds merge into the mystery of night and
stars"

(l) *Blood:*

"The crimson stain of courage"
"The velvet blood of his slit throat"
"The velvet blood of roses streams from the dark
subway stand"

(m) *Rose:*

"The dangerous perfection of the rose"

(n) *Cold:*

"The fir tree stately in its sparkled ice"

(o) *Mountain:*

"Mountain, magnanimous overseer of snows
Its pillared wings
Towering toward God"

(p) *Spring:*

"The cool freedom of new violets"
"Freedom of the blossomed Spring"
"The waterfall blossoms over the green plain"
"The green renascence of waters"

(q) *Autumn:*

"Leaves falling in the vagabond Autumn"
"The halting loneliness of the twangy Autumn"
"The yellow witchcraft of bacteriological decay"
"The wind crunching through fantasy of leaves piled and rusty"

(r) *Ocean:*

"The secret immensity of the ocean"
"The darkness of the meditating ocean"

(5) There follows a list of words and their associations arrived at by collective action in three separate classes. Draw up a list of 50 words from this group (they may be associated with several key words on the list) that, in your opinion, constitute the most effective associations for one idea that you have selected. Attempt to create five syntheses from these associations.

(a) *Hunger*—animality, hollow-cheeked, sunken-eyed, fear, pity, gaunt, child's cry, silent, entreaty, jobless, bones

(b) *Food*—essential, multitudinous, bread, life, strength, milk, rotund

(c) *Wealth*—corpulence, strongbox, oil portrait, penthouse, Florida, Country Club, conspicuous consumption, opulence, luxury, jewels, mahogany, library, poodle dog, lack of privacy, needless obligations, power, Republican, gold mansion, dowager, furs, sheared beaver coat, convertible car, security, sadness, destruction, small family, splendor, chandelier, flowered gown, success, capitalism

(d) *Poverty*—staring eyes, tired hands, slum, cynical, alone, hopelessness, paper money, cold dirt, no tree no green, cigar butt on toothpick, patched trousers, "Lend me five," emaciation, delinquency, sudden, aloneness, runaway despair, Europe, St. Francis, nakedness, disheveled hair, not at home, shack by the railroad

(e) *Birth*—expectancy, promise, fulfillment, cigars, doctor, baby, hospital, pain, man, wife, death, love, tenderness, nursery, joy, rejuvenation, confusion, black bag, frontier, tub, washing clothes, screams, pink-and-blue crib

(f) *Death*—scent of roses, wakes, girl outside building, black, subdued voices in a small room, stone, staring, hopeless, emptiness, absorbing, bleakness, decisive, parting, eternity, void, burst, hush, inevitable, pattern, coffin, morgue, finality, flowers, rain, stairway, bedroom, door, candles, priest, whisky, necessity, sadness, winter, white sheet, lamenting, veil, the Mass, stone

(g) *Peace*—justice, books, countryside, meditation, broad fields, high mountains, snowfall, Christmas Eve, serenity, laurel, dove, easy chair, evening, summer, men returning, sleep, oars docked in a rowboat, lake-summer, music, waters, valley, homemade pie, peacepipe, haven, home town, normal routine, tranquillity, assurance, yellow wheat fields

(h) *War*—mud, confused motion, troop ship, seasickness, separation, frustration, railroad train, flash in the night, prison walls and a white face, boy in field void of feeling, pile of stiffened bodies, ideology, waste, havoc, misery, error, tension, heart, rotting vegetation, blackout, rigidity, vacuum, boredom, time, schedule, limit, wristwatch, mandatory, cosmology, eternity, timelessness, motionless, mountain, infinite, ocean, music

(i) *Dawn*—milk wagon, fog-laden, awakening, dew, piercing, ship, top of cliff, streak of lightning, sleep, wet grass, orange cloth, alarm clock, stealthy, horizon, below, eastern, boat at anchor, rays, rebirth, rooster, fence, sun behind mountain, newness, sun burning stream, mountain streaming, bridges, quietness and pale skies

(j) *Sunset*—prayer, settling, sadness, shadowing, quiet, loneliness, cattle, river, hungry, worker, home returning, glowing shadow, rim of ocean, streaks of cloud, railroad tracks, barren trees against gray sky, tired beauty, red on the roof of the store across the way, call of birds

(k) *Night*—solitude, clear, cold, peace, sightless, streak of lampposts, sleep and stars, wind in the trees, shadows must fall, stillness, fear, rest, black, hidden, moonlit mist in the valley, railroad whistle in distance, cats, lighted windows, high water at the dock, *clair de lune,* canoe, car, roses, silhouette, terrace, brushing winds in mountain forest, waters' edge, cricket's song, mystery, sleep, stars

(l) *Blood*—opening, death, pain, concern, patience, catastrophe, crimson, nausea, violence, donor, salt, vein, tension, gushing, corpuscles, obnoxious, needle

(m) *Crimson*—sanguine, banner, daring sin, sacrifice, martyrs, sticky, stained, toreador, roses in wallpaper, fury, velvet, cardinal, brilliance, exciting, slit throat, caravan, horses on a hill, bull fighting, Spanish cape, startling

(n) *Rose*—dangerous, loving, velvet, perfection, thorn, evil, noisy darkness of black roses, prom, white dress, picture hat, graduation, bees, Carmen singing, tenderness, bugs, happiness, poetry, death, funeral, warm weather, exquisite, delicate, petals, Romeo and Juliet, tall, slender vase with one yellow rose, velvet touch, cool, a stand in the subway

(o) *Cold*—Stiffness, barren, anguish, emptiness, attitude, skating, gray lights, hands, thermometer, fuel, ice, bathrobe, a shivering whale, frosted window, cellar, Canada, frost, frozen toes, thawing by a fireplace, wool, heartless, snow-laden branches, stately, needles

(p) *Mountain*—snow, upheaval, pillar, magnanimous, overseer, wings, tower, towering, God, trail, red house, thick, tract, pine trees, blackberries, brook, deer, rushes, trout, green mold, treacherous, ropes, grooves from running waters, snow spilling, grace, stature, goats, impassable, picket fence

(q) *Whiteness*—purity, piercing, baptism, immaculate, hospital, cloud, soul, shock, shroud, sleigh-riding, starched, wave-foam, chalk, sheets, nurse's uniform, sun, penetrating, spring, green renascence

(r) *Spring*—cool, rock, sweet, violet, blossoming, freedom, moss, forecast, new hat, running water, Easter, cooling soda and beer bottles in cold water, piling rocks to keep them from floating downstream, leap, Seltzer water, fishing, trickling of water, baseball, cool water bubbling from a piece of ground shaded by trees, balmy, Paris, park, poem, scent in the air, dirt roads, ground shaded by trees, church steeple, school-house, pasture, waterfall zooming to a green, flat land

(s) *Joy*—home, flash, sparkle, fear, speech, race track, relief, friends, Christmas, family dinner, cork, sparkling bubbles, champagne, gaiety, stained glass, pink elephants, Midnight Mass, turkey and cranberry sauce, Mardi Gras

(t) *Autumn*—sadness, leaves, twangy, loneliness, halting, artist, return to school, early twilight, leaves, wind, hunting, rust, bare trees, withering plants, red leaves falling, burning leaves, raking lawn, caretaker, large house, vagabond, absence of color, bare ground, crisp, football, walking through dry leaves, bacteriological decay, yellow witches, fresh paint, windy fantasy of leaves.

(u) *Ocean*—danger, absent feeling, free, joy, pounding death, warm sand, whitecaps, vastness, lonely prison, mutiny, crack of waves against rocks, palm trees, seaweed, crabs, silk from China, heavy chains, schooner before the wind, silver rays beaming downward and drawing droplets of water, distant shore, exploration, immensity, raft, adventure, thirst, lifeboat, old board, South Seas, whirling, shipwreck, light-house, crumbling mast, iceberg, barnacles, ladder, reef, coral, clash, cargo, swing, pathway, torment, violence, signals, debris, survival of the fittest, treasure chest, darkness of high waves

(v) *Charity*—St. Vincent de Paul, begging nuns, March of Dimes, money, good works, orphans, CARE packages, collections, church, love, help, kindness, faith, hope, virtue, poor people,

resentment, horror, relief, Red Cross, ragged people, crip-
ples, love of neighbor, nun, pennies, benefits, church, rare,
Sisters of Charity, dirty-faced children, baskets of food, pity,
American Legion, St. Paul, a sweet face, basketball game,
blind, social worker, poor district, "begins at home," sending packages to Europe, seven virtues

(6) Attempt a piece of impressionistic writing (see p. 128),
in which you incorporate some of the selections of associations you have made.

(7) A mental association should be distinguished from a
conceptual translation. The conceptual translation simply
gives the *denotation* of the word in alternative phraseology.
A mental association is strictly an *association*—that is, something distinctly different from, yet related to, the word evok-
ing the association. In the following list, which is a conceptual translation, which an authentic mental association?

Word   Association or Conceptual Translation
Hunger—desire to eat, ashcan
Food—dinner table, nourishment
Wealth—frivolity, abundance of riches
Poverty—shanty, want of material goods
Birth—new life, pain
Death—departure from life, black
Peace—no trouble, waving grain
War—battle, catch in the throat
Dawn—sun over housetops, another day
Sunset—setting of sun, quieting down after a hard day
Night—end of day, lights aglow
Blood—essential for life, arteries
Crimson—colorful, martyr
Rose—nice to smell, stained glass
Cold—starlit sky, low temperature
Mountain—high elevation of land, permanency
Joy—graduation, happiness
Charity—gift of alms to needy, Christmas in the slums

NOTE ON COLLECTIVE SYNTHESES

The key words on page 112 were given to a class of men and women on September 23, 30, 1949. Following the formation of mental associations in the classroom, and the drawing up of a master list of associations, syntheses were formed at the next meeting.

The instructor acted extemporaneously, pointing out that these words were before the class, and that they were to write down any combination or suggested combination arising from them. Embryo poems and powerful individual expressions were formed as follows for some of the words in the list:

> *Poverty:* Almost unheard of in America
> the drafty and unmended holes
> the ragged and illiterate tatters
> of a homeless St. Francis
> in his shanty of poverty

(The overtone here may or may not be ironic.)

> Poverty must learn
> must learn to appreciate values
> the quiet charm of hunger
> the unwashed smell of the abandoned home . . .
> learn the shame of the famished bone
> the inward and empty house of loneliness

(These lines definitely contained ironic overtone.)

> *Birth:* A mother suffering in birth the joyful
> renewal of eternity

> *Death:* The undertaker conserving finality in the
> closed solitude of death
> A patch of silence behind a collapsing wall

> *Peace:* The waving stability of grain in the tranquil fields
> The green oblivion of the still pastures

(Note the transference of "waving" from *grain* to *stability*—a "transferred epithet" that is particularly successful; note also the transference of "green" from *pastures* to *oblivion*.)

> *War:*   Pale urgency demanding exuberance of blood

>   (See section on color symbolism.)

>> The bleak tumult of chaos caught in the throat
>> The cries of the shambles spread in the quiet farms

The instructor pointed out that the words *peace* and *war* are already associated by contrast and opposition. Frequently, therefore, the syntheses formed for the one word can be artistically united in terms of contrast with the other. Thus, an embryo poem can be constructed as follows:

>> amid the waving stability of grain in the tranquil fields
>> amid the green oblivion of the still pastures
>> the bleak tumult of chaos caught in the throat
>> the cries of the shambles spread in the quiet farms

> *Dawn:*   the quiet resurrection of the cool sunrise
>   the train whistling through the soft light of golden fields

> *Sunset:*   the somber tranquillity of the myriad-colored solitude
>   survival of cool lights in the hush of day

> *Night:*   the sleeping tomb of the frightened night
>   mysterious stars blacked out in the forbidden night
>   the panther night that stalks the city streets

> *Blood:*   the life-stream of Christ in crimson and loyal surrender of essential blood

> *Mountain:* the inaccessible glory of the hidden mountain
>   challenging the permanent barrier of the mountain
>   to climb its wooded treasury of height

> *Spring:*   the fertilizing laughter of spring dancing through the meadows

Ocean: God's mercy cruising its black waters, its unbounded
dimensions, the illimitable roar of its immensity

Following are two examples of students' adaptations of the
syntheses included on pages 110-112. These passages, though
containing elements of confusion, manifest an emotive power
which could not be reached by merely rational or intellectual processes.

> For me the prairie is a place
> of wonder and delight,
> like the opening of a white picket fence
> to the far-off mountains stately and impassable.
> The tranquil assurance of yellow wheatfields
> under the quiet of pale skies
> blends with the green renascence
> of waters deep in a marsh
> but best of all is the cricket's song
> and the call of birds by the waters' edge
> which merge into the mystery of night and stars.
>
> —M. B.

When the quiet and tired beauty of the sunlight sinks
from the pale skies and spreads itself over the
tranquil assurance of the yellow wheatfields, I open
my door upon a far-off mountain, stately and impassable.
My weary feet drag this lonely being away from the
hunger and desolation of that shack by the railroad.
Whether I am greeted by the wind crunching through a
fantasy of piled and rusty leaves, or by the penetrating
whiteness of newly fallen snow, these jobless bones
of poverty trudge on and on to where the green
renascence of waters reflect the gentle, velvet touch
of the sunset, until the cricket's song and the call of
birds by the water's edge merge into the mystery of
night and stars. Hope once again renews my soul
and her petals flower above the finality of stone.

—F. G.

MENTAL ASSOCIATION AND DESCRIPTION

What do we mean by saying that we have *really* seen something? The answer is not obvious; when we come to the world of art, difficulty is increased by the fact that the artist is as frequently interested in his own *perception* of the object as in the *object itself.* Labels are not of great value here; for all art, as we have said elsewhere, is made up of symbols, of conventions. A realistic painting and an abstract painting are equally distinct from the immediate order of reality which art imitates. Both have to be understood by the intelligence, by a knowledge of the conventions of art. Labels merely emphasize certain aspects of the artist's interpretation of reality. Some labels emphasize the subjective element in the beholder's view of the world; others denote an increased effort to see the object, disassociated, as far as this is possible, from the beholder's emotional reaction. Thus, you may speak of *impressionism* in description as an effort to give a view of reality in which the reality of emotion is emphasized at the expense of the reality of objective contour and line. Art, after all, has its own laws, and the very meaning of "heightened" in "heightened imitation" would be lost— in fact, emphasis would be impossible—if all aspects of reality were given their scientifically due weight and proportion. If you like, you might say that art is handicapped by the necessity of dealing with only one kind of reality at one time. *Realism* will stress contour and line, the objective relations of lines and planes, but, for this very reason, must tend to ignore the artistic expression of emotion, itself a reality no less valid than contour and plane.

In order to write creatively, you must alert the five senses (touch, sight, smell, taste and hearing) that in modern life tend, paradoxically, to become anaesthetized under the constant pressure of radio, television, advertising, and other mass media. It is possible to build a protective indifference to sights, sounds, odors, tastes, so great that our senses seem scarcely alive. In fact, the greater our insensibility, the wilder grows the bombardment of the senses by commercial interests overcompeting for "captive audiences." Even students in college may have succumbed to the massed attack upon their inert senses. The senses need discipline—in the sense of a more proper focusing and sharpening, but they must neither be rendered callous nor abnegated.

Many are so underprivileged in this respect that they are incapable of experiencing the elemental richness of sights and smells, color and taste, sound and touch. Their ears may be dead to the drift of a leaf, to the non-pushbutton laugh, the splash of spring rain—to any sound that cannot shriek above the city traffic or the blaring jukebox. Their hands are insensitive to the variegated textures of warm bread, stone, a baby's curl. At least they do not think to express the subtleties of sense experience in their writing—that is, until their senses are reawakened and sensitized by proper education.

One problem of the beginning writer whose imagination has been channeled in conventional grooves revolves about how to handle with originality experiences that tend to echo a thousand previous experiences already described. It is the problem of "life imitating art." Imaginative deadness may also result from seeing life through the blur of mediocre reading.

One student asked: "How would I describe Mulberry Street, on the lower east side of New York City, except as a dozen previous writers have already pictured it? How can I avoid the descriptive clichés that inevitably pop up—smells, dirt, heat, poverty, pushing crowds, sidewalk pushcarts, foreign accents?"

One method of combatting the tendency to rehash hackneyed memories of random readings that may prejudice our own creative insight is to try to see a frequently described scene or incident from a new angle. A native of Mulberry

Street, for example, like the Madwoman of Chaillot, might regard the street as the exciting center of his own particular universe, a place to make a big sale, to meet his old friends, to strike a good buy in a fine piece of salami—a street warm with familiar associations.

Another device is to describe sensory experiences through unusual sense channels—that is, colors through smell; sights through sound; noise through touch. The senses are deliberately "kaleidoscoped."

"He tasted the freshness of the day on his lips."

"The wild greenness of the spring was a gnawing hunger."

"The throbbing pavements resisted the pressure of his tired feet."

"The chortle of the seas amid the rocks, the pounding of the surf in sparkling rush."

"From the denuded wood the crow caws sullenly."

The writer must be able to say with Edith Sitwell, "my senses are like those of a primitive people, at once acute and uncovered—and they are interchangeable."

A third method is to find a fresh, new-coined image—an unusual combination of words—to express a universal and common experience. For example, instead of including a cliché like "the scent of pine needles" in a description of a mountain scene, one might reawaken one's reader's jaded senses by a new combination of words like "the pine-fresh dawn"—a combination that stimulates the reader's memories of the freshness, the quiet, the pine air of a mountain scene.

Experiment

Show how the different sensory impressions are fused to increase the effectiveness of the description in the following extracts from student themes.

(1) The emaciated child of the ghettoed grain
a threadbare trappist in a barren field
huddled in the mourning rain of sadness.

(2) The blue lips of winter muffled in dead earth.

(3) A silver bridge spanning the river, a harp dropped
from the sky and silenced for a hundred years or more.

(4) The horses galumped on the cobblestoned street.

(5) Looking down on the crimson blotch of sunset
in the harbor—
the glassy tilt of oars touching red solitude
gulls curtseying to the serenity of the
ceaseless ocean.

(6) Dawn comes on soft white wings of snow
Sweeps the hills from the rim of night.

(7) The spinning, spiraling gift of snow
Like the eloquence of unloosed bells.

(8) It is night; a heavy fog rolls coldly in from an angry,
swollen sea and envelops the fishing village of Suffolk in a
dank, eerie embrace. Situated upon a jagged, white stretch
of sandy beach, the clusters of houses and huts are tightly
shuttered in a flimsy attempt to escape the anger of the foam-
ing sea which is noisily gathering its strength and roaring
close to its goal—destruction. There is a peal of bells, mysterious, submerged bells which seem to cry out from the very
heart of the sea.

(9) The sky is sadly gray. The rain drips down in quiet
misery, splashing into little pools of grief.

(10) The creaking silence of the untilled farm.

Actually, the methods of poetry and of descriptive writing
quite often cover the same area. The techniques explained

in this book in reference to mental associations apply to description as well.

Once you have become conscious of the methods and values of mental association, your ability to write description will be enormously increased. Description as a distinct form of writing is not very common in contemporary literature, but descriptive power serving purposes of intellection, action, and climax (point of highest tension) is fundamental to all creative work.

Artistic description is not a matter of listing characteristics or features of the thing observed. What the creative writer sees is not merely the object, but the object plus his own mood or interpretation. Entering description is metaphor, or the transference and presentation of one experience in terms of another through the usual methods of mental association.

Powerful descriptive effects can be obtained by expressing simultaneously the universal and the particular, the abstract and the concrete, the general and the individuated. Thus, in the list of syntheses to be found in this book, a phrase such as "pity the gaunt-cheeked animality of hunger" combines the abstract idea of animality with the concrete image, *gaunt-cheeked*. It is a noteworthy fact that in this type of combination the universal idea gains in universality by association with a concrete and individuated image. The image, in turn, gains in sharpness and focus by its union with the abstract. Such a phrase as "the Mass flowering from the finality of stone" gains beauty and significance from the hard and abrupt image of *stone*. "The cool freedom of new violets" is a powerful combination of the abstract idea with the concrete imagery of the violet.

Very productive, both in poetry and descriptive writing, is the use of "action" words in relation to forms and colors which are often considered to be contemplative. Actually, many colors suggest movement of various kinds. Thus, Keats says in "The Eve of St. Agnes": "Sudden a thought came like

EL GRECO: *View of Toledo*

Subjective, Impressionistic, Leading
to Climax of Mood

VERMEER: *View of Delft*

Objective, Direct, Leading to Predetermined Effect

a full-blown rose." What does this line really mean? On a purely rationalistic level it would mean nothing at all. But if you think of the rose as possessing powerful and streaming color and coming in all its fullness and perfection ("full-blown"), it provides a good symbol for sudden and unexpected violence, both of thought and emotion. The suggestion of "sudden fruition" in the image of the rose as "full-blown" adequately symbolizes instantaneous and complete certainty in the "thought."

One student approximated this effect in the synthesis, "the waterfall blossoms over the green plain." Another writer captured the emotional power of color in the phrase, "the shock of the immaculate shroud of whiteness." Still another wrote: "The velvet blood of roses streams from the dark subway stand."

Technical problems in description are fairly simple. Choose the method that suits your purpose best. Among the most common methods are:

(1) The *direct and climactic,* in which you proceed in an orderly way to a climax (or "culmination of force"). The following description of Killarney is an example of the direct and climactic:

Is there a greater surprise in the British Isles? With a suddenness that takes the breath away you are faced by one of the grandest views in Europe! There is no warning. You emerge from the wilderness as suddenly as a man leaving a dark tunnel comes into the light of day. You do not expect it! You can hardly believe! Behind you the abomination of desolation; below you an earthly paradise—the three blue Lakes of Killarney.

I rested on a stone wall and stayed in a kind of dream, gazing down at the amazing bird's eye view of the lakes, the blue mountains, and the green woods. It was a warm, sunny day. The lakes were the colour of the sky and as still as glass. A boat smaller than a leaf moved slowly over the water, and I could see men pulling at a salmon net.

Every graciousness and softness that nature has denied the

mountains have been poured out into the rich Valley of Killarney. It is almost too good to be true; almost too opulent
to be quite credible. You feel, as you look down on it, that it
might at any moment dissolve into mist, leaving you in the stern
reality of the hills . . .[2]

To what extent do you have objective imagery, subjective
impression, in the piece you have just read?

(2) The *impressionistic,* in which you follow the technique
present in the work of writers like Walt Whitman or Thomas
Wolfe and gain your end by amassing somewhat disordered
but accumulative details that create the atmosphere you
want. An example of the impressionistic is Whitman's "A
Song of Joys":

Another time mackerel-taking
Voracious, mad for the hook, near the surface,
   they seem to fill the water for miles;
Another time fishing for rock-fish in Chesapeake bay,
   I one of the brown-faced crew;
Another time trailing for blue-fish off Paumonok,
   I stand with braced body,
My left foot is on the gunwale, my right arm throws far out
   the coils of slender rope,
In sight around me the quick veering and darting of fifty skiffs,
   my companions,
O boating on the rivers,
The voyage down the St. Lawrence, the superb scenery, the
   steamers,
The ships sailing, the Thousand Islands, the occasional timber-
   raft
   and the raftsmen with long-reaching sweep-oars,
the little huts on the rafts, and the stream of smoke
   when they cook supper at evening.

What general impression do you get from Walt Whitman's
free verse? Are there too many details? Or do they combine
well for a total effect?

[2] H. V. Morton, *In Search of Ireland,* New York, Dodd, Mead & Co.,
1931, pp. 169-170.

(3) The *highly selective,* a particularly useful form in relation to psychological situations in which a number of implications and moods are bound up with one significant object. An example of the highly selective follows:

But my emotion, so far as I could undestand it, seemed to attach itself more particularly to the willow bushes, to these acres and acres of willows, crowding, so thickly growing there, swarming everywhere the eye could reach, pressing up the river as though to suffocate it, standing in dense array mile after mile beneath the sky, watching, waiting, listening. And quite apart from the elements, the willows connected themselves subtly with my malaise, attacking the mind insidiously somehow by reason of their vast numbers, and contriving in some way or other to represent to the imagination a new and mighty power, a power, moreover, not altogether friendly to us.

Great revelations of nature, of course, never fail to impress us in one way or another, and I was no stranger to moods of this kind. Mountains overawe and oceans terrify, while the mystery of great forests exercises a spell peculiarly its own. But all these, at one point or another, somewhere link on intimately with human life and human experience. They stir comprehensible, even if alarming emotions. They tend on the whole to exalt.

With this multitude of willows, however, it was something far different, I felt. Some essence emanated from them that besieged the heart. A sense of awe awakened, true, but of awe touched somewhere by a vague terror. The serried ranks, growing everywhere darker about me as the shadows deepened, moving furiously yet softly in the wind, woke in me the curious and unwelcome suggestion that we had trespassed here upon the borders of an alien world, a world where we were intruders, a world where we were not wanted or invited to remain—where we ran grave risks perhaps! [3]

This is practically the method of symbolism, where an external object is used as a token representation of a much greater and larger force behind it. How is the effect of menace secured in this description?

[3] Algernon Blackwood, "The Willows," *Tales*, New York, E. P. Dutton & Co., 1939.

All artistic description, of course, depends upon mental association for its emotional effect. Scientific description more properly falls under the heading of exposition, but its objective is not to stimulate the emotions, but to amass information for use. In writing artistic description, your interest is not inclusive or unselective, but you choose your details for emotional impact, whether you are writing the straight description of a travel book, or the psychologized description of a short story.

It is possible, especially in poetry, to present a description that is more or less justified in itself. It is not subordinate to any other purpose; it stands or falls on its own beauty alone.

Could the following description be regarded as complete and justified in itself?

Far off
in the cold mountains the immaculate snow
is lit by stars as cold. The terraced trees
move not, but hoard their perfume all the night,
till, with the dawn released, green flautists, they
stir all the air of the valley to a tune.
The cowherd climbing to the Alpine hut
stands for an instant with the green counterpoint
entranced. Then, as the cowbells overtake
the high, ecstatic trebles of the snow,
he takes his alpenstock and trudges on.[4]

Experiment

(1) Write a description based on one of the following suggestions; you may use the riddle technique (p. 133).

(a) An abstract quality—such as Joy, Hope, First Love, Military Honor, The Ideal of the Gentleman

[4] Humbert Wolfe, *The Uncelestial City*, New York, Alfred A. Knopf, 1930, p. 240.

(b) A place of special interest—such as Home Town, The Old Schoolhouse, The Cathedral, Favorite Fishing Spot, Office Building, Suspension Bridge

(c) A natural force—such as Dawn at Sea, Dusk in the Northwoods, Rainfall in the Mountains, Blizzard on the Railroad

(2) A rewarding type of descriptive writing comes from following "snapshot" technique through the use of the word in place of the camera lens. As you go about your town, city, or countryside, jot in your notebook impressions of the external world that stimulate you for their beauty, irony, contrast, or social significance.

Attempt three snapshot descriptions in free verse of aspects of the city in which you are now living.

THE IMAGE AND THE RIDDLE

An interesting experiment in description is the attempt to give in a succinct, even abrupt, way the most general characteristics of a species, group, or class. You might consider this an experiment in "abstractionism" or in "essentialism." You winnow away anything in the way of the individualistic so that what is most generally characteristic will alone bear emphasis. It is a method that readily lends itself to humorous or satiric overtones. "Generic description," as we call this process, can provide a complete artistic unity of its own.

The following two generic descriptions serve to isolate the essential components of a general idea. The reader's response depends largely upon his perception of overtone (p. 37) and of *motif* (p. 138).

If this material is read too quickly or inattentively, its meaning may easily be lost, for the various statements demand, through overtone, a sympathetic insight on the part of the reader into the writer's implied values. In the first piece, *though he doesn't belong to my club* suggests a value by which to measure the other attributes of Atterbury Jocelyn Peabody. In "I am Society at Its Best," the word *suffering* is a key to the assessment of the values otherwise expressed in the piece.

Atterbury Jocelyn Peabody

I am Atterbury Jocelyn Peabody
And the world takes me seriously—
As indeed it should.

I have done my bit to leave
the world a better place than I found it.
I headed the *Red Cross List* at St. Bartholomew's
And founded the *Peabody Memorial Home*
in honor of Atterbury Jocelyn.
I patronized the arts
And my later years have been troubled by gout.

But I don't complain.
I believed in democracy and the League of Nations
when they existed.

But now I spend most of my time at my club
And soon, my doctors inform me, I shall meet God.
I shall be pleased to meet him
though he doesn't belong to my club
and have a quiet conversation.

—W. J.

I Am Society at Its Best

I am Society at its Best
I give pattern and purpose
to a thousand aspirations and petty ambitions
I weave them into a punctilious design
of *sheer* surface
more delicate and nicely balanced
than convent needlework.

I am the leader of those gracious ladies
whose excellent taste terrifies the uninitiated.
I stand in the forefront
of a thousand select virgins and matrons
who wear jewels well on chaste skins
who have found life beautiful
and *always* amusing.

I am Society at its Best
I stand at the forefront of a regiment of women
sensitive to the occasional pathos
in the lives of the common people.

I wear my gracious smile
and jewels—as usual—
as I touch delicately
with tapering fingers
Suffering.

—W. J.

An interesting experiment in the use of imagery is to be found in that ancient literary form known as the *riddle* in Anglo-Saxon poetry. The power of imagery both in poetry and in creative prose comes from the vivid and dramatic effect, very often from the surprise, both just and apt, that accompanies a good image. To tell a good story, for example, you should "keep to the point of interest with a minimum of revelation." Keep the audience interested by withholding the answer to the main problem. That is the art of climax. Good writing, both in poetry and in creative prose, consists in "pacing" effects. Pace, whether in a horse race, an essay, or a poem, implies a deliberate control on the part of the artist, a deliberate decision regarding the exact points at which to spring effects or divulge information. Generic description as used in the riddle technique paces its effects in this way.

The generic description is one of the most interesting forms in writing, a form simple enough to master quickly. In this form you concentrate the most universal qualities of an idea, a person, a situation, and then present these qualities through a speaker in the first person who describes himself as a symbol of these qualities. "I am Hunger," "I am Death," "I am Music," "I am Joy." An application of this method to advertising is to be seen in the plate, "I am Industry— 1952."

The Anglo-Saxon riddle is an example of generic description. From the viewpoint of the audience the fun was to guess what the object was that spoke in the first person and gave an account of its generic qualities:

> My robe is silent, when I rest on earth,
> Or run by the shore, or ruffle the pools:
> But oft on my pinions upward I mount
> Borne to the skies on the buoyant air,
> High o'er the haunts and houses of men,
> Faring afar with the fleeting clouds.
> Then sudden my feathers are filled with music.
> They sing in the wind, as I sail aloft
> O'er wave and wood, a wandering sprite.[5]

What is the answer? In this case it is "The Swan."

A student used this technique, which permits climax by withholding the explicit statement of the subject matter until the reader has been psychologically prepared for it.

The Third Horseman

I am the unwelcomed guest of the world, the perennial man who came to dinner. To America I am a stranger, but the rest of mankind knows me all too well. I am the scourge that is never checked, the insidious blight that knows no bounds. My victims run before me, pleading, praying, protesting. But inexorably my tentacles reach out and ebb their life away. I am of the Apocalypse. I am starvation.

In America I am a legendary figure existing only in newspaper

[5] Translated by J. Duncan Spaeth in *Old English Poetry*, Princeton, Princeton University Press, 1927.

I am Industry—1952

Ushered into a new world,
I had a bustling, brawling, bruising youth.
I was a potential giant awakening in a world of giants.
People were hurt when I first stirred in life;
Then I grew and learned;
 Then I matured and knew that
Though I work with water and metal and chemicals and fire,
I am more than these things.
  I am the people's work!
  I am the people's dream!
  I am the people!

With maturity, I have grown, too, in social responsibility
To the people.
  To America!
  And even to those beyond our shores.
My efforts are not in selfish interest;
Rather, all my brain and brawn strives for the good of the many.
I am the American way!

  Now, I have sworn that these things shall be:
I shall deliver ever-better products to those who use my fruits!
I shall offer equal opportunity to those who work at my side
  Whatever their race!
  Whatever their creed!
  Whatever their color!
  Whatever their national origin!
I shall forever do my part to keep America great!

And why?
Because only in this way can I remain a healthy force in our free world.
  For when I am healthy, America prospers
  And tyrants tremble before my might.

I am America's life-blood!
I am America's strength!
I am the bulwark of the World's freedom!

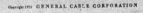

headlines. But the Chinese coolie, the Yugoslav peasant, the Hindu farmer are not so fortunate. They have to face realities. They have to face me. Their babies cry with hunger, their wives beg for bread or weeds. They are in a strange world of inertia, the world of in-between. For I am the sneak thief that steals their will power, wipes out their initiative, destroys their desire to struggle on.

And then I complete my task. It may be a cold street corner in Naples or on a winding dusty road leading to the countryside, the countryside where there should be food. But how can there be food when soldiers have torn each other's heart out, where the machines of war have worn the soil thin, where death is planted instead of wheat? The farmers, struggling against me, shutter their windows and bar their gates as if the Black Plague of the Middle Ages was sweeping down the road. Quietly and peacefully they lie down to wait for my companion who rides constantly with me. At last in death they are beyond my power.

—J. C.

How adequate is the following generic description symbolizing an abstract idea?

Despair

I come by night, a halter around my throat, to wrap your limp form in black velvet. My hollow eyes mock you, my thin white hands reach out and clutch your dry heart. I bring emptiness clothed in a shroud. I tear your head from your hands. My bitter sigh echoes down narrow halls. I close the great oak door.

—B. E. G.

A humorous version of the riddle technique can be seen in the following example. A complete artistic effect, though, of course, simple and limited, is thus achieved.

I am a Woman. I wait until the Big Chase in a Wild West movie or the Big Kiss in a torrid love picture before removing my coat. I try to pick up subway change with my gloves on during the rush hour. I drop packages in revolving doors. I have violent coughing spells during Sunday's sermon. I stall the car when the light turns green. I hard-boil soft-boiled eggs. I allow my wet umbrella to drip down the leg of a fellow bus passenger. I lose library cards. I trump my partner's ace in a bridge game. I "adore" hats with twelve-inch feathers. I am watery-eyed at the sight of one black kitten in the midst of nine white ones. I serve salads with uncut lettuce leaves. I always need stockings. I discover blond hairs on dark suits. I "fall for" glib-voiced salesmen. Yes, I am a Woman!

—J. K.

Experiment In Description

(1) Explain in detail all that you visually see in the photograph of a painting by an old master. Use a new paragraph for every major aspect of the picture.

(2) Having physically described the picture, express any possible meaning it may have for you, historical, associative, suggestive, fanciful. In the case of a portrait, imagine what characteristics you would normally associate with such physical features.

(3) Write a description as a key to human character, attempting to indicate a meaning, ironical or sentimental, that will appeal to the reader's emotions.

(4) Present a character making a sudden discovery of an object which leads to a train of memory, as, for example, coming across an old photograph within the leaves of a book.

(5) Describe any curious mannerism of a person that has interested you. Achieve a climactic effect by suddenly stressing its biographical and psychological meaning as if it had just dawned on you.

(6) Show two people viewing the same object from two entirely different perspectives because of their clashing characteristics.

(7) Go to a definite spot in your town or city, and write down the mental associations you experience on viewing aspects of the scene. Write an impressionistic description in terms of your associations.

(8) Using the riddle technique, present a generic description of such familiar types as a salesman, a policeman, a politician.

MOTIF

One of the most successful conventions for deepening emotional impact in writing is *motif*. Motif is basically a repeated pattern of some sort—frequently, the repetition of a key image. It is not necessarily a logical or intellectual pattern, but, by restatement at climactic points (points of highest tension) in a discourse, this pattern deepens emotional intensity and becomes the artistic means of conveying intensity. It frequently consists in using an external object or situation to symbolize an internal, psychological tension. It may also consist in the ironic repetition of a key phrase.

For example, Macbeth, under the dynamic pressure of his own wife, nerves himself to commit a murder for which he is temperamentally unsuited. Having killed his king and guest, he looks at his hands and sees blood on them. For his wife, the reaction to the murder is very simple. "A little water clears us of this deed," she says. But for Macbeth himself, the bloody hands become a symbol of the enormity of his crime. At this point he realizes what Lady Macbeth, with her more extrovert mentality, does not, that the blood on the hands is the visible sign of inner spiritual guilt.

> Will all great Neptune's ocean wash this blood
> Clean from my hand? No, this my hand will rather
> The multitudinous seas incarnadine,
> Making the green one red.

This symbol of the bloody hands is used by Shakespeare as a *motif*. Later in the same play, Lady Macbeth, having lost her reason in the course of brooding over the mutual disasters that have overtaken herself and her husband, thinks again of the night of the murder and of blood on her hands. "All the perfumes of Arabia will not sweeten this little hand," she says. The hands, by means of connotation deliberately reinforced, carry all the associated meaning previously stated in the work of art. The motif illustrated in *Macbeth* is a motif of great imaginative power. The motif concentrates symbolically emotional and spiritual experience.

This very concentration, however, creates the need in the reader to see what has been concentrated, what has been implied, but not explicitly stated. The ability to see the motif and to catch the overtone that goes with it, to read between the lines, does not merely increase one's pleasure in the subtlety of art. Generally speaking, the motif-overtone is *essential* to the meaning. In order that the artist's communication may be fully understood, he has to be *over*heard, as well as heard.

MACBETH *(Act II, Scene ii)*

Enter Lady Macbeth

Lady M. That which hath made them drunk hath made me bold;
What hath quench'd them hath given me fire.
Hark! Peace! It was the owl that shriek'd,
The fatal bellman, which gives the stern'st good-night.
He is about it: The doors are open;
And the surfeited grooms Do mock their charge with snores:
I have drugg'd their possets,
That death and nature do contend about them,
Whether they live, or die.

Macb. *(Within.)* Who's there? what ho!

Lady M. Alack, I am afraid they have awak'd,
And 'tis not done. The attempt and not the deed

Confounds us. Hark! I laid their daggers ready;
He could not miss 'em. Had he not resembled
My father as he slept, I had done't.
　　　　　　Enter Macbeth.
　　　　　　　　　　　　　　　My husband!

Macb. I have done the deed. Didst thou not hear a noise?

Lady M. I heard the owl scream and the crickets cry.
Did not you speak?

Macb.　　　　　　　When?

Lady M.　　　　　　　Now.

Macb.　　　　　　　　　　As I descended?

Lady M. Ay.

Macb. Hark!
Who lies i' the second chamber?

Lady M.　　　　　　　　　　　Donalbain.

Macb. This is a sorry sight. *(Looking on his hands.)*

Lady M. A foolish thought, to say a sorry sight.

Macb. There's one did laugh in's sleep,
And one cried 'Murder!' that they did wake each other.
I stood and heard them; but they did say their prayers,
And address'd them again to sleep.

Lady M.　　　　　　　There are two lodg'd together.

Macb. One cried 'God bless us!' and 'Amen' the other,
As they had seen me with these hangman's hands.
Listening their fear, I could not say 'Amen,'
When they did say 'God bless us!'

Lady M.　　　　　　　Consider it not so deeply.

Macb. But wherefore could not I pronounce 'Amen'?
I had most need of blessing, and 'Amen'
Stuck in my throat.

Lady M.　　　　　　　These deeds must not be thought
After these ways; so, it will make us mad,

Macb. Methought I heard a voice cry 'Sleep no more!
Macbeth does murder sleep,'—the innocent sleep,
Sleep that knits up the ravell'd sleave of care,
The death of each day's life, sore labour's bath,
Balm of hurt minds, great nature's second course,
Chief nourisher in life's feast,—

Lady M.   What do you mean?
Macb.   Still it cried 'Sleep no more!' to all the house:
      'Glamis hath murder'd sleep, and therefore Cawdor
      Shall sleep no more; Macbeth shall sleep no more.'
Lady M. Who was it that thus cried? Why, worthy thane,
      You do unbend your noble strength, to think
      So brainsickly of things. Go get some water,
      And wash this filthy witness from your hand.
      Why did you bring these daggers from the place?
      They must lie there; go carry them, and smear
      The sleepy grooms with blood.
Macb.   I'll go no more.
      I am afraid to think what I have done;
      Look on't again I dare not.
Lady M.   Infirm of purpose!
      Give me the daggers. The sleeping and the dead
      Are but as pictures; 'tis the eye of childhood
      That fears a painted devil. If he do bleed,
      I'll gild the faces of the grooms withal,
      For it must seem their guilt.
                  (Exit. Knocking within.)
Macb.   Whence is that knocking?
      How is't with me, when every noise appals me?
      What hands are here? Ha! they pluck out mine eyes.
      Will all great Neptune's ocean wash this blood
      Clean from my hand? No, this my hand will rather
      The multitudinous seas incarnadine,
      Making the green one red.

Experiment

(1) *Macbeth.*

(a) Show how the fact that Lady Macbeth retains some traces of humanity helps to create tension ("Had he not resembled My father as he slept, I had done't"). Show how her emotional reluctance to accept the accomplished fact of murder deepens the irony of the scene.

(b) Explain how the image of sleep has become an ironic and transcendent symbol of peace of conscience that is forever lost.

(c) Can you show how Macbeth is isolated as a tragic figure (in spite of his wife's affection) by the contrast between her attitude to emergency ("Go get some water") and his own ("They pluck out mine eyes").

(d) In how many different ways is "the hands" image used in this scene?

(e) What further emotional force does the image of "hands" gather with its subsequent recurrence?

(2) Locate any uses of *motif* approaching this standard in any other piece of writing with which you are acquainted.

(3) Take a common occurrence—a clock ticking, rain falling on the roof, a telephone bell ringing, dying embers falling from a fire—and use it as a *motif* in a brief narrative of an incident or situation (minimum, 300 words). Repeat the *motif* three times—at the beginning of your piece, in the middle and at the end. Each time, the *motif* should have an added meaning. Conceive, for example, a person awaiting impatiently for a telephone call, a conversation tapering off late at night, a person isolated in the country, someone awaiting a doctor's decision about a sick friend.

Chapter 4

CREATIVE COMPOSITION AND BEAUTY

EXPERIMENTS IN CRITICISM

You come to enjoy something when you understand it. This is particularly true of the art of literature. Even if you yourself do not excel in creative activity, a certain amount of practice enables you to understand, and therefore to enjoy, the productions of others. In this connection, you must not be afraid to form your own opinions. It is true that, as you gain experience, you may alter your views, perceiving certain crudities and misunderstandings. By forming your own views, rather than by merely bringing together the established views of critics, you will grow and develop.

Some knowledge of basic principles increases the possibility of enjoyment. Ecstasy cannot be communicated, but knowledge can. Robert M. Hutchins says in regard to "the communication of ecstasy":

. . . reduced to its lowest terms it may be described in the words of one of my professors at Yale who told us that the excellence of a work of art could be measured by the thrill it sent down your spine. This may be called the chiropractic approach to literature. Persons with spines of peculiar rigidity or toughness would be denied the privilege of artistic comprehension, and an X-ray examination of the vertebrae would be a prerequisite to employment as a literary critic.[1]

The experiments in criticism that follow are designed to help you see the object as it really is—a prerequisite to any enthusiasm you may have for it.

[1] Robert Maynard Hutchins, *Education for Freedom,* Baton Rouge, Louisiana State University Press, 1943, p. 55.

143

Before setting out to write a critical essay it is necessary to form some concept of the purpose of criticism.

The neo-classical tradition has particularly stressed judgment or evaluation as the main end of criticism. Other traditions, including the romantic, have particularly stressed interpretation as the main aim, evaluation being made implicit rather than explicit.

The basis for the classical precepts of art is to be found in Aristotle's *Poetics,* wherein Aristotle defines art as the heightened or selective imitation of life (mimesis). He meant that the artist's business is to create a special world (art) related to, but different from, the world of experience. It is not the same world, but one that has been selected and heightened from experience and reshaped according to the lines and designs of art.

It is important to observe that Aristotle connects art directly with life. His commentators, in subsequent history, often departed from his contextual realism and took an increasingly bookish view of art. Art began to be considered not as a mimesis of life (the authentic Aristotelian view), but as an imitation of previous works of art. Criticism of this kind tended to be unsympathetic to any work with an entirely new spirit or a new technique.

It is not necessary for a modern student to follow any one school of criticism. He should profit by the experience of all of them and attempt to synthesize their most valid principles and techniques.

With classical critics we believe that there are permanent standards of criticism based on solid principles of the nature of art. These we call criteria (plural of the Greek *criterion,* meaning standard of judgment). But, unlike so many "classical" critics, we should not apply these standards according to a one-sided or mechanistic pattern. A classical critic like Matthew Arnold in the nineteenth century emphasized the need for perceiving the great principles of art concealed under a variety of forms and techniques. He stressed the thesis that all great works of art have unique forms; they do not merely repeat a universal form or archetype; they are distinct; they are individual. The danger in applying criteria arises from the fact that the critic may not understand these principles in a sufficiently universal sense and may apply them in a merely mechanical way.

The method in this book is designed to assure understanding and accuracy. It is assumed, first of all, that the critic combines within himself the dual role of artist and scientist. It is particularly in his scientific role that the critic checks on the validity of his conclusions and presents what Samuel Johnson once called "examinable particulars." As an artist, the critic makes a mimesis of the work of art just as the artist makes a mimesis of life, but as a scientist he takes pains to be acquainted with the means and techniques of the work of art, so that he can explain technically what went into the making of the work of art. He should proceed from scientific analysis to judgment. He is primarily interested in showing *what* the work of art is and *how* it is what it is. After this demonstration has been accomplished, he can please himself whether he should make his judgment implicit or explicit. Judgment, of course, revolves around whether a work of art was worth creating in the first place on the basis of its intrinsic, aesthetic, moral, and social influences.

To illustrate critical procedure within a limited but definite area, we shall consider an experiment in the criticism of a poem and in the criticism of a picture or visual object in terms of the beautiful. These experiments present "examinable particulars" to the critic, so that he may proceed from scientific analysis to judgment. It is a method that combines both the artistic and scientific roles of criticism.

GENERAL PROCEDURE FOR ANY CRITICISM

(1) As a preliminary to writing the criticism of any work of art, you must first of all form a point of view based on your

intuition of it. But this point of view you should regard as tentative.

(2) As you note and collect the particulars about the work of art in answering "How is this work of art what it is?" you will find occasion to check and perhaps correct your initial point of view.

(3) The answer to these first two questions constitutes a criticism in itself. If circumstances call for an explicit judgment (implicit judgment is present by inference in the answer to the first two questions), be careful to place it in a third separate division.

CLASSIFYING SYNTHESES AS A PRELIMINARY TO CRITICISM OF A POEM

The syntheses (p. 49) in poetry vary according to the work they perform. Some are purely decorative, some intuitive, and others symbolic. Also, syntheses may be predominantly emotional, predominantly intellectual, or predominantly musical and pictorial. Other types of classification may occur to you. What are presented here are not meant by any means to be inclusive.

It will be helpful for you to realize that the discovery and classification of syntheses is a useful step in understanding, appreciating, and criticizing a poem. In classifying syntheses, you are forced to examine particulars.

In order to illustrate how you may collect and label syntheses, let us assume that you are going to interpret Keats's "The Eve of St. Agnes." First of all, read the poem stanza by stanza. At the conclusion of each step in the reading, put down in your notebook what you consider to be the syntheses in each stanza. Also put down any pertinent remarks or observations about the syntheses that may occur to you.

After you have collected the syntheses, your next step is to label each synthesis according to kind—decorative, intuitive, or symbolic; emotional, intellectual, or musical. You will now have made the tentative beginning of critical analysis. The syntheses you have gathered constitute a heightened selection of the content of the whole poem; they are the basis of your artistic criticism. By this procedure you are making a heightened imitation of the poem, just as the poet was making a heightened imitation of life.

Here is a possible list of syntheses from the poem:

"The hare limp'd trembling"—*pictorial*.
Note the double exaggeration. Not only was it so cold that the hare limp'd. He was also trembling.

"The sculptured dead, on each side, seem to freeze,
Emprisoned in black, purgatorial rails"—*pictorial*.

Again note exaggeration. Even the "sculptured" dead "freeze."

"The silver, snarling trumpets"—*musical*.
Notice also the symbolism of the music as inimical, "snarling." Sound and music are the symbols of the outside "revelry" that threatens the safety of the lovers.

"The music, yearning like a god in pain"—*musical*.
The music yearns not only "like a god," but "a god in pain."

"Beside the portal doors
Buttress'd from moonlight, stands he"—*musical* and *pictorial*.
Notice the contrast between labial and nasal consonants, and the harsh separating "buttress'd."

"He found him in a little moonlight room
Pale, lattic'd, chill and silent as a tomb"—*musical*.

"Feebly she laughed in the languid moon"—*musical*.
Notice the contrast between shrill trochaic foot, "feebly" and long vowels, resonant iambics.

"Sudden a thought comes like a full-blown rose"—*intellectual.*

Note the brilliant image of thought flashing upon the mind as a luxurious rose would hit the sense of sight.

"Innumerable of stains and pleasant dyes
As are the tiger-moth's deep damask'd wings"—*pictorial.*
Note music and tone-color.

"Rose-bloom fell on her hands"—*pictorial.*
Here the poet particularizes color in the manner of a painter.

"As though a rose should shut, and be a bud again"—*pictorial* and *intellectual.*
Note the brilliance of the image and its perfect appropriateness.

"These delicates he heap'd with glowing hand"—*pictorial.*
"Glowing hand" crystallizes the poet's love of color and light.

". . . sumptuous they stand
In the retired quiet of the night"—*pictorial.*
Crystallizes poet's love of contrasting colors.

". . . he arose
Ethereal, flush'd and like a throbbing star"—*pictorial.*
The image suggests the energy of fast-moving color.

"Into her dream he melted, as the rose
Blendeth its odour with the violet"—*emotional* and *pictorial.*
Note the symbolic use of color to present action.

When you have made your list of syntheses and labeled them, you may no longer regard "The Eve of St. Agnes" primarily as a story. (Actually, it may lack some of the elements of a good story—character interest, fast-moving action, and suspense—or may be deficient in them in some degree.)

In going over your list of syntheses, you will be immediately struck by the importance of color in the poem and the conscious use of color by the poet to achieve his desired effects. This will enable you to understand Keats's main purpose in the poem—to present a picture of rich and varied tone, to create atmosphere even more than to recount a narrative.

This collection of syntheses will not only give you immediate insight into a poem; it will also serve the useful purpose of helping you to remember the poem. With each of the syntheses, you will be able to recall the circumstances with which it is associated. For example, the synthesis "the hare limp'd trembling" will recall to you the whole winter scene and its attendant circumstances. Or "as the rose blendeth its odour with the violet" might indicate to you the situation of lovers as well as their respective characters. You can discipline yourself to reconstruct the story and its connecting links from keys such as these. As you come to recognize that all syntheses are not equally great or effective, you will consider the quality of the syntheses with special attention.

The value of this method of criticism is, of course, limited. The structure of the poem, the influence of previous works upon it, and its purpose must also be given attention. In combination with these other factors—and not regarded merely by itself—this classification of syntheses is very helpful, especially when you first attempt to analyze and criticize poetry.

In criticism, your objective is to see the work as it really is. It is possible to give other people's reports of what the work really is without your ever having seen the work in its concrete individual aspect. The following guide (in this specific sense—in regard to a poem) will help you to write an honest, direct criticism. Such criticism will be specific, and concentrated on the *one* work that you are actually looking at.

WRITING A CRITICAL ESSAY ON A POEM

(1) Look at the work of art before you (the actual poem). For the purpose of this experiment do *not* consult reference books or works of literary criticism. Look at the work of art in its own light.

(2) Read the poem through (aloud, if possible). Mark off the syntheses as you go along.

(3) Enter the syntheses individually on separate sheets of paper. This will permit you to reshuffle them for purposes of classification.

(4) Examine and classify the syntheses.

(5) See what leads they give to the specific nature of the poem.

(6) With the syntheses and leads organized, begin the writing of a critical essay, answering the following points.

(a) What do the syntheses indicate about the poem? What do they tell you about the use of color, of sound, of intellectual overtone? What do they suggest about the predominant *motifs,* the predominant ideas?

(b) How are these syntheses used in building up the poem?

(c) What is the total effect of the poem? Can you define the essential characteristics of the poem from the results of your analysis?

(d) Estimate the general value and importance of the poem on the basis of your answer to (c).

7. Aim for integration in your critical point of view. Try to see the work as a whole.

It takes a little time for the beginning critic to avoid "cant" and unconscious dishonesty in criticism. In various papers submitted on "The Eve of St. Agnes" the following observations were made. They are representative of common errors in carrying out this exercise.

In the following remark the student departs from his subject and ceases to be specific. The important thing for the embryo critic is to see the poem, not to give the work a comparative rating in relation to the rest of Keats's poetry.

Although the plot is not a very important or impressive one, the poem is one of the best of Keats's poems.

In the following lines the critic departs from specific criticism to introduce remarks about the author's life.

At the time he wrote this poem he was very much in love with a young girl and it could be that his love gave color and expression as pictured in "The Eve of St. Agnes."

The critic could have made the following statement, with its generous but vague terms, without reading "The Eve of St. Agnes" at all.

All that Keats stands for is revealed in "The Eve of St. Agnes" —sheer beauty of form, imagery, and expression.

The following statement confuses art (a heightened imitation of experience) with experience itself.

A very appealing section of "The Eve of St. Agnes," especially to a gourmet, is the stanza describing the various types of food arrayed on the table in Madeline's bedroom.

The observation below assumes that a certain kind of subject matter must inevitably carry with it certain artistic qualities. The critic overlooks the fact that the handling of the subject is also important.

"The Eve of St. Agnes" expresses universality because of its very subject, love.

The following observations do not sufficiently define terms. They are confused and overstated.

"The Eve of St. Agness" is a medieval love story. Its basis is religion, mysticism, and unplumbed mystery.

In conclusion I would like to bring out that, although "The Eve of St. Agnes" does not possess deep moral or intellectual values, it is an outstanding piece of poetry. If the poem had nothing else, it would always stand out among all other famous poems as a perfect and unsurpassable study in pure color and clear melody.

Experiment

Write a criticism, according to the method presented, of one of the following poems. Attach separately to your essay your list of syntheses (minimum, 500 words).

> Tennyson, "Morte D'Arthur"
> Browning, "A Grammarian's Funeral"
> Keats, "The Pot of Basil"
> Shelley, "Hymn to Intellectual Beauty"
> Coleridge, "Christabel"

WRITING A CRITICAL ESSAY ON A VISUAL OBJECT OR PICTURE IN TERMS OF THE BEAUTIFUL

What is the beautiful? Is it something that pleases on sight? Do not many things please on sight that are not really beautiful? Is something really beautiful in itself or does it merely seem beautiful to a particular observer? Is the beautiful, in fact, merely the creation of the observer, a projection of his own mind or does the beautiful exist in the thing itself? Are all beautiful things equally beautiful? May the beautiful shine through destitution, suffering? Are there different kinds of beauty, spiritual, moral, physical? Can a work of art show the frequently real struggle of experience, its anguish, its frustrations, and still be beautiful?

These are some of the questions raised in any discussion

of the beautiful. On some points there is agreement. A beautiful object is *one,* in the sense that it is integral—it has all the parts necessary for its own particular being, whether it be a rose, a torso, or a cylinder. It has a harmony among its parts determined by their relationship to the integrity of the whole. Dante's "Hell" in this sense is harmonious with *The Divine Comedy.* The beautiful has "individuality"— the uniqueness of its own particular being. Beautiful objects differ in the degree of their depth, their intensity.

Artists have considered beauty as necessary for the soul as food is for the body. Perhaps we do not speak nearly enough of man's need for beauty, partly because the concept of beauty is difficult to explain. In fact the concept of beauty for other than superficial treatment needs careful philosophical introduction. Nor have the philosophers fully explored the problems of beauty.

A transcendent or universal value is to be found in the beautiful. But no less important is the concrete and unique aspect of the beautiful. It is particularly this concrete individuality that is so hard to define.

There has been previous discussion, in explaining synthesis (p. 49), of the importance of the unique image, often arrived at by mental association (p. 45). The individuated (or "individualized") and unique symbol is especially the creation of great art.

We might say that the keener our understanding of concrete individuality, the keener, frequently, our perception of the transcendent and the universal. The great artists, for example, were never vague; they were characterized by an intense awareness of the individuated and the real. The artistic life too, as Chesterton saw it, had as its objective to see things *really.* When things were really seen, one discovered the "submerged sunrise of wonder" that is at the heart of things.

. . . no man knows how much he is an optimist even when he calls himself a pessimist, because he has not really measured the depths of his debt to whatever created him and enabled him to call himself anything. At the back of our brains, so to speak, there was a forgotten blaze or burst of astonishment at our own existence. The object of the artistic and spiritual life was to dig for this submerged sunrise of wonder; so that a man sitting in a chair might suddenly understand that he was actually alive, and be happy! [2]

Yet human intuition (p. 32), while not a material principle, is partly dependent upon perception of the material world for its activity. As much as we may study or learn, vast areas of knowledge remain beyond our immediate comprehension. They seem to us, by analogy, to be like great sweeps of the ocean or of the skies or of the depths of the stellar places. The artist's act of creation is often conducive to insights and intuitions into this world of mystery. Such areas of knowledge, while not completely assimilable by our intelligence in its present state, can at least be made "companionable" to us by art. Art, because it touches the transcendent world, taps these vast areas of meaning. At the same time, because it is wedded to the concrete and the individuated, it is expressed in symbols whereby a specific form created by the artist stands for overtones and transcendentals of meaning not subject to merely logical penetration.

THE COMPLEXITY OF BEAUTY

It is the concept of the unique, of what in philosophy is called the individuated, that deepens religious sensitivity to the beauty of the human person, that enables us to see in our neighbor the image of the Creator. Through awareness of the unique and the individuated one may rise joyfully to the transcendent vision:

The world is charged with the grandeur of God,
It will flame out, like shining from shook foil;

[2] *Autobiography of G. K. Chesterton*, New York, Sheed and Ward, 1936, pp. 90-91.

It gathers to a greatness, like the ooze of oil
Crushed.

Under this transcendent light, one's neighbor appears beautiful. But does this imply that one is no longer really aware of what one's neighbor is really like? Not at all. The charity of St. Paul is not blind, but like beauty itself, it embraces, assimilates, and transcends limitations and oppositions.

Think of the beautiful as perceiving and incorporating the real, the actual fact, if you like. The beautiful should not be limited to the idea of simple harmony; it may also admit of a disharmony that it transcends. It may not always be symmetrical; it may permit asymmetry.

Even the appearance of the ugly by way of contrast may be introduced into a work of art in order to emphasize the beautiful that transcends it. Nor does the beautiful have to be presented explicitly. Irony (p. 193) may be present in the beautiful. Irony implies a method of sharp and conflicting contrasts. Irony, like humor, often states on the surface of the writing the opposite of its real meaning beneath the surface, not in order to deceive an audience, but in order to drive home emphatically its message by the conflict of surface form and real interior meaning. The artistic method of irony is such that a value is made conspicuous either by its absence or by the deliberate statement of its opposite. Because art often works on more than one level of thought simultaneously, a truth can sometimes be made more penetrating by leaving it unstated on the direct level of communication.

Let us take an example. Is *King Lear* beautiful?

Yes, it will appear beautiful to one if one perceives the use of disharmony, asymmetry, and irony in the service of the beautiful that transcends and incorporates the real. The heath scene, the blinding of Gloucester, the cruelty of some of the characters, the pessimism and stupidity of others contribute in the dynamics of this work of art to the transcendence of truth, justice, and beauty. As one recent critic puts it:

Sentimentality would be to consider the play cynical and "pessimistic" and unendurable. This sentimentality, which is not unfamiliar today, is that of finding evil too unpleasant to face. To the sentimentalist who prefers to see reality in some more comforting guise, Shakespeare may seem "bitter" or "morbid." [3]

It is true that the evil and the ugly are presented in *King Lear*. But first of all it should be remembered that they are presented under conditions of aesthetic distance or "heightened imitation," so that they are not exactly the same forces as in real life. Secondly, they are assimilated and transcended by the total purpose of the work of art or its integrity. It is this integrity that makes a work beautiful. In the case of *King Lear,* the integrity is one of conflict, and in *conflict* evil as well as good must be presented. This integrity organically binds a work together and it is purely a forced and rationalistic interpretation to consider component parts of a work of art as divorced from the total life-giving stream of meaning. So considered, some elements might be considered objectionable, but such a consideration ignores the whole meaning of art.

King Lear will not appear beautiful to one if one fails to realize that the concept of the beautiful is complex. A mass culture society tends to follow a *fixed pattern* of the beautiful, an *archetype*. Mass-produced archetypical "beauty" lacks the essence of the beautiful which is dependent, among other things, upon *individuation.* An archetype in this sense is merely a mechanical pattern that can be endlessly imitated without the soul or the intelligence of a craftsman entering into it. To take a common illustration, cover girls provide an almost mechanical interpretation of beauty in terms of regular features, approved physical dimensions, and stereo-

[3] Robert B. Heilman, *This Great Stage,* Baton Rouge, Louisiana State University Press, 1948, p. 289.

typed emotional attitudes. In our society we are conditioned to think that one should never grow old, and one should never die. Youth is often idealized beyond any proper bounds. A cover girl must never be a middle-aged woman, least of all an old woman. Yet these cover girls are often monotonous and insipid, and an old woman by a great artist like Rembrandt is forever beautiful:

> . . . as though
> Rembrandt had charged her quiet, ruined face
> with difficult beauty, and would not let her go.[4]

Why is she beautiful? Her face is indeed "ruined," judged by "surface" standards. But she possesses individuation and transcendence, whereas the cover girl has still to be reborn. Rembrandt does not disguise the fact and meaning of physical decay. The old woman is indeed old, but her beauty has assimilated and transcended what is asymmetrical and opposed to it. The beautiful embraces reality; it does not seek escape from it.

Traditionally, the beautiful is said to be identified by *integrity, harmony* (or proportion), and *radiance* (or "individuation of matter and form through which beauty shines").

Art that is primarily meant to be contemplated (the lyric, for example) can easily be distinguished in these terms. But art that presents aspects of evil, of ugliness in experience at first sight, presents difficulty.

Art presenting conflict (the drama, the short story) does not fit in so easily. In painting, for example, a work by Fra Angelico may present no difficulty, because in his work only freshness and innocence are present. But the problem is different when we come to the work of Albert Dürer.

Now, drama, the short story, the novel, the epic are arts of conflict. Good cannot conflict with the good, the true with the true; therefore, if we present conflict, we must also within the terms of our work of art make a heightened imitation

[4] Humbert Wolfe, *The Uncelestial City*.

(*mimesis*) of what is evil and ugly as well as what is good and beautiful. Otherwise conflict and the art that represents it are quite impossible.

But the purpose of all art is to be beautiful, and the end of the beautiful is contemplation. It is the integrity of a work of art that ultimately establishes it as a fit subject for contemplation. Harmony, therefore, must always be viewed in relation to integrity. Harmony is to be determined by organic contribution to the integrity of the total design. In an art of conflict, harmony is not a surface harmony, but one that assimilates and transcends, with reference to the integrity of the whole work, what in itself may be inharmonious, what may be asymmetrical as well as symmetrical. It is on this level that irony, so characteristic of Shakespeare, can enter the constitution of the beautiful.

Dürer's woodcut (see page 35) is a visual demonstration of beauty arising out of an art of conflict. The grotesque figures of Death and the Devil do not diminish the beauty of the whole composition by their own ugliness. In fact, the stern nobility of the Knight gains in emphasis by contrast with these opposing forces. They actually contribute to the beauty of the work by making the assertion of the Knight possible and vivid. The Knight demonstrates the higher harmony that assimilates the ugly and asymmetrical.

In regard to *radiance,* the philosophical tradition originating in Aristotle regards the actual matter in the beautiful object as contributing to its beauty—matter shines through the form, matter is an essential component of the beauty of a human creation. In the tradition deriving from Plato, art is a shadow of a shadow of a transcendent divine idea (*Republic,* Book X). A simple illustration will show the difference as it pertains to us here. A carpenter makes a table, let us say, and makes it well—he has a sense of "difficulty overcome" —yet the actual wood, according to Plato, has prevented him from a completely adequate expression of the beautiful. For Aristotle's followers, the actual wood has made an integral

Which Contains Greater Elements of Beauty? Why?

contribution to the beauty of the table. Beauty is for them individuated and concrete, it is not an imperfect reflection of a divine archetype.

In other words, in determining whether a given work is beautiful, and the degree of its beauty, you must realize the work as a whole. You must be aware that in an art of conflict there must be a heightened imitation of what is evil, ugly, and inharmonious, in order to assert, in terms of this conflict, the true and the beautiful. The individuation, the concreteness, of a work of art is an important consideration, as the exercises in mental association, illustrating the way of the imagination, have evidenced. James Joyce, in *A Portrait of the Artist as a Young Man,* incorporated an essay on the beautiful that is a synopsis of the traditional Aristotelian philosophy. Integrity and harmony were easy enough for Joyce to explain, but he found the translation of the Latin *claritas* as "radiance" unsatisfactory. Joyce himself is forced to use another Latin equivalent for *claritas* in *quidditas.* The last word is literally a combination of the Latin interrogative, "what," and the noun suffix, "ness." *Claritas* is therefore the *whatness* of the beautiful, the individuated unique substance.

Examine the student experiments on pages 170-184. Measure the extent of your agreement and disagreement with their ideas of the beautiful.

TENSION IN A WORK OF ART

When we say that a work of art is meant for contemplation, we do not imply in any way that the work of art is static. Often one thinks of great works of art as possessing a kind of permanence, a sort of immobility. But, more properly, what a work of art possesses is *balance,* a bringing together and harmonizing of various dynamicisms. Works of art are distinguished by tension, all that is opposed to flaccidity and limpness. Balance and tension go together. Balance gives a sense of the permanent, the stable. Tension reminds one that the forces in a work of art are all intensely alive. Tension that is the result of a balance of forces gives a work of art its value no less than to a tennis racket or a violin string.

We think easily enough of tension in the short story, the novel, the drama. But it is no less characteristic of other forms of art that are quieter and more reflective. Coleridge, in speaking of the imaginative power, says that it reveals itself

in the balance or reconciliation of opposite or discordant qualities: of sameness, with difference; of the general with the concrete; the idea with the image; the individual with the representative; the sense of novelty and frankness, with old and familiar objects; a more than usual state of emotion, with more than usual order; judgment ever awake and steady self-possession, with enthusiasm and feeling, profound or vehement . . .

It is not always easy to pin down the exact tensions that you would find, let us say, in specimens of poetry. Such tensions depend upon mental association and the psychological factors entering such association. But, frequently, a little analysis will indicate a tension ending in the balance or "reconciliation" of opposite qualities. Take these lines from Wordsworth:

> The silence that is the starry sky
> The sleep that is among the lonely hills.

At first you might say that no lines could suggest more complete relaxation, more complete "escape." But there are overtones of other elements (and opposed elements) beside those of silence and sleep. *The starry sky* suggests a clarity, an expansion, a vitality that create an opposition to *silence*. The phrase *lonely hills* provides an opposed overtone to *sleep*. *Sleep* may be a symbol of escape, it is true, but the idea of loneliness suggests the need to "escape from escape" back to the society of men.

Sometimes this tension is much more obvious, as in statements that are clearly in terms of contrast, ironic or dramatic, as in the famous lines from Chaucer's "Knight's Tale":

> What is this world? What asketh men to have?
> Now with his love, now in his colde grave
> Allone, withouten any companye.

It might be said that every work of art is the theater of "contrast and struggle, the drama of this synthesis and harmony." In major works, such as *Antigone* or *Hamlet,* the tensions are on a cosmic level, in which great spiritual deeps and calms are in violent contrast to the turbulent confusion of the surface storms of fate and chance and accident.

The tension that results from a balance of forces often results from bringing together, as in simile and metaphor, associations that are remote or opposed to one another. In the following student exercises in mental association, the images of *ocean* and *snake* are brought together to give adequate tension:

> Tapping insistently
> on May-warmed rocks
> dark green wave
> a snake arched gracefully
> rippling green the whole length of you
> silver-scaled and hissing
> poised to crash.
>
> —B. D.

The following description in a student elaboration of a news extract strikes an effective balance in creative prose between security symbols and menace symbols:

Gulls circled restlessly in the shadowy nave of evening . . . only lit by the candles of the villagers a mile away. Down by the water the darkness lapped at the clean keel of silence. The fishing boat tied up at the wharf was deserted and its sails flapped idly. The world slept in solemn harmony, but clear chords of foreboding sounded in the far reaches of the wide

wind. Quiet, quiet. It dared not break the shimmering silence
of the moon rise. But still the undertone blended with the
lonely twilight and changed it somehow. I could almost hear
it now, far away. It stalked in over the sea. It gurgled and
slipped in under the water. It sneaked along under the cliffs on
the hard-packed sand. I could hear it tremble under the broken
quay. The trees came alive in the night wind and took up the
song. The whole cathedral of abandoned night rung loudly
with the tolling of the bells.

—H. O'R.

Very simple ideas, if presented with tension, gain an
interest far beyond what the subject matter would seem to
warrant. A series of contrasts heightens this generic description:

I am the color red
        the crimson flash to accompaniment of baying hounds
        the velvet pride of pomp and royalty
I am red
        the hectic death-pillow of the tubercular patient
        the torrent of life spilled in battle
        and poppied slumber in alien earth
I am red
        the gleeful scorching of Dante's hell
        the crackling heat of virgin woodland aflame
I am the red of full-blown love,
        the breast of winged spring,
        the ruby's heart
I am the Creator's pastel subdued in sunset,
        His palette run wild in fall
I am excitement and victory and conflict
I am the color red.

—M. Z.

The harmony of beauty is intimately connected with
tension, or Coleridge's "reconciliation of discordant qualities." With this idea in mind, consider this short essay on
the beauty of an amphora:

Let us take a Greek amphora, which may be described as a vessel with a pear-shaped body surmounted by a short neck splayed like a bugle and, at two points diametrically opposite, continuing into the handles that meet the body where it attains its greatest width.

But when I sit and concentrate my mind even upon the "flat" lines of the amphora then that bald description seems so inadequate that it leaves out all that is momentous in what I contemplate. First I see the outlines of the sides spring upward from the narrow base each imitating the other so sedulously, though in a reverse direction, that the evidence of a conspiracy is irresistible. At first the conspiracy seems mysterious and the evidence self-contradictory, for they have apparently agreed to diverge. But presently I observe that their paths are gently convex and their divergence gradually lessening and then, with rising excitement, that the lessening of that divergence is itself continuously increasing as the curvature of the outlines becomes tenser and ever tenser. And now at their greatest distance apart the lines march for a moment parallel, yet only to increase the inward curve of the shoulder on which they are at last converging as if impatient for their meeting. Yet a moment later, when about to sweep directly to their confluence harshly and with tragic finality they for ever repudiate its possibility. Abruptly but *together* they turn short and unpausing swerve upward again, but this time in sharp curves that, bending outwards from one another, are the abnegation of their own union.

But despair yields to perplexity as I see them persevering with their curves beyond the lip of the neck into the lines of the handles, and at last to wonder as each sinks and falls and merges, not into the other, but into itself at that point where it had begun to converge towards its fellow. And considering that point of reunion I perceive the necessity of that dizzy and seemingly ruinous swing into the sky that traced the outline of that neck. For, whatever the relentless mathematician may conclude, the eye can discern no reason why the curve, hitherto hardly perceptibly increasing in sharpness, should there increase with just that *speed*. In order to exploit fully its potentialities as discerned by the eye it needed to prove experimentally its freedom by continuing in another and gentler curve at that point along the line of the handle. Now that the adventurous thrusts describing the neck have lapsed through these gentler spirals of the handle into their lower parts I see that no line remains unterminated at another for continuance and development. And, seeing that each curve has manifested its capacity for development and resulted in a finished figure intrinsically predestined as a whole by any part of itself, I am relieved and gratified and love the very lines of the amphora for the gallantry of their achievement.[5]

The language here, though somewhat technical, is of interest in showing the dynamicism of line in the particular illustration, and in indicating the harmony that is the result of tension and a balance of forces.

Simplicity in writing is the result of balance, of tension. We might call an arch simple, or the amphora previously

[5] Arthur Little, *The Nature of Art or The Shield of Pallas*, London, Longmans Green, 1946, pp. 9-11.

sketched. Actually, nothing is merely "simple" when you look at it closely. The arch meets through a balance of forces. In layman's language, we might say that it is actually supported by its very inclination to collapse. The Greek amphora is the result of the compromise and union of opposing lines.

Simplicity indicates the capacity human intuition has for unity and synthesis. It is this sense of unity that we frequently and justly call simplicity, but it is not really "simple" in the colloquial sense of the word.

Simplicity, because of the intuitive power and coordinating force behind it, may conceal from us the years of study, conviction, and reasoned experience, as well as technical skill that have entered into it. Dante's line is very simple: "In your will, O God, is our peace." The word *peace* here touches many levels of meaning—not merely political peace, but interior peace, the peace of a good conscience, intellectual peace arising from free comformity to what is for Dante spiritual reality. The thought is complex, though the resulting artistic expression is one of simplicity.

PRESENTING EVIL IN ART

The problem of presenting evil in art has specific difficulties. Evil has a certain kind of attractiveness; otherwise, we would not yield to temptation. In order to convey the meaning of sin and evil—a meaning which also includes attractiveness—the artist must not create a source of temptation for the beholder. This demands that the order of direct experience yield to aesthetic transformation, the "aesthetic distance" (*mimesis*) from the order of direct experience. Aesthetic distance, or the selective process in the *mimesis,* evaluates the true nature of evil at the same time that it presents evil. An artist may present evil realistically. But the very way in which he presents an evil act in the context of his work will imply an evaluation of that act. For example,

Macbeth murders his king. His hands are bloody with gore. He tries to fasten his crime on innocent men—the drunken grooms whom he smears with blood. But Macbeth's hesitation, his guilty conscience, his fear and anxiety and eventual despair indicate clearly to the audience that murder is evil, that the murder of a guest is particularly heinous. In *Antony and Cleopatra,* the attraction between the noblest soldier of the Roman Empire and the Empress of Egypt, whose charms "age cannot wither nor custom stale," is presented as immensely strong and compelling, but it is presented, too, as the passion that leads to destruction, not to fruition. Maritain, in speaking of the novelist's art, puts the problem in this way:

> The essential question is not to know if a novelist can or cannot paint a particular aspect of evil. The essential question is to know *at what height* he places himself to make this painting, and if his heart and his art are pure enough, and strong enough, to make it without connivance.[6]

We should be careful not to condemn a work of art as immoral because of its subject matter alone. The presentation of evil does not in itself constitute immorality. Always to be borne in mind is the distinction between the evil which the artist imitates and the *viewpoint* (herein, connivance is found or is not found) which he brings to the evil he represents. It does not follow that a *mimesis* of sin and evil in a work of art implies that an artist approves of them or that he intends the reader to approve of them. Immorality in a work of art becomes evident only when an artist "glorifies" evil and suggests it as a suitable pattern for human conduct. A moral work of art may present evil no less "realistically" than an immoral work, but the moral work of art, in contrast to the immoral work, implies an adverse criticism of such evil. Such criticism need not be explicit; it is sufficient that it is implicit.

[6] *Art and Scholasticism,* London, 1930, p. 224 (Note 154).

We may say that the morality of the work of art does not depend upon the raw material that it handles, but upon the way that this raw material is subject to a heightened imitation and upon the purpose which the imitation serves. Anything that may legitimately be considered a part of human experience (this would include suffering, death, sin, tragedy) is a matter suitable for the artist's handling.

It is true, of course, that certain kinds of material carry with them special dangers and difficulties. An artist, like a teacher, has a responsibility in prudence to his audience. A teacher, for example, should not assign literature to his students for which they are intellectually and emotionally unprepared. But in this matter a careful distinction should be made between literature that should not be allowed to fall into the hands of the immature and literature that is immoral in itself. We should not, for example, determine the morality of literature by the norm, let us say, of what is fit for children. The audience for creative writing, from the point of view of a norm, should be an adult audience of reasonable education and critical capacity.

James Joyce makes a point about the beautiful that also bears upon the problem of morality in art. For Joyce, the beautiful creates a contemplative experience—a *stasis* (literally, "a standing still"), rather than a *kinesis* (literally, a "movement"). When art produces a stimulation in the kinetic sense rather than a stasis in the contemplative sense, for Joyce it is not pure or moral. The handling of the nude, for example, in art can be criticized on this basis. In many altar pieces of the Middle Ages and of the Renaissance, Adam and Eve are presented naked. The nude appears in many great works of religious art. Some of the most beautiful sculptures in the world, those of the Greeks, present the nude. These works are perfectly moral. They are interpreted contemplatively. On the other hand, one has only to compare the *kinetic* type of portrayal of the human figure sold in vulgar publications on newsstands throughout the country for the purpose of exciting the adolescent imagination toward improper desire to see the difference between moral and immoral art. Joyce makes the distinction in these words:

The feelings excited by improper art are kinetic, desire or loathing. Desire urges us to possess, to go to something; loathing urges us to abandon, to go from something. The arts which excite them, pornographical or didactic, are therefore improper arts. The aesthetic emotion (I used the general term) is therefore static. The mind is arrested and raised above desire or loathing.[7]

Didacticism (direct and overt instruction) is inartistic when such material is not sufficiently absorbed into the unity, the integrity of the total work. Moral value should be fused with the mimesis of life constituting the work of art, rather than introduced extraneously.

Experiment

(1) Select a photograph of a painting or of a sculpture and attach it to your report paper. Write an essay answering the question: Is this beautiful? In your essay, (300 words, minimum), answer the following questions:

(a) In what ways does this work of art imitate experience?

(b) What kind of symbols does it use? Explain their meaning.

(c) Is it a work of art that presents conflict, or is it an art that appeals directly to contemplation?

(d) If this work of art indicates an art of conflict, does it possess a harmony that transcends and assimilates its opposites? (Such conflict, for example, is presented in Dürer's "The Knight, Death, and the Devil." The Knight symbol-

[7] James Joyce, *A Portrait of the Artist as a Young Man*, New York, Viking Press.

izes a good man freely opposing evil: the devil and death—
the inevitable obstacles to life. But the figure of the Knight
predominates and unifies the picture. Coherent meaning is
present, in spite of discordant elements.)

(e) Does the work of art possess individuation and concreteness? Does the actual material of the work of art contribute to its "radiance"?

(f) Does the work possess an over-all integrity?

(g) From your answers to these questions can you call this
work of art beautiful?

(This experiment is even more interesting if you use as
your selection work that is apt to be controversial and to
cause a conflict of views.)

(2) How far do you agree with the following student as-
sessments?

(a) Piet Mondrian: "Composition in White, Black, and
Red"

This painting claims to be a composition in white, black, and
red. It *is* that. Its elements are so arranged as to produce a
harmonious whole. Proportion is clearly its theme and its one
perfection. In fact, the clarity and perfection exist only in terms
of the proportion. But the elements of beauty, to *be* beauty,
must be balanced. Clarity and perfection must exist in their
own right.

Mondrian's oil work is stark, cold, hard. It means and por-
trays merely proportion, which, of itself, awakens no strong
emotion. It is pleasing only in its harmony. There is no message or moral save the importance of balance. Its beauty is too
obvious and shallow and does not increase on examination.
There are no shadows, no subtle shades of color. There are no
symbolic figures, nothing to suggest to the mind of the observer
a myriad of associations. It is not an imitation of life, for life
is not so orderly or so blank.

—B. D.

MONDRIAN: *Composition in White, Black and Red*

(b) "Card Game"

This sketch of a "Card Game" is classified as Modern Art. In determining whether this is beautiful or not, one does not condemn or glorify Modern Art generally, but at least one can give some standards whereby all such art can be judged.

Let us analyze the concept of the beautiful and apply it to this particular sketch.

Beauty consists of three fundamentals: Integrity—soundness, completeness, virtue; Harmony—a sense of proportion and connected whole; Clarity—whatness or brilliance in which the object manifests itself to a contemplator.

With regard to clarity, no strenuous contemplation is necessary to grasp this picture's "whatness"—namely, a card game among six players. However on further meditation it is noticed that the forms are vague. They are human, it is true, but lacking in individual characteristics. All the characters seem alike and cold as the benches on which they are seated. Thus its quality, its "whatness," strikes the eye immediately but fades on closer study.

In regard to harmony, the picture seems to possess dynamicism. There's a sense of rhythm and movement in the lines—circular and rectangular—real geometric harmony. The hands seem grotesque and clumsy, but taken in conjunction with the large hats and boots, a certain pattern is achieved. The drab shade of color is also in keeping with the lack of vitality; the atmosphere of cold intensity is dominant, certainly not inviting, but harmonious.

Wherein lies its integrity? It is an honest attempt to represent truth in a sensible form—no propaganda is seen here. However, it gives an effect of a rough cartoon done in a hurry and thus lacks completeness so necessary for integrity. There is an effort to catch and record something vital, something experienced, to record the atmosphere around a card game. It partially conveys the idea, but lack of vitality prevents perfection. A pleasing sketch but not beautiful.

—S. J.

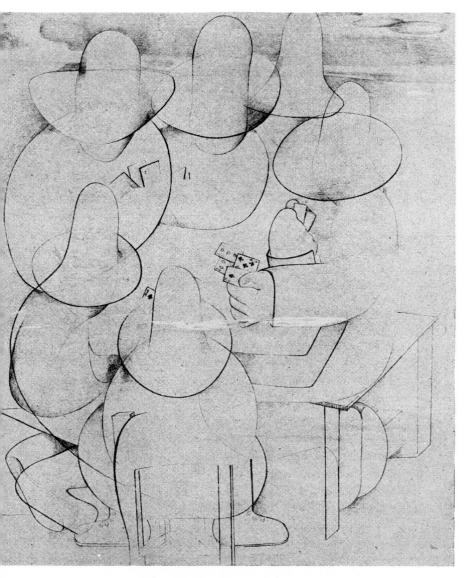

DEL CASAL: *Card Game*

(c) Pablo Picasso: "The Frugal Repast"

At first glance this picture did not please me. On further study I began to see first one good point and then another. Before putting down my reactions on paper, I decided to question one or two other persons.

The first reaction of one woman was a faint smile, followed by the comment that she thought it to be two persons suffering from a "hangover." It suggested sadness to the other woman, coupled with a remark about drinking. Without a doubt, the bottle on the table was a very significant factor for both of these observers.

Upon further examination, I could see that the title suited the picture; the wine bottle is part and parcel of everyday living for the Spanish, and Picasso is a Spanish artist. The man and woman certainly depict starvation with resulting lack of vitality. There is a standing still or "stasis," especially significant in the woman. To me, the limpness of her breasts physiologically fits in with malnutrition. The man seems to be anticipating an arrival or some foreboding event, so that I'm not sure whether there is a sense of "kinesis" or "stasis" here. The long slender fingers of both show sensitivity as well as malnutrition.

The picture can be said to have integrity, harmony, individuation, and the universal. It certainly makes for contemplation. The background gives the impression of a dark, damp cellar room, but despite the somber idea presented, there is beauty in its contemplation. I see a loving husband protecting his wife in a war-torn country or one where totalitarian rule has taken place. On the other hand, it could be significant of economic strife during any stage of life.

—S. A. H.

THE FRUGAL REPAST.
Pablo Picasso, Spanish, 1881-.

(d) Picasso: "Guitar and Fruits"

I will discuss this picture in terms of the general elements of beauty: unity, truth, and goodness; also in terms of its particular elements: completeness (*integritas*), proportion (*consonantia*), and splendor (*claritas*).

The most universal feature in the various definitions of beautiful or pleasing objects is "unity amid variety."

The apprehension of this unity is an intellectual act. In this work of art my intellect refuses to behold this perfection present. The fault may be due to the incompleteness of intellectual education and appreciation on my part, but I cannot consider the work as one whole. I can recognize certain parts, but I do not get the impression of unity.

Truth also forms a general element of beauty. There must be truth in the object itself. An object is therefore true in the sense of "being" or "ontology," if it conforms to the proper concept or idea of itself. To be beautiful a thing must be "ontologically" true. Dr. Emmanuel Chapman, in dealing with the particular element of beauty, *integritas* or "completeness," brings out this thought more clearly. "A particular torso of Venus, for example, though a fragment, may have the unity, wholeness, completeness, perfection or integrity proper to the nature of a torso, and hence be beautiful to the degree that it possesses these as well as the other co-ingredients of beauty." Yet, though taxing the imagination, I can perceive no completeness, wholeness, perfection or integrity in the picture, proper to the nature of a guitar or fruits.

Another element of the beautiful is proportion or harmony. We usually connote by this: symmetry, balance, orderly association, assonance. Yet the real meaning is much deeper. Each being has its due proportion or harmony in so far as its confluent parts are arranged in accordance with its intrinsic end determined by its form. This may require asymmetry or dissonance as well as the more accepted kinds of proportion. In seeking to achieve its end, which is also to achieve its form, each being seeks its good. To the degree that each being is good, that is,

PICASSO: *Guitar and Fruits*

desirable, suitable or agreeable to its own nature or essence, conforming to the purpose or end determined by its form, it has due proportion or harmony. According to what has been stated above, even the picture must be said to have some proportion because the artist certainly made it conform to the purpose or end he determined.

Claritas is the shining out of all the transcendentals united in the beautiful. This requires that an object of beauty possess qualities that give it luster and splendor, make it impressive, lend vividness and charm to its appearance, so that the object stimulates contemplation on the part of the observer.

Applying Joyce's definition to the picture, I do not think it possesses this essential *claritas*. Without its title underneath, and indeed in spite of the title, it may be interpreted as practically anything one wishes to see in it. St. Thomas Aquinas spoke of *claritas* as a "resplendent ray of light irradiating a being from within and belonging to it by its very nature." I find this *claritas* altogether non-existent in the picture.

The true is any adequation of intellect and thing; but the truth of a beautiful thing is an "agreeable, satisfying, gratifying, joyful, lovable, reposeful, peaceful, tranquil adequation. Truth, or that in things which can be known, is seen. Beauty, or that in things which makes us enjoy knowing them, is seen and loved."

This certainly cannot be said of the picture above. It neither placates upon being seen, nor does it possess that desirableness, lovableness, and delectability of apprehensible being which it is enough just to behold in itself.

Beauty is as wide and deep as being itself and its co-extensive transcendentals. Beauty is indefinable, but presents its own evidence superabundantly. Beauty lights up the other transcendentals, enhancing their intrinsic importance, whether in the lowest or highest degree of being. To the degree that the right art form is made to shine out through its appropriate matter, actualizing its potentialities, realizing its essence, integrating, perfecting, completing, unifying, proportioning and harmonizing its existence, the object made will have its own kind of truth, goodness, and beauty. To the degree that these do not shine out as fully as the nature of the thing made requires, the work of art will be relatively false, bad, and ugly.

I do not claim to be a connoisseur of art. The painting has been recognized as beautiful by competent critics. Yet, I do not see "Guitar and Fruits" as beautiful because it has not achieved the form or actuality which its nature requires.

—J. C.

DAUMIER: *Convicting Evidence*

(e) Honoré Daumier: "Convicting Evidence"

The question which arises first in my mind upon looking at this picture is, "Why was the Crucified Christ shown in this scene?" Obviously, it need not have been. Obviously, too, while the Judge seated in the middle is seated so as to be the center of the picture, the lines in the picture converge on the painting of Christ which, as seems to be customary in France, hangs on the wall behind the bench of justice.

The evidence on the small table before the judges is "convicting." It does not interest the judge on my left: he is apparently asleep. Nor does it affect the judge on my right: he is obviously bored. What of the judge in the center?

The judge on the left, the judge on the right, represent callous indifference—an aspect of man's inhumanity to man. The judge in the center represents legal justice: not harsh, but cold. The artist has placed his left eye in the shadow, as much as to say, "This man is half-blind." He is Pilate. The others are the men who once said, "He has blasphemed; what further need have we of witnesses?"

Behind these three men is Mercy and Justice Himself, unjustly condemned, punished without mercy. The judges have their backs towards Him.

There is more humanity—"anger and clamorous accord"—in the evidence lying on the table than in the human figures behind the cold, drab bench. The artist asks the question: "Who will receive mercy at the hands of the Divine Judge: these descendants of those who crucified Him or he who did the deed of passion?"

—C. W. E. P.

REDON: *Silence*

(f) Odilon Redon: "Silence"

The artist imitates life because he presents a human emotion as experienced by the woman in the painting. The imitation is heightened, for, although the beholder is touched by the tragedy depicted, the artist has known how to raise this tragedy from direct experience to a heightened level; he has given it "aesthetic distance."

In my opinion the artist has meant to convey how injury, inflicted by the outside world on a sensitive being, may forever render that individual silent, silent in the sense that never again will this woman express her emotions verbally, nor will she let them penetrate the protective wall of her face.

To project the mood which to me radiates from this picture, the artist used partly familiar symbols and partly abstract ones.

The human face, mirroring a bruised soul and turbulent emotions, is a familiar symbol to us, whereas the thick fog which seems to come closer, and which, in my opinion, will envelop her completely, is an abstract symbol. She cannot face life again. Her childlike vulnerability is unprotected, and she is therefore lacking defenses, those defenses which are termed "maturity" and differentiate us from children. She will not recover from the blow she has received. The enveloping fog is her protection, is bringing her relief, and, by drawing a screen between her and reality, lets her live in the dream world in which she can exist.

The painting possesses integrity and harmony. The artist does not advocate insanity as a solution to life's problems, nor does he arouse in us the temptation to cease struggling, facing life. The beauty of this woman's soul, her purity, her childlike defenselessness transcend her defeatist attitude toward life and, in fact, enhance her beauty.

Odelon's painting, "Silence," appeals quite definitely to the contemplative faculty. It does not instruct. It should be contemplated by one's imaginative and intuitive faculties, rather than grasped by means of one's intellectual conceptions. The more one allows oneself to become invaded by the mood of the painting and the longer the picture is contemplated, the stronger will grow the awareness of its beauty.

The painting has individuation and concreteness. The artist has put into being what has not existed before. The picture bears the stamp of the artist, for it has true originality. By means of his symbols, he has expressed a definite intellectual meaning. Therefore, his painting is motivated and concrete.

The actual matter of the work contributes its "clarity." The artist has clearly defined his symbols. Each symbol forms a complete unit, is assigned its special role, and, without fusing, the symbols blend, comparably to the different instruments in an orchestra, which although playing their own parts, expressed by their individual tone-mechanisms, are subordinated to the main theme and, joining together, can make the music rise, until this theme finds the desired climax in a crescendo.

—S. R.

Review Questions

(1) Explain the relationship of color to mental association.

(2) Explain the "riddle" technique.

(3) What is meant by *motif?*

(4) What is the purpose of criticism?

(5) Explain the general procedure for any criticism.

(6) How does the collecting of syntheses help in the criticism of poetry?

(7) What problem is presented by *harmony* as applied to an art of conflict?

(8) Explain how you would criticize a visual object in terms of the beautiful.

Chapter 5

THE FORMS OF CREATIVE PROSE

THE FORMS OF CREATIVE PROSE

The forms of creative prose are distinguished by the part that mental analysis, plot construction, logical connection play in their creation. They are poetry in the sense that all creative art is poetry. They are creative prose in the technical sense that logic, construction, analysis are predominant rather than intuition, imagination, synthesis.

Humor, irony, satire are forms in which the play of intellect is paramount, in which the imaginative symbol, the fusion of image and idea, is less evident. In such forms as the fantasy, the short story with plot, the short story without plot, poetical elements in the technical sense become extensive, but not so great as to upset the predominance of the qualities of creative prose.

There are degrees of predominance in these forms. The short story with plot will have a higher degree of plotting, "construction," than the short story without plot, which will tend to have more symbolism, more imagery. Fantasy will have more elements of poetry than satire possesses.

Experiment

Contrast the amount and impact of poetic elements in Benét's "By The Waters of Babylon" with those present in Leacock's "Buggam Grange."

186

HUMOR

It is practically impossible to be a first-class writer—or at least a first-class writer whose interests are not channeled in one direction—without mastering the techniques of humor. Humor is achieved by a deliberate distortion of a mutual scale of values established between an artist and his audience, for the purpose of emphasis and amusement and not of deception.

First, it must be noted that the human mind is frequently active on more than one level at the same time. When we perceive that something is disproportionate or distorted, we are able to make a judgment because we possess mentally a concept of true proportion. When we say that a door hangs crookedly, we are at the same time thinking of the abstract idea of "straightness."

It is possible to present a distortion merely with the end in view of emphasizing the accompanying sense of proportion. If, however, you distort with the intention of having your distortion accepted as true, you deliberately lie. But when you present a distortion with the purpose of having the true proportion clarified, you are using the method of humor.

The title of De Quincey's essay "Murder as a Fine Art" is humorous because, although De Quincey distorts the true value associated with murder by assuming that it is a fine art rather than a moral evil, he does so with the intention to amuse—not to deceive. This title would not appear humorous to a group of lunatics who considered murder a fine art, or to a gathering of people convinced that De Quincey was in dead earnest. The value distorted in this title is the moral value that murder is an intrinsic evil. This value is distorted by the assumption (for purposes of amusement, not of deception) that murder is a fine art.

Herein you meet a basic artistic problem. You are always in danger of encountering an audience who, for one reason or another, does not grasp your real meaning. The "surface" meaning of your distortion is accepted as your real meaning. The inner spirit of what you say is missed.

In this regard, it may be noted that humor of a distinctly national or regional character is not always understood beyond national or regional boundaries. The reason is simple. The value distorted may be a value only understood within local boundaries. It may be a social convention, local etiquette, or custom. A national of another country, not understanding the implications of this particular value, cannot appreciate the ridiculousness involved in its distortion.

On the contrary, when humor distorts (in "presentation" only, of course, not in reality) a universal value like justice, it can be understood by everyone, irrespective of nationality or local environment. An American would have no difficulty understanding Jonathan Swift, but he might require a certain acclimatization to appreciate London's *Punch*.

Humor is an outstandingly successful literary mode because it permits the audience to share a secret, to enjoy reading between the lines, to contrast the inner meaning of what you say with the surface meaning.

Read the following page of dialogue from Marc Connelly's *The Green Pastures*. Note how the subtle effects of humor are obtained. There is the distortion of the customary ritual of respect for Deity, which has been replaced here by a frank, neighborly, even folksy approach. The concept of God as Himself a Negro humorously reflects man's tendency to remake God to his own image. On the other hand, there is also a distortion of this distortion, for God in this passage can also act here very much as God, insisting on *one* keg of liquor for Noah, and backing up his injunction by the roll of thunder.

God. I ain't gonter destroy you, Noah. You and yo' fam'ly, yo' sheep an' cattle, an' all de udder things dat ain't human I'm gonter preserve. But de rest is gotta go. (*Takes a pencil and a sheet of paper from his pocket.*) Look yere, Noah. (*Noah*

comes over and looks over his shoulder.) I want you to build me
a boat. I want you to call it de "Ark," and I want it to look like
dis. (*He is drawing on the paper. Continues to write as he
speaks.*) I want you to take two of every kind of animal and bird
dat's in de country. I want you to take seeds an' sprouts an'
everythin' like dat an' put dem on dat Ark, because dere is
gonter to be all dat rain. Dey's gonter to be a deluge, Noah, an'
dey's goin' to be a flood. De levees is gonter bust an' everything
dat's fastened down is comin' loose, but it ain't gonter float long,
caize I'm gonter make a storm dat'll sink everythin' from a hen-
coop to a barn. Dey ain't a ship on de sea dat'll be able to fight
dat tempest. Dey all got to go. Everythin'. Everythin' in dis
pretty worl' I made, except one thing, Noah. You an' yo'
fam'ly an' de things I said are going to ride dat storm in de Ark.
Yere's de way it's to be. (*He hands Noah the paper. Noah takes
it and reads.*)

    Noah. (*Pause. Looks at paper again.*) Yes, suh, dis seems to
be complete. Now 'bout the animals, Lawd, you say you want
everythin'?

    God. Two of everythin'.

    Noah. Dat would include jayraffes an' hippopotamusses?

    God. Everythin' dat is.

    Noah. Dey was a circus in town las' week. I guess I kin fin'
dem. Co'se I kin git all de rabbits an' possums an' wil' turkeys
easy. I'll sen' de boys out. Hum, I'm jest wonderin'—

    God. 'Bout what?

    Noah. 'Bout snakes. Think you'd like snakes, too?

    God. Certainly, I want snakes.

    Noah. Oh, I kin git snakes, lots of em. Co'se, some of 'ems
a little dangerous. Maybe I better take a kag of likker, too?

    God. You kin have a kag of likker.

    Noah. (*Musingly.*) Yes, suh, dey's a awful lot of differ'nt kin's
of snakes, come to think about it. Dey's water mocassins, cot-
ton-moufs, rattlers—mus' be a hund'ed kin's of other snakes
down in de swamps. Maybe I better take two kags of likker.

    God. (*Mildly.*) I think de one kag's enough.

    Noah. No. I better take two kags. Besides I kin put one on
each side of de boat, an' balance de ship wid dem as well as
havin' dem fo' medicinal use.

God. You kin put one kag in de middle of de ship.
Noah. (Buoyantly.) Jest as easy to take de two kags, Lawd.
God. I think one kag's enough.
Noah. Yes, Lawd, but you see forty days an' forty nights—
    (*There is a distant roll of thunder.*)
God. (Firmly.) One kag, Noah.
Noah. Yes, Lawd, one kag.[1]

Humor may deliberately distort in one direction, then in another. In the passage quoted, it is humorous to present God as a rather democratic neighborly overseer. But the humor reverses direction, and gains intensity, when this familiar figure acts very much as God with unquestionable and final authority.

The "drier" the humor, the more concealed is the standard or mean from which the deliberate distortion arises. Also, the danger of misunderstanding is the greater. The Irish clergyman mentioned in Samuel Johnson's *Life of Swift* said, on reading *Gulliver's Travels,* that he did not believe that Gulliver ever took those travels. Either the clergyman missed the point of the book, or else his remark was very dry, indeed. It is wise in writing for a general audience to provide a key or mean to your standard of judgment.

Humor is an underlying quality of evaluation, more or less hidden and implicit in writing. Take Dryden's line in *MacFlecknoe:* "mature in dullness from his tender years." The hidden assumption here is that the subject of Dryden's work, a poet named Thomas Shadwell, actually *must* have *studied* and *aimed* at dullness to achieve the dullness he did. The "deliberate distortion" for the purpose of amusement that Dryden maintains is the assumption that this dullness on the part of Shadwell is a heroically maintained achievement:

> The rest to some faint meaning makes pretence
> But Shadwell never deviates into sense.

[1] Marc Connelly, *The Green Pastures,* New York, Rinehart, I, viii.

Again the assumption is continued—Shadwell is so *perfected* in dullness that he never "deviates." The "mutual scale of values" distorted here is the value that dullness is not something we approve of or strive for. The distortion consists in the assumption that dullness is a noble aim.

Humor is a much more protracted technique than what is commonly referred to as *wit*. Wit consists, as Samuel Johnson once said, in "a sudden and violent collision of ideas." That means the bringing together of ideas that would not normally go together. They are brought together accidentally as in a pun, where the same verbal sound symbolizes two distinct ideas at once. Such ideas, almost accidentally brought together, are then perceived to have unexpected but just relationships. Alexander Pope's pun about the "Divine Right of Kings to govern wrong" plays upon the two meanings of *right*—right in the legal sense, and right as the opposite of wrong. A higher form of wit is the epigram, the antithetical statement, in which two contrasting aspects of the same idea are placed sharply side by side. Such examples of *wit* are to be found throughout Andrew Marvell's "To His Coy Mistress." He reminds his lady that love must be fulfilled before Time's "winged charriot" has run its course:

> The grave's a fine and private place,
> But none I think do there embrace.

Dr. Johnson's dictionary definition of *patriotism* as "the last refuge of a scoundrel" is an example of wit in the sense that it is unexpected, apparently unrelated, yet, in another sense, appropriate and relevant. Johnson, whose close friend and biographer was James Boswell, a Scotsman, loved to poke fun at the Scotch. The *Dictionary* contains this witticism at their expense: "*oats:* a grain which in England is generally given to horses, but in Scotland supports the people."

To contrast humor with wit we can do no better than to take up the friendly feud between Johnson and Boswell about the Scotch. Note the humor of Boswell's famous first encounter with Johnson. Underlying the entire paragraph is the sense of values in which Boswell pokes fun at his own impressionability as well as the social dominance of Dr. Johnson.

At last, on Monday the 16th of May, when I was sitting in Mr. Davies's back-parlour, after having drunk tea with him and Mrs. Davies, Johnson unexpectedly came into the shop and Mr. Davies having perceived him through the glass-door in the room in which we were sitting, advancing towards us,—he announced his aweful approach to me, somewhat in the manner of an actor in the part of Horatio, when he addresses Hamlet on the appearance of his father's ghost, "Look, my Lord, it comes." I found that I had a very perfect idea of Johnson's figure, from the portrait of him painted by Sir Joshua Reynolds soon after he had published his *Dictionary*, in the attitude of sitting in his easy chair in deep meditation, which was the first picture his friend did for him, which Sir Joshua very kindly presented to me, and from which an engraving has been made for this work. Mr. Davies mentioned my name, and respectfully introduced me to him. I was much agitated; and recollecting his prejudice against the Scotch, of which I had heard much, I said to Davies, "Don't tell where I come from."—"From Scotland," cried Davies roguishly. "Mr. Johnson, (said I) I do indeed come from Scotland, but I cannot help it." I am willing to flatter myself that I meant this as light pleasantry to sooth and conciliate him, and not as an humiliating abasement at the expence of my country. But however that might be, this speech was somewhat unlucky; for with that quickness of wit for which he was so remarkable, he seized the expression "come from Scotland," which I used in the sense of being of that country; and, as if I had said that I had come away from it, or left it, retorted, "That, Sir, I find, is what a very great many of your countrymen cannot help." This stroke stunned me a good deal; and when we had sat down, I felt myself not a little embarrassed, and apprehensive of what might come next.

Experiment

Write a straightforward exposition on how to win friends and influence people (250 words). Having done this, take your completed material and reverse the approach, aiming for humorous effects. Write 250 words on "How *not* to win friends and influence people."

IRONY

Irony may be interpreted on two levels. On one level it is merely a rhetorical device in which the surface statement is the opposite of the intended inner meaning. In this sense it is allied to humor.

But irony also has a much deeper sense. This deeper irony is implicit in human experience. It is the irony that John Ruskin indicated in his essay, "Of the Pathetic Fallacy." Ruskin realized that many poets traditionally like to assume that external nature shares the moods and sympathies of men. When the waters claimed a victim, they might be called the "cruel, creeping foam." But, in strict fact, waters do not know cruelty or generosity or any human attribute.

If you want to achieve irony, you reverse this poetic tradition and re-emphasize the lack of correspondence between man and nature. In actuality, the cosmic universe carries on regardless of your privations and suffering as a human person. You may suffer an intense personal tragedy, but the sun will rise in the spring and the flowers will bloom as usual.

In other words, in the very existence of man himself there is an ironic situation. By emphasizing this situation, an artist wins sympathy for the plight of man—immortal yet subject to death, dual citizen of time and eternity. This irony and the sympathy and shock arising from it tend to be dissipated somewhat by the use of the pathetic fallacy, with its consoling assumptions.

If as a writer you wish to achieve a stark or somber effect, your best method is merely to express the keen irony present in human life itself.

In *Romeo and Juliet,* for example, the morning Romeo takes leave of Juliet, never to see her again, is a free, joyous morning when "jocund day stands tiptoe on the misty mountain tops," despite the intense anguish of the lovers' parting.

In expressing this implicit irony, Shakespeare reveals a more consummate mastery than does Byron who, as Sir Arthur Quiller-Couch pointed out, would employ "an earthquake to dismiss a short *amour.*" Irony, on its strongest levels, may be said to rest on the contrast between the world as we actually experience it and the world of love and sympathy that we eternally desire.

Such is the irony Shakespeare presents in *Othello* (II, ii), when Othello has been so overjoyed to meet again his beloved Desdemona:

> I cannot speak enough of this content,
> It stops me here; it is too much of joy:
> And this, and this, the greatest discords be
> *(kissing her)*
> That e'er our hearts shall make!

Iago, the villain, standing apart, says in an aside:

> O, you are well tuned now!
> But I'll set down the pegs that make this music . . .

Even deeper is the irony of Goethe's Faust, who is aware of his own spiritual frustration:

> You must tremble before all that does not happen,
> And must always weep for the things you will never lose.

Irony is so deeply part of human experience that it is a major theme in all the arts that imitate conflict.

English and American literature are especially rich in various types of irony, from the studied anger of Swift to the polished understatement of Jane Austen or the subtle analysis of Max Beerbohm. Irony frequently pursues the same literary mode as that of humor, but it is capable of more tragic overtones. We have such an overtone in Dante's *Inferno*, when Dante meets the ghost of the proud Florentine patrician, Farinata. Farinata is sitting in a coffin burning to white heat. But even under these circumstances he loses neither his poise nor his conviction of superior ancestry. The first question he addresses to Dante is a demand to know what family Dante comes from. This situation borders on the grotesque and the ridiculous, but at the same time it is infused with tragedy. Farinata, even in Hell, does not care to know the wrong people—and that is one reason why he is in hell.

THE METHOD OF SATIRE

It has been debated whether there is a distinct form called the satire, or whether satire is a method in writing which may be adopted in any form whatsoever. In Latin literature there is such a distinct form, but on the whole in English, with the exception of a few classical imitations, satire is a method rather than a form.

It is a method that is distinctly artificial, that is premeditated, contrived, sophisticated. It is primarily a weapon of the intelligence.

Satire seeks to cultivate the overtones in writing. It is basically allied to humor, which we defined as the deliberate distortion, for the purpose of amusement and not of deception, of a mutual scale of values established between an artist and an audience. As we pointed out, the human mind functions on more than one level at once. When we perceive distortion it is because we are simultaneously aware of the principle of proportion. The principal business of the satirist is to indicate (not directly but indirectly) the norm from which the deliberate distortion is made. As with irony, the satirist emphasizes what he really has to say by appearing to be in sympathy with its opposite. The satiric method is normally not direct, although satires based closely on classical forms occasionally use direct invective. It does not generally present its meaning on the surface, but proceeds by *studied indirection.* And this studied indirection is achieved by the use of variations in the forms of humor—all the way from mere mental reserve to deliberate irony.

What are some of the advantages of the satiric method?

First, from the point of view of audience reaction, it gives the reader the pleasure of sharing a secret. He knows that he has the "inside track" of the satirist's mind, and delights in a kind of intellectual game in which his mind is active in "reading between the lines." Satire both stimulates and flatters the reader's intelligence. The perception of incongruity maintained throughout the satiric method gives the audience a certain pleasurable shock and creates permanent interest.

Secondly, from the point of view of the writer, it is a method that permits a great deal of verve, "nuance," overtone. This method is especially suited to the exposition of moral values. In fact, the specific aim of the classical satire was to defeat folly and vice by presenting them to the cleansing ridicule of the human intelligence. By this method the moralist or, to use a more favored expression today, the person with "a social conscience" is enabled to avoid the clumsiness of direct denunciation, vindictiveness of tone, and the other qualities which by injecting the personality of the writer between what he wishes to say and his audience tend to make him either offensive or boring. Chaucer's satire is, for example, the more effective in that he lets the facts speak for themselves, and by indirection suggests a humorous understanding of them. At the same time he sets a scale of values, a *norm,* through characters like the Parson, the Plowman, the Knight, with which are contrasted the Monk, the Friar, the Wife of Bath.

Satire as a specific literary form generally uses the mode of humor. In fact, wherever humor is directed toward adverse criticism, it is practically impossible to distinguish it from satire. In fact, one can only determine that a given piece of work is a satire by examining the total design. When Chaucer says of the Friar in the *Prologue* that it may not advance a man to have contact with the poor, in fact, "it is not honest," we have irony, humor, satire—all in one statement. Chaucer as a satirist distorts the "mutual scale of values" by appearing on the surface to approve of persons whom he deplores in terms of real interior meaning. The Shipman, for example, was "certainly a good fellow." One aspect of his good fellowship was to send the victims of his piracy "home to every land by water"—that is, make them walk the plank.

Parody might be considered to fall within the scope of satire. It is designed to ridicule affectations of literary style by exaggerating them or placing them in an absurd context. There is, of course, hardly any maliciousness in parody; it is just good fun. "Buggam Grange: A Good Old Ghost Story" is a fine example of parody, of humor, at the same time that it has quite an element of excitement as a story.

Experiment

Write a satire (minimum, 400 words) on one of the following suggestions:

(1) Television as an ideal means of educating children.

(2) Glamor as an indispensable aid to achievement.

(3) Why well-tailored clothes make a successful man.

(4) Why higher taxation aids prosperity.

(5) The dangers of stressing intellectual objectives in a college.

STEPHEN LEACOCK [2]

Buggam Grange: A Good Old Ghost Story

The evening was already falling as the vehicle in which I was contained entered upon the long and gloomy avenue that leads to Buggam Grange.

A resounding shriek echoed through the wood as I entered the avenue. I paid no attention to it at the moment, judging it to be merely one of those resounding shrieks which one might expect to hear in such a place at such a time. As my drive continued, however, I found myself wondering in spite of myself why such a shriek should have been uttered at the very moment of my approach.

I am not by temperament in any degree a nervous man, and yet there was much in my surroundings to justify a certain feeling of apprehension. The Grange is situated in the loneliest part of England, the marsh country of the fens to which civilization has still hardly penetrated. The inhabitants, of whom there are only one and a half to the square mile, live here and there among the fens and eke out a miserable existence by frog fishing and catching flies. They speak a dialect so broken as to be practically unintelligible, while the perpetual rain which falls upon them renders speech itself almost superfluous.

Here and there where the ground rises slightly above the level of the fens there are dense woods tangled with parasitic creepers and filled with owls. Bats fly from wood to wood. The air on the lower ground is charged with the poisonous gases which exude from the marsh, while in the woods it is heavy with the dank odors of deadly nightshade and poison ivy.

It had been raining in the afternoon, and as I drove up the avenue the mournful dripping of the rain from the dark trees accentuated the cheerlessness of the gloom. The vehicle in which I rode was a fly on three wheels, the fourth having apparently been broken and taken off, causing the fly to sag on one side and drag on its axle over the muddy ground, the fly thus moving only at a foot's pace in a way calculated to enhance the dreariness of the occasion. The driver on the box in front of me was so thickly muffled up as to be indistinguishable, while the horse which drew us was so thickly coated with mist as to be practically invisible. Seldom, I may say, have I had a drive of so mournful a character.

The avenue presently opened out upon a lawn with overgrown shrubberies and in the half darkness I could see the outline of the Grange itself, a rambling, dilapidated building. A dim light struggled through the casement of a window in a tower room. Save for the melancholy cry of a row of owls sitting on the roof, and croaking of the frogs in the moat which ran around the grounds, the place was soundless. My driver halted his horse at the hither side of the moat. I tried in vain to urge him, by signs, to go further. I could see by the fellow's face that he was in a paroxysm of fear and indeed nothing but the extra sixpence which I had added to his fare would have made him undertake the drive up the avenue. I had no sooner alighted than he wheeled his cab about and made off.

Laughing heartily at the fellow's trepidation (I have a way of laughing heartily in the dark), I made my way to the door and pulled the bell-handle. I could hear the muffled reverberations of the bell far within the building. Then all was silent. I bent my ear to listen, but could hear nothing except perhaps the sound of a low moaning as of a person in pain or in great mental distress. Convinced, however, from what my friend Sir Jeremy Buggam had told me, that the Grange was not empty, I raised the ponderous knocker and beat with it loudly against the door.

But perhaps at this point I may do well to explain to my readers (before they are too frightened to listen to me) how I came to be beating on the door of Buggam Grange at nightfall on a gloomy November evening.

A year before I had been sitting with Sir Jeremy Buggam, the present baronet, on the verandah of his ranch in California.

"So you don't believe in the supernatural?" he was saying.

"Not in the slightest," I answered, lighting a cigar as I spoke. When I want to speak very positively, I generally light a cigar as I speak.

"Well, at any rate, Digby," said Sir Jeremy, "Buggam Grange

is haunted. If you want to be assured of it go down there any time and spend the night and you'll see for yourself."

"My dear fellow," I replied, "nothing will give me greater pleasure. I shall be back in England in six weeks, and I shall be delighted to put your ideas to the test. Now tell me," I added somewhat cynically, "is there any particular season or day when your Grange is supposed to be specially terrible?"

Sir Jeremy looked at me strangely. "Why do you ask that?" he said. "Have you heard the story of the Grange?"

"Never heard of the place in my life," I answered cheerily, "till you mentioned it to-night, my dear fellow, I hadn't the remotest idea that you still owned property in England."

"The Grange is shut up," said Sir Jeremy, "and has been for twenty years. But I keep a man there—Horrod—he was butler in my father's time and before. If you care to go, I'll write him that you're coming. And since you are taking your own fate in your hands, the fifteenth of November is the day."

At that moment Lady Buggam and Clara and the other girls came trooping out on the verandah, and the whole thing passed clean out of my mind. Nor did I think of it again until I was back in London. Then by one of those strange coincidences or premonitions—call it what you will—it suddenly occurred to me one morning that it was the fifteenth of November. Whether Sir Jeremy had written to Horrod or not, I did not know. But none the less nightfall found me, as I have described, knocking at the door of Buggam Grange.

The sound of the knocker had scarcely ceased to echo when I heard the shuffling of feet within, and the sound of chains and bolts being withdrawn. The door opened. A man stood before me holding a lighted candle which he shaded with his hand. His faded black clothes, once apparently a butler's dress, his white hair and advanced age left me in no doubt that he was Horrod of whom Sir Jeremy had spoken.

Without a word he motioned me to come in, and, still without speech, he helped me to remove my wet outer garments, and then beckoned me into a great room, evidently the dining room of the Grange.

I am not in any degree a nervous man by temperament, as I think I remarked before, and yet there was something in the vastness of the wainscotted room, lighted only by a single candle, and in the silence of the empty house, and still more in the appearance of my speechless attendant which gave me a feeling of distinct uneasiness. As Horrod moved to and fro I took occasion to scrutinize his face more narrowly. I have seldom seen features more calculated to inspire a nervous dread. The pallor of his face and the whiteness of his hair (the man was at least seventy), and still more the peculiar furtiveness of his eyes, seemed to mark him as one who lived under a great terror. He moved with a noiseless step and at times he turned his head to glance in the dark corners of the room.

"Sir Jeremy told me," I said, speaking as loudly and as heartily as I could, "that he would apprise you of my coming."

I was looking into his face as I spoke.

In answer Horrod laid his finger across his lips and I knew that he was deaf and dumb. I am not nervous (I think I said that), but the realization that my sole companion in the empty house was a deaf mute struck a cold chill to my heart.

Horrod laid in front of me a cold meat pie, a cold goose, a cheese, and a tall flagon of cider. But my appetite was gone. I ate the goose, but found that after I had finished the pie I had but little zest for the cheese, which I finished without enjoyment. The cider had a sour taste, and after having permitted Horrod to refill the flagon twice, I found that it induced a sense of melancholy and decided to drink no more.

My meal finished, the butler picked up the candle and beckoned to me to follow him. We passed through the empty corridors of the house, a long line of pictured Buggams looking upon us as we passed, their portraits in the flickering light of the taper assuming a strange and lifelike appearance as if leaning forward from their frames to gaze upon the intruder.

Horrod led me upstairs and I realized that he was taking me to the tower in the east wing in which I had observed a light.

The rooms to which the butler conducted me consisted of a sitting room with an adjoining bedroom, both of them fitted with antique wainscotting against which a faded tapestry fluttered. There was a candle burning on the table in the sitting room but its insufficient light only rendered the surroundings the more dismal. Horrod bent down in front of the fireplace and endeavoured to light a fire there. But the wood was evidently damp, and the fire flickered feebly on the hearth.

The butler left me, and in the stillness of the house I could hear his shuffling step echo down the corridor. It may have been fancy, but it seemed to me that his departure was the signal for a low moan that came from somewhere behind the wainscot. There was a narrow cupboard door at one side of the room, and for the moment I wondered whether the moaning came from within. I am not as a rule lacking in courage (I am sure my reader will be decent enough to believe this), yet I found myself entirely unwilling to open the cupboard door and look within. In place of doing so I seated myself in a great chair in front of the feeble fire. I must have been seated there for some time when I happened to lift my eyes to the mantel above and saw, standing upon it, a letter addressed to myself. I knew the handwriting at once to be that of Sir Jeremy Buggam.

I opened it, and spreading it out within reach of the feeble candle light, I read as follows:

"My dear Digby,

In our talk that you will remember I had no time to finish telling you about the mystery of Buggam Grange. I take for granted, however, that you will go there and that Horrod will put you in the tower rooms, which are the only ones that make any pretense of being habitable. I have, therefore, sent him this letter to deliver at the Grange itself. The story is this:

On the night of the fifteenth of November, fifty years ago, my grandfather was murdered in the room in which you are sitting, by his cousin Sir Duggam Buggam. He was stabbed from behind while seated at the little table at which you are probably reading this letter. The two had been playing cards at the table and my grandfather's body was found lying in a litter of cards and gold sovereigns on the floor. Sir Duggam Buggam, insensible from drink, lay beside him, the fatal knife at his hand, his fingers smeared with blood. My grandfather, though of the younger branch, possessed a part of the estates which were to revert to Sir Duggam on his death. Sir Duggam Buggam was tried at the Assizes and was hanged. On the day of his execution he was permitted by the authorities out of respect for his rank, to wear a mask to the scaffold. The clothes in which he was executed are hanging at full length in the little cupboard to your right, and the mask is above them. It is said that on every fifteenth of November at midnight the cupboard door opens and Sir Duggam Buggam walks out into the room. It has been found impossible to get servants to remain at the Grange, and the place —except for the presence of Horrod—has been unoccupied for a generation. At the time of the murder Horrod was a young man of twenty-two, newly entered into the service of the family. It was he who entered the room and discovered the crime. On the day of the execution he was stricken with paralysis and has never spoken since. From that time to this he has never consented to leave the Grange where he lives in isolation.

Wishing you a pleasant night after your tiring journey,

I remain,

very faithfully,

JEREMY BUGGAM."

I leave my reader to imagine my state of mind when I completed the perusal of the letter.

I have as little belief in the supernatural as anyone, yet I must confess that there was something in the surroundings in which I now found myself which rendered me at least uncomfortable. My reader may smile if he will, but I assure him that it was with a very distinct feeling of uneasiness that I at length managed to rise to my feet, and, grasping my candle in my hand, to move backward into the bedroom. As I backed into it something so like a moan seemed to proceed from the closed cupboard that I accelerated my backward movement to a considerable degree. I hastily blew out the candle, threw myself upon the bed and drew the bed clothes over my head, keeping, however, one eye and one ear still out and available.

How long I lay thus listening to every sound, I cannot tell. The stillness had become absolute. From time to time I could dimly hear the distant cry of an owl and once far away in the building below a sound as of someone dragging a chain along a floor. More than once I was certain that I heard the sound of moaning behind the wainscot. Meantime I realized that the hour must now be drawing close upon the fatal moment of midnight. My watch I could not see in the darkness, but by reckoning the time that must have elapsed I knew that midnight could not be far away. Then presently my ear, alert to every sound, could just distinguish far away across the fens the striking of a church bell, in the clock tower of Buggam village church, no doubt, tolling the hour of twelve.

On the last stroke of twelve, the cupboard door in the next room opened. There is no need to ask me how I knew it. I couldn't, of course, see it, but I could hear, or sense in some way, the sound of it. I could feel my hair, all of it, rising upon my head. I was aware that there was a presence in the adjoining room, I will not say a person, a living soul, but a presence. Anyone who has been in the next room to a presence will know just how I felt. I could hear a sound as of someone groping on the floor and the faint rattle as of coins.

My hair was now perpendicular. My reader can believe it or not, but it was.

Then at this very moment from somewhere below in the building there came the sound of a prolonged and piercing cry, a cry of a soul passing in agony. My reader may censure me or not, but right at this moment I decided to beat it. Whether I should have remained to see what was happening is a question that I will not discuss. My one idea was to get out and to get out quickly. The window of the tower room was some twenty-five feet above the ground. I sprang out through the casement in one leap and landed on the grass below. I jumped over the shrubbery in one bound and cleared the moat in one jump. I went down the avenue in about six strides and ran five miles along the road through the fens in three minutes. This at least is an accurate transcription of my sensations. It may have taken longer. I never stopped till I found myself on the threshold of the Buggam Arms in Little Buggam, beating on the door for the landloard.

I returned to Buggam Grange on the next day in the bright sunlight of a frosty November morning, in a seven cylinder motor car with six local constables and a physician. It makes all the difference. We carried revolvers, spades, pickaxes, shotguns and a ouija board.

What we found cleared up forever the mystery of the Grange.

We discovered Horrod the butler lying on the dining room floor quite dead. The physician said that he had died from heart failure. There was evidence from the marks of his shoes in the dust that he had come in the night to the tower room. On the table he had placed a paper which contained a full confession of his having murdered Jeremy Buggam fifty years before. The circumstances of the murder had rendered it easy for him to fasten the crime upon Sir Duggam, already insensible from drink. A few minutes with the ouija board enabled us to get a full corroboration from Sir Duggam. He promised moreover, now that his name was cleared, to go away from the premises forever.

My friend, the present Sir Jeremy, has rehabilitated Buggam Grange. The place is rebuilt. The moat is drained. The whole house is lit with electricity. There are beautiful motor drives in all directions in the woods. He has had the bats shot and the owls stuffed. His daughter, Clara Buggam, became my wife. She is looking over my shoulder as I write. What more do you want?

Experiment

(1) Explain how the apparent imperturbability of the story teller helps the impact of the humor here.

(2) Show how Leacock has deliberately parodied literary description.

(3) Specify other elements of parody that you find in the story.

(4) What is the humorous value of this type of definition?

I was aware that there was a *presence* in the adjoining room. I will not say a person, a living soul, but a *presence*.

(5) What normal effects in ghost stories are deliberately exaggerated in Leacock's parody?

(6) Why is the following narrative humorous?

I am not nervous (I think I said that), but the realization that my sole companion in the empty house was a deaf mute struck a cold chill to my heart.

Horrod laid in front of me a cold meat pie, a cold goose, a cheese, and a tall flagon of cider. But my appetite was gone. I ate the goose, but found that after I had finished ・ the pie I had but little zest for the cheese, which I finished without enjoyment. The cider had a sour taste, and after having permitted Horrod to refill the flagon twice, I found that it induced a sense of melancholy and decided to drink no more.

After you have had some practice with exercises in motif, humor, irony, and satire, you will probably have been impressed by the importance of the social theme in writing. If your value-judgments are keen and strongly held, you will become interested in the problem of presenting moral or social judgments without seeming to teach directly. You will want to avoid what has been traditionally called didacticism (direct teaching in a work of art), so jarring in a creative work. In a creative work, points must be made implicitly and not explicitly. In exposition or argumentation, direct exhortation or denunciation have their places, but in creative work you can be as morally effective without encountering as large a number of possibilities of resistance and of offended readers. Such argumentative writers as T. S. Eliot, H. L. Mencken, and G. K. Chesterton have written a large number of short pieces, both in verse and prose, in which their instruction is subordinate to the aesthetic contemplation encouraged by the work. The social theme may often take the form of satire, which by its own method avoids the overtly direct approach. Satire is very often strengthened in proportion to its brevity and tension. The following piece by W. H. Auden compacts a criticism of "statism" that could be extended into a volume.

THE UNKNOWN CITIZEN
(To JS/07/M/378
This Marble Monument
Is Erected by the State)

He was found by the Bureau of Statistics to be
One against whom there was no official complaint,
And all the reports on his conduct agree
That, in the modern sense of an old-fashioned word, he was a
    saint
For in everything he did he served the Greater Community
Except for the War till the day he retired
He worked in a factory and never got fired,
But satisfied his employers, Fudge Motors Inc.
Yet he wasn't a scab or odd in his views,
For his Union reports that he paid his dues,
(Our report on his Union shows it was sound)
And our Social Psychology workers found
That he was popular with his mates and liked a drink.
The Press are convinced that he bought a paper every day
And that his reactions to advertisements was normal in every
    way.
Policies taken out in his name prove that he was fully insured.
And his Health-card shows he was once in hospital but left it
    cured.
Both Producers Research and High-Grade Living declare
He was fully sensible to the advantages of the Instalment Plan
And had everything necessary to the Modern Man,
A phonograph, a radio, a car and a frigidaire.
Our researchers into Public Opinion are content
That he held the proper opinions for the time of year;
When there was peace, he was for peace; when there was war,
    he went.
He was married and added five children to the population,
Which our Eugenist says was the right number for a parent of
    his generation,
And our teachers report that he never interfered with their
    education.

Was he free? Was he happy? The question is absurd:
Had anything been wrong, we should certainly have heard.[3]

Experiment

Write a short piece, with satiric overtones, on one of the
following topics:

(1) Graft in Local Government (as suggested by an item
in the news).

(2) The Intellectual Value of a Specific Television Pro-
gram.

(3) A Recent Advertising Slogan.

(4) Net Results of Attending a School of Charm.

(5) How to Win as a Democrat in a Republican District.

(6) The Social Effects of Marrying the Boss's Daughter.

FANTASY

Traditionally in English literature a distinction has been
made between fancy and imagination. Fancy is concerned,
not with the compression of experience, but with decoration
and measurement. By "measurement" is implied the type
of interest we find in a fairy story like "Jack and the Beanstalk"—the size of the Giant, the height of the beanstalk, Jack
as a "giant-killer." We have many examples of fancy in *A
Midsummer Night's Dream,* with its insistence on diminu-
tiveness and whimsicality. For instance, the fairy says:

> I must go seek some dewdrop here
> And hang a pearl in every cowslip's ear.

and Titania states:

> Come, now a roundel and a fairy song;
> Then, for the third part of a minute, hence;

[3] *The Collected Poetry of W. H. Auden,* New York, Random House, 1945.

Some to kill cankers in the musk-rose buds,
Some war with rere-mice for their leathern wings
To make small elves' coats, and some keep back
The clamorous owl that nightly hoots. . . .

The reaction of an audience might be stated colloquially in the phrase, "How cute!" Fancy and the particular form of writing known as fantasy, which derives from it, emphasize dimensions, color contrasts, imagistic surprises that have charm but do not have, and are not meant to have, underlying depth.

If you were to elaborate such suggestions as the following, you would proceed by the method of fantasy; and *motif*— in this type of writing, of which the fairy story is an example ("Jack and the Beanstalk," "Beauty and the Beast")—would consist in the repetition of certain key colors and dimensions:

Visiting the Bottom of the Monstrous World
The Rose Garden on the Other Side of the Moon
A Date in the Gardens of the Caliph
Following Pink Elephants
A Night with a Banshee

Grimm's "The Story of the Youth Who Went Forth to Find Out What Fear Was" is an example of fancy dependent upon repetitive motif, "If I did but know what it was to shudder!" A series of macabre but humorous occurrences, like those in a dream sequence, follow, constituting a basic pattern with surface variations. As in most fairy stories, the situation can only continue as long as the surface variations have the quality of surprise. The storyteller, on the other hand, has the advantage of being able to terminate his story at any time, since the initial situation has not been really and organically complicated by the events narrated. The Beast can always turn into a Handsome Prince; Jack can always kill the Giant; The Youth can always learn to shudder.

Fantasy, because of its insistence on measurements—"pearls in cowslips' ears," "warring with rere-mice" (bats), the gigantic hero (Gulliver in Lilliput), or the diminutive hero (Gulliver in Brobdingnag)—easily allies itself with the method of humor, which consists in a play of proportion against distortion. In Grimm's story, one of its delights is the humor underlying and softening the macabre fantasy.

The structure of a fantasy resembles the outlines of an actual dream. Occurrences do not have to result from any obvious logical cause. In fantasy, things "just happen." Jack's beanstalk just keeps on growing and takes Jack into another country. The laws of scientific reality, of natural phenomena, are suspended. On a midsummer night the woods become alive with diminutive creatures. An island is governed by a magician who sends a spirit light as imagination to control the winds and the waves. Frequently, however, an indirect symbolic meaning, even a penetrating criticism of life, becomes obvious amid the fanciful, irregular, impossible details of the fantasy. In Giraudoux's *The Madwoman of Chaillot,* for example, the "madwoman" has a wisdom that the "sane" modernists cannot achieve. Giraudoux implies that the "irrational"—intuition, imagination, emotion—are no less valuable than logic.

Fantasy, like imagination, has form, organization, direction, but it does not attempt to symbolize meaning directly. The symbolic image compresses meaning. Macbeth's hands, for example, form a symbol of transcendent guilt. But fancy, in contrast to imagination, approaches intellectual meaning indirectly. In this sense it is "playful." Hanging "a pearl in every cowslip's ear" is not a direct symbol of any sort, though the total world of Oberon and Titania in Shakespeare's play has symbolic and imaginative meaning. Just as in a natural dream we have a kaleidoscope of scenes and events to which we react emotionally, though we do not respond to them through the intellect (it is "asleep") except to be amused, in retrospect, by their incongruity—so, in the written fantasy, we stress sequence rather than logic, emotion rather than intellect.

JACOB AND WILHELM GRIMM [4]

*The Story of the Youth Who Went Forth
To Learn What Fear Was*

A certain father had two sons, the elder of whom was smart and sensible, and could do everything, but the younger was stupid and could neither learn nor understand anything, and when people saw him they said: "There's a fellow who will give his father some trouble!" When anything had to be done, it was always the elder who was forced to do it; but if his father bade him fetch anything when it was late, or in the night-time, and the way led through the churchyard, or any other dismal place, he answered: "Oh, no, father, I'll not go there, it makes me shudder!" for he was afraid. Or when stories were told by the fire at night, which made the flesh creep, the listeners sometimes said: "Oh, it makes us shudder!" The younger sat in a corner and listened with the rest of them, and could not imagine what they could mean. "They are always saying: 'It makes me shudder, it makes me shudder!'" "It does not make me shudder," thought he. "That, too, must be an art of which I understand nothing."

Now it came to pass that his father said to him one day: "Hearken to me, you fellow in the corner there, you are growing tall and strong, and you too must learn something by which you can earn your bread. Look how your brother works, but you do not even earn your salt." "Well, father," he replied, "I am quite willing to learn something—indeed, if it could but be managed, I should like to learn how to shudder. I don't understand that at all yet." The elder brother smiled when he heard that, and thought to himself: "Good Heavens, what a blockhead that brother of mine is! He will never be good for anything as long as he lives! He who wants to be a sickle must bend himself betimes."

The father sighed, and answered him: "You shall soon learn what it is to shudder, but you will not earn your bread by that."

Soon after this the sexton came to the house on a visit, and

[4] Translated by Margaret Hunt. Copyright, Pantheon Books, Inc.

the father bewailed his trouble, and told him how his younger son was so backward in every respect that he knew nothing and learnt nothing. "Just think," said he, "when I asked him how he was going to earn his bread, he actually wanted to learn to shudder." "If that be all," replied the sexton, "he can learn that with me. Send him to me, and I will soon polish him." The father was glad to do it, for he thought: "It will train the boy a little." The sexton therefore took him into his house, and he had to ring the church bell. After a day or two, the sexton awoke him at midnight, and bade him arise and go up into the church tower and ring the bell. "You shall soon learn what shuddering is," thought he, and secretly went there before him; and when the boy was at the top of the tower and turned around, and was just going to take hold of the bell rope, he saw a white figure standing on the stairs opposite the sounding hole. "Who is there?" cried he, but the figure made no reply, and did not move or stir. "Give an answer," cried the boy, "or take yourself off, you have no business here at night."

The sexton, however, remained standing motionless that the boy might think he was a ghost. The boy cried a second time: "What do you want here?—speak if you are an honest fellow, or I will throw you down the steps!" The sexton thought: "He can't mean to be as bad as his words," uttered no sound and stood as if he were made of stone. Then the boy called to him for the third time, and as that was also to no purpose, he ran against him and pushed the ghost down the stairs, so that it fell down ten steps and remained lying there in a corner. Thereupon he rang the bell, went home, and without saying a word went to bed, and fell asleep. The sexton's wife waited a long time for her husband, but he did not come back. At length she became uneasy, and wakened the boy, and asked: "Do you not know where my husband is? He climbed up the tower before you did." "No, I don't know," replied the boy, "but someone was standing by the sounding hole on the other side of the steps, and as he would neither give an answer nor go away, I took him for a scoundrel, and threw him downstairs. Just go there and you will see if it was he. I should be sorry if it were." The woman ran away and found her husband, who was lying moaning in the corner, and had broken his leg.

She carried him down, and then with loud screams she hastened to the boy's father. "Your boy," cried she, "has been the cause of a great misfortune! He has thrown my husband down the steps so that he broke his leg. Take the good-for-nothing fellow out of our house." The father was terrified, and ran thither and scolded the boy. "What wicked tricks are these?" said he; "the devil must have put them into your head." "Father," replied he, "do listen to me. I am quite innocent. He was standing there by night like one intent on doing evil. I did not know who it was, and I entreated him three times either to speak or to go away." "Ah," said the father, "I have nothing but unhappiness with you. Go out of my sight. I will see you no more."

When day dawned, therefore, the boy put his fifty talers into his pocket, and went forth on the great highway, and continually said to himself: "If I could but shudder! If I could but shudder!" Then a man approached who heard this conversation which the youth was holding with himself, and when they had walked a little farther to where they could see the gallows, the man said to him: "Look, there is the tree where seven men have married the ropemaker's daughter, and are now learning how to fly. Sit down beneath it, and wait till night comes, and you will soon learn how to shudder." "If that is all that is wanted," answered the youth, "it is easily done; but if I learn how to shudder as fast as that, you shall have my fifty talers. Just come back to me early in the morning." Then the youth went to the gallows, sat down beneath it, and waited till evening came. And as he was cold, he lighted himself a fire, but at midnight the wind blew so sharply that in spite of his fire, he could not get warm. And as the wind knocked the hanged men against each other, and they moved backwards and forwards, he thought to himself: "If you shiver below by the fire, how those up above must freeze and suffer!" And as he felt pity for them, he raised the ladder, and climbed up, unbound one of them after the other, and brought down all seven. Then he stoked the fire, blew it, and set them all around it to warm themselves. But they sat there and did not stir, and the fire caught their clothes. So he said: "Take care, or I will hang you up again." The dead men, however, did not hear, but were quite silent, and let their rags go on burning. At this he grew angry, and said: "If you will not take care, I cannot help you, I will not be burnt with you," and he hung them up again each in his turn. Then he sat down by his fire and fell asleep, and the next morning the man came to him and wanted to have the fifty talers, and said: "Well, do you know how to shudder?" "No," answered he, "how should I know? Those fellows up there did not open their mouths, and were so stupid that they let the few old rags which they had on their bodies get burnt." Then the man saw that he would not get the fifty talers that day, and went away saying: "Such a youth has never come my way before."

The youth likewise went his way, and once more began to mutter to himself: "Ah, if I could but shudder! Ah, if I could but shudder!" A waggoner who was striding behind him heard this and asked: "Who are you?" "I don't know," answered the youth. Then the waggoner asked: "From whence do you come?" "I know not." "Who is your father?" "That I may not tell you." "What is it that you are always muttering between your teeth?" "Ah," replied the youth, "I do so wish I could shudder, but no one can teach me how." "Enough of your foolish chatter," said the waggoner. "Come, go with me, I will see about a place for you." The youth went with the waggoner, and in the evening they arrived at an inn where they wished to pass the night. Then at the entrance of the parlor the youth again said quite loudly: "If I could but shudder! If I could but shudder!" The host who heard this, laughed and said: "If that is your desire, there ought to be a good opportunity for you here." "Ah, be silent," said the hostess, "so many prying persons have already lost their lives, it would be a pity and a shame if such beautiful eyes as these should never see the daylight again."

But the youth said: "However difficult it may be, I will learn it. For this purpose indeed have I journeyed forth." He let the host have no rest, until the latter told him, that not far from thence stood a haunted castle where any one could very easily learn what shuddering was, if he would but watch in it for three nights. The King had promised that he who would venture should have his daughter to wife and she was the most beautiful maiden the sun shone on. Likewise in the castle lay great treasures, which were guarded by evil spirits, and these treasures would then be freed, and would make a poor man rich enough. Already many men had gone into the castle, but as yet none had come out again. Then the youth went next morning to the King, and said: "If it be allowed, I will willingly watch three nights in the haunted castle." The King looked at him, and as the youth pleased him, he said: "You may ask for three things to take into the castle with you, but they must be things without life." Then he answered: "Then I ask for a fire, a turning-lathe, and a cutting-board with the knife."

The King had these things carried into the castle for him during the day. When night was drawing near, the youth went up and made himself a bright fire in one of the rooms, placed the cutting-board and knife beside it, and seated himself by the turning-lathe. "Ah, if I could but shudder!" said he, "but I shall not learn it here either." Towards midnight he was about to poke his fire, and as he was blowing it, something cried suddenly from one corner: "Au, miau! how cold we are!" "You fools!" cried he, "what are you crying about? If you are cold, come and take a seat by the fire and warm yourselves." And when he had said that, two great black cats came with one tremendous leap and sat down on each side of him, and looked savagely at him with their fiery eyes. After a short time, when they had warmed themselves, they said: "Comrade, shall we have a game of cards?" "Why not?" he replied, "but just show me your paws." Then they stretched out their claws. "Oh," said he, "what long nails you have! Wait, I must first cut them for you." Thereupon he seized them by the throats, put them on the cutting-board and screwed their feet fast. "I have looked at your fingers," said he, "and my fancy for card-playing has gone," and he struck them dead and threw them out into the water. But when he had made away with these two, and was about to sit down again by his fire, out from every hole and corner came black cats and black dogs with red-hot chains, and more and more of them came until he could no longer move, and they yelled horribly, and got on his fire, pulled it to pieces, and tried to put it out. He watched them for a while quietly, but at last when they were going too far, he seized his cutting-knife, and cried: "Away with you, vermin," and began to cut them down. Some of them ran away, the others he killed, and threw out into the fish-pond. When he came back he fanned the embers of his fire again and warmed himself. And as he thus sat, his eyes would keep open no longer, and he felt a desire to sleep. Then he looked around and saw a great bed in the corner. "That is the very thing for me," he said, and got into it. When he was just going to shut his eyes, however, the bed began to move of its own accord, and went over the whole of the castle. "That's right," said he, "but go faster." Then the bed rolled on as if six horses were harnessed to it, up and down, over thresholds and stairs, but suddenly hop, hop, it turned over upside down and lay on him like a mountain. But he threw quilts and pillows up in the air, got out and said: "Now any one who likes, may drive," and lay down by his fire, and slept till it was day. In the morning the King came, and when he saw him lying there on the ground, he thought the evil spirits had killed him and he was dead. Then said he: "After all it is a pity,—for so handsome a man." The youth heard it, got up, and said: "It has not come to that yet." Then the King was astonished, but very glad, and asked how he had fared. "Very well indeed," answered he; "one night is past, the two others will pass likewise." Then he went to the innkeeper, who opened his eyes very wide, and said: "I never expected to see you alive again! Have you learnt how to shudder yet?" "No," said he, "it is all in vain. If some one would but tell me!"

The second night he again went up into the old castle, sat down by the fire, and once more began his old song: "If I could but shudder!" When midnight came, an uproar and noise of tumbling about was heard; at first it was low, but it grew louder and louder. Then it was quiet for a while, and at length with a loud scream, half a man came down the chimney and fell before him. "Hullo!' cried he, "another half belongs to this. This is not enough!" Then the uproar began again, there was a roaring and howling, and the other half fell down likewise. "Wait," said he, "I will just stoke up the fire a little for you." When he had done that and looked round again, the two pieces were joined together, and a hideous man was sitting in his place. "That is no part of our bargain," said the youth, "the bench is mine." The man wanted to push him away; the youth, however, would not allow that, but thrust him off with all his strength, and seated himself again in his own place. Then still more men fell down, one after the other; they brought nine dead men's legs and two skulls, and set them up and played at nine-pins with them. The youth also wanted to play and said: "Listen you, can I join you?" "Yes, if you have any money." "Money enough," replied he, "but your balls are not quite round." Then he took the skulls and put them in the lathe and turned them till they were round. "There, now they will roll better!" said he. "Hurrah! now we'll have fun!" He played with them and lost some of his money, but when it struck twelve, everything vanished from his sight. He lay down and quietly fell asleep. Next morning the King came to inquire after him. "How has it fared with you this time?" asked he. "I have been playing at nine-pins," he answered, "and have lost a couple of farthings." "Have you not shuddered then?" "What?" said he, "I have had a wonderful time! If I did but know what it was to shudder!"

The third night he sat down again on his bench and said quite sadly: "If I could but shudder." When it grew late, six tall men came in and brought a coffin. Then said he: "Ha, ha, that is certainly my little cousin, who died only a few days ago," and he beckoned with his finger, and cried: "Come, little cousin, come." They placed the coffin on the ground, but he went to it and took the lid off, and a dead man lay therein. He felt his face, but it was cold as ice. "Wait," said he, "I will warm you a little," and went to the fire and warmed his hand and laid it on the dead man's face, but he remained cold. Then he took him out and sat down by the fire and laid him on his breast and rubbed his arms that the blood might circulate again. As this also did no good, he thought to himself: "When two people lie in bed together, they warm each other," and carried him to the bed, covered him over and lay down by him. After a short time the dead man became warm too, and began to move. Then said the youth, "See, little cousin, have I not warmed you?" The dead man, however, got up and cried: "Now will I strangle you."

"What!" said he, "is that the way you thank me? You shall at once go into your coffin again," and he took him up, threw him into it, and shut the lid. Then came the six men and carried him away again. "I cannot manage to shudder," said he. "I shall never learn it here as long as I live."

Then a man entered who was taller than all others, and looked terrible. He was old, however, and had a long white beard. "You wretch," cried he, "you shall soon learn what it is to shudder, for you shall die." "Not so fast," replied the youth. "If I am to die, I shall have to have a say in it." "I will soon seize you," said the friend. "Softly, softly, do not talk so big. I am as strong as you are, and perhaps even stronger." "We shall see," said the old man. "If you are stronger, I will let you go— come, we will try." Then he led him by dark passages to a smith's forge, took an axe, and with one blow struck an anvil into the ground. "I can do better than that," said the youth, and went to the other anvil. The old man placed himself near and wanted to look on, and his white beard hung down. Then the youth seized the axe, split the anvil with one blow, and in it caught the old man's beard. "Now I have you," said the youth. "Now it is your turn to die." Then he seized an iron bar and beat the old man till he moaned and entreated him to stop, when he would give him great riches. The youth drew out the axe and let him go. The old man led him back into the castle, and in a cellar showed him three chests full of gold. "Of these," he said, "one part is for the poor, the other for the king, the third yours." In the meantime it struck twelve, and the spirit disappeared, so that the youth stood in darkness. "I shall still be able to find my way out," said he, and felt about, found the way into the room, and slept there by his fire. Next morning the King came and said: "Now you must have learnt what shuddering is?" "No," he answered; "what can it be? My dead cousin was here, and a bearded man came and showed me a great deal of money down below, but no one told me what it was to shudder." "Then," said the King, "you have saved the castle, and shall marry my daughter." "That is all very well," said he, "but still I do not know what it is to shudder!"

Then the gold was brought up and the wedding celebrated; but howsoever much the young King loved his wife, and however happy he was, he still said always: "If I could but shudder —if I could but shudder." And this at last angered her. Her waiting-maid said: "I will find a cure for him; he shall soon learn what it is to shudder." She went out to the stream which flowed through the garden, and had a whole bucketful of gudgeons brought to her. At night when the young King was sleeping, his wife was to draw the clothes off him and empty the bucketful of cold water with the gudgeons in it over him, so that the little fishes would sprawl about him. Then he woke up and cried: "Oh, what makes me shudder so?—what makes me shudder so, dear wife? Ah! now I know what it is to shudder!"

Experiment

(1) What does this story gain by emphasizing (from the very beginning) the motif, "If I could but shudder"?

(2) Explain the humor resulting from the fact that the unshuddering boy is more than adequate in every emergency.

(3) Show how the narrative gains in value from the number and unpredictability of the hero's experiences.

(4) Give examples of where humor and fantasy are simultaneously present in the piece.

(5) The following dialogue is highly humorous because of the youth's unusual sense of values: "Then," said the King, "you have saved the castle and shall marry my daughter." "That is all very well," said he, "but still I do not know what it is to shudder." Locate other examples of such humorous contrasts.

(6) Does the story end according to a logical scheme or arbitrarily?

(7) Show how numbers and measurements are used in the story.

(8) In what ways does the course of the story resemble the course of a dream?

PRELIMINARIES TO STORY WRITING

Experiments with creative prose include such forms as artistic narration based on fact, short stories without plot including the methods of *motif*, fantasy, thematic contrast, pathos.

Artistic unity can be achieved through the forms mentioned. Quite often, these forms provide greater artistic achievements than those that are secured by plotted narrative. As a matter of fact, the plotted story may run into the danger of being too contrived, of being too artificial. Life does not always run in such carefully demarcated compartments as the motivation, climax, and denouement of a plotted short story suggest. The temptation in the plotted story is to sacrifice experience to technical ingenuity. This is the great defect of the "slicks," and partly accounts for the increased emphasis, by way of reaction, on what we call the "slice of life" short story. *The Atlantic Monthly*, in its comments on the college short stories submitted for the 1949-50 contest, stated that "Hollywood and pulp fiction appear to have made heavy inroads on college creation. Sentimentality as a substitute for emotion, feeble characterization, triteness, and imitation of shoddy models marred many of the stories." Obviously, experience and its interpretation must not be sacrificed to trick devices and to cleverness. Emotional depth and sincerity are basic requirements of art, and, in this sense, characterization must not be sacrificed to plot. It is, of course, quite possible to write what is a "plot" story without sacrificing characterization.

Your first problem as a storyteller is to determine whether you will place the greater emphasis on the plot situation or on characterization. But whichever choice you make, you must never forget for one moment the correlation between character and action. It is the mark of Western literary tradition that, even if a people have a philosophy or religion of determinism, their creative writing is still postulated on the principle of free will and free choice—even when the story-teller introduces a philosophy of determinism in his work. It is a person's character, rather than outside forces, that causes him to act in the way he does. Suspense arises from free choice. A modern short-story writer may even consider free will an illusion, but in his story he creates suspense and tension by at least supporting for the time being what he considers an illusion.

The primary requirement of a short-story writer is a knowledge of human emotions and of human psychology, not necessarily on a scientific or technical level, but based on experience. Your characters must be recognizably human and humanly motivated. If they are presented in some extraordinary light, the conditions must be thoroughly explained and motivated.

Some basic knowledge of the nature of the emotions is prerequisite to undertaking creative writing of this kind. Some emotions are not in themselves well suited for short-story treatment. These emotions deal with their objects without reference to accompanying difficulties of attainment. For example, love which desires an object for its own sake may be a very suitable emotion for a lyrical poem or a reflective essay. When Shakespeare meditates on love, as in Sonnet 116, he thinks of the nature of love, not of love in conflict:

> . . . it is an ever-fixed mark
> That looks on tempests and is never shaken . . .

But in *Romeo and Juliet,* love is expressed in terms of conflict, with reference to all the difficulties that may bar its attainment. An emotion such as hope—which implies love in a certain sense, but love in a state of tension as to the attainment of its desire—is an appropriate emotion for the short story. Hatred, an emotion directed to what the observer perceives to be evil, is a suitable emotion for a sermon or a satire (as in Swift's *Gulliver's Travels*). Fear, which implies not only the hatred of evil, but the suspenseful situation in which evil may actually affect one personally, is far better adapted to the short story, as in Walpole's "The Tarn." It is to be borne in mind that the emotions in the short story are emotions that arise not in the contemplative world but in the world of immediate action and consequence, for this form of art is closely allied to suspense and action. Lyrical or pensive moods do not predominate in these art forms; rather, the fulfillment or frustration of highly motivated desires in the face of practical contingencies. We have no examples of a short story with plot that is primarily contemplative or reflective.

Experiment

What emotions motivate the characters named below who appear in short stories included in this volume?

(1) Luigi in "The Bishop's Beggar"

(2) Fenwick in "The Tarn"

(3) Uncle Luke in "Luke Baldwin's Vow"

(4) The Son of the Priest in "By the Waters of Babylon"

If you are emphasizing the novelty, speed, or climax of a plot situation, you can afford to be a little more indifferent to characterization than if your aim is basically psychological. In spite of any technical proficiency, the ultimate value of your story will depend on the adequacy of your characterization.

It is most important, therefore, for you to present a recognizable character, to whom your audience can respond emotionally, either in love or hate, fear or admiration. Obviously, an audience cannot be interested in what happens to a person who does not arouse its interest.

Action springs from character. Action in turn affects the

development of character. Action might be considered the outward symbol of internal emotional and intellectual change. Action is closely connected with character in a short story because action implies a single chain of cause and effect having its origin in a character's specific reaction to a given situation—by his affirmation, negation, or even by his indecision. An action must be whole and complete—to quote Aristotle, "with its several incidents so closely connected that the transposal or withdrawal of any one of them will disjoin and dislocate the whole." In a short story without plot, one incident is sufficient to indicate the crisis of character—in affirming, denying, or evading. In a short story with plot, a series of interrelated incidents is required.

Some short stories are psychologically very penetrative. In such stories a sensitive account is given of what takes place in the internal nature of the character in the light of his external experience. A story possessing unusual depth in this respect is Stephen Benét's "The Bishop's Beggar," wherein the Bishop's whole interior life is transformed by his experience with the beggar.

On the other hand, many popular stories concentrate almost exclusively on action. The characters do not undergo any internal change from the initial positions they assume in the story. This type of story is of a lower order artistically than the first.

Characterization in the short story should be achieved not by direct explanation but by the interaction of one character with another, or by the character with circumstance. The hero of a short story is generally "sympathetic" from the reader's viewpoint. The reader tends to identify himself in imagination with the central character of a story who serves as the focal point from which the action radiates. The hero does not necessarily have to be a model of perfection so long as the reader can sufficiently accept him to feel for him and at least to pity him. The hero of Benét's story, for example, is admirable in his ability to progress spiritually. The hero of Walpole's "The Tarn," on the other hand, is a murderer, but, like Shakespeare's tragic hero Macbeth, an understandable one and one who can excite pity in us.

One may write a short story in which the hero is villainous and stands morally condemned. But in this case the story will be one emphasizing plot almost to the exclusion of psychological subtlety. Such is Poe's "The Cask of Amontillado." Even here, however, the hero-villain is not without an admirable quality. He is at least a perfectionist, though in revenge. Poe's story lacks depth and is almost purely a creation of technique. We can scarcely afford to take it sufficiently seriously on the psychological level to say that it glorifies crime and criminals. It belongs to what in the theater would correspond to melodrama rather than to tragedy. Hugh Walpole's "The Tarn," because of its more serious and complex characterization, is of a higher order of art than Poe's story. Both stories present similar themes, but one is merely clever; the other, comparatively deep. A short story may present a character who is obnoxious and to whom justice is done. But most stories of this type are "fictionalized" documentaries in which the effort merely to maintain "news value" is apparent, as in magazines recounting police investigations and "true" stories.

THE SHORT STORY WITHOUT PLOT

Before writing a short story with plot, you should have considerable experience in writing the short story without plot—not that the short story without plot is easier to write. It is not. In fact, it is sometimes deceptively easy to think of a good plot. But a good plot without the foundations of good characterization and sound psychology will never in itself make an effective short story.

Some of the greatest achievements in the modern short story are not based on formal plot narrative at all. The short story without plot is a method of writing in which a unity of impression, or a unity of mood, leads to a climax, or point of highest tension, and to the conclusion or "resolution" of this point. This climax is not necessarily related to a reversal of narrative situation, that is, to the turns, twists, and surprises that cause suspense in the short story with plot. Rather, the climax in a short story without plot is the expression of an ironic or symbolic or intellectual overtone. By overtone we mean the essential implication beyond the surface meaning of the explicit situation. Since the short story without plot, more particularly than the short story with plot, depends on irony, to write this type of story well you must master the use of overtone. In creating such overtone, you must be sensitive to the emotional power that you may achieve through *restraint*. Where in a short story with plot details often must be explicitly clarified, the short story without plot often succeeds for the reverse reason. It may leave the motive for an act uncertain. In fact, one way to create climax in this type of writing is to present the surface explanation as apparently acceptable, while at the same time it is suggested that the reverse, submerged explanation is really true. Your reader's imagination and intelligence will be stimulated by this device.

This form, less unwieldy than that of the short story with plot, permits a greater freedom of approach, and often for this very reason leads to a production of great emotional force.

Favorite forms of the short story without plot are the thematic contrast—often ironic, humorous, satiric—and the form dependent on pathos, an unresolved emotional situation. These forms are subsequently explained. Generic description, already presented (see p. 131), will in itself form a short story without plot if it is connected with episode or incident.

In writing any kind of story you must realize that the aesthetic objective is *intensity* resting on emotional depth and climactic effect. As stated in the section on *motif*, climax can often be indicated by repeating an initial pattern in relation to a growing seriousness of mood. Such a procedure is exemplified in the jingling of the bells in Edgar Allan Poe's well-known "A Cask of Amontillado." This short story has been continuously reproduced in anthologies largely because of the efficient economy of the style. It also possesses a perfectly studied irony in relation to the subject matter. The story is told in the first person by a murderer planning the perfect crime. His victim is dressed for the pre-Lenten carnival. "The man wore motley. He had on a tight-fitting, parti-striped dress and his head was surmounted by a conical hat and bells. I was so pleased to see him that I thought I should never have done wringing his hands." The victim wore the fancy dress of a medieval jester. But the natural hilarity of the bells served to mark a somber procession to doom. These bells jingle when the victim drinks his first glass of Medoc on his search for the Amontillado. The bells jingle again in death: "I thrust a torch through the remaining aperture and let it fall within. There came forth in return only a jingling of the bells." The murderer has walled up his victim alive, and with quiet, malicious irony he concludes: "Against the new masonry I re-erected the old rampart of bones. For the half of a century no mortal has disturbed them. *In pace requiescat.*"

The really powerful writer, however, does not have to seek for sensational, unusual, or garish situations. In fact, a story often is more powerful for its basic simplicity of situation—whether or not to open a closed door, to drop a letter in the mailbox, or to acknowledge or disregard an old acquaintance may be the basis of the most acute penetration into experience.

With the growth in psychological acuteness in modern writing, with a greater awareness in concrete particulars of the frustrations to which an individual may be subjected in an overmechanized society, writers on all levels have come to realize the value of symbolism in heightening tension. The symbol, as has been stated, is primarily an aesthetic device for carrying a burden of meaning in a compressed package. The writer need not expose this full burden of meaning, but any sensitive reader can follow in the train of his own thinking all the implications contained in the package.

The short story without plot can make use of the simplest incident, but the incident should be connected with values and psychological realities that are universal. Hugh Mooney's short story without plot, "Wait'll I Write Mom," enlarges a very simple incident—the dropping of an identification bracelet—so that various ironic values entering the war situation are indicated.

HUGH J. MOONEY

Wait'll I Write Mom

It was early morning, a thick grey mist hung low over the clearing, and the rain, which had begun a week ago, still came down, coursing down the tree trunks and falling from the branches to the mushy ground with a constant loud "plop, plop." It soaked through packs, ran down rifle bores, rolled down up-turned coat collars, dripped from helmet brims and extinguished cigarettes. Here and there throughout the clear-- ing, by the light of flashlights, sergeants checked the rosters of the departing replacements.

"Ryan, Andreone, Polizzi, Vachris, Murray, Wuensch, Berg. Riley, DeMane, Angelo, Werbe, Werner, Goodman and Barrett. Baker Company, load into this truck." The sergeant's voice was harsh yet weary as he assigned the men to the various groups.

The men, made clumsy by their overcoats, packs, gas masks and rifles, struggled into the six by six he had indicated. Each man was absorbed in his own thoughts and an unnatural quiet prevailed as they twisted into more comfortable positions and lit their cigarettes. The rain beat down savagely on the truck's canvas and the dark interior resembled a cave lit by a dozen glowing red eyes.

The darkness was abruptly shattered by the sergeant's flashlight. It moved relentlessly from face to face as he counted them again.

"Fourteen, Baker Company, right." He stepped aside and called to the driver. "O.K., take off."

The motor whined, sputtered and then caught with a roar. The truck rumbled off between the trees, jolting and swaying, and in the back the men were thrown from their seats. Their sudden outburst of curses seemed to ease the tension and as they sat back someone said:

"You know this may not be such a bad deal. I heard this division is supposed to come off the line for thirty days to rest and reorganize. They may be out of the lines before we even get there."

"Baloney," said another. "You hear that all the time."

"How far have we got to go, anyway?"

"The driver said it's about twenty miles, then we walk a mile."

The truck lurched out from between the trees and into the road, a trough of liquid yellow clay hemmed in on both sides by mud-spattered evergreen trees. The truck wallowed on through the mud and, as the mist lifted, the rain poured down in cold torrents that strummed loudly on the canvas and gradually forced its way through in different spots.

At the back of the truck a soldier cursed softly.

"Damn that lousy mud." Using his sleeve, he wiped the mud thrown by the churning wheels from his face. Twisting in his place, he produced a pack of cigarettes and offered one to the man next to him.

"Cigarette?"

"Yeah. Thanks."

Putting the pack away, he lit a match and sheltering it in muddy hands held it to the other's cigarette. "My name's Murray, Joe Murray. It looks as though we're going to be together. What's yours?"

"Barrett, Tom Barrett. Yeah, it looks as though we'll be in the same outfit. I sure hope we hit the second platoon. I got a kid brother in the second platoon of this outfit."

"No kidding. What a break. That's sure a coincidence. You sure you got the right outfit?"

Barrett smiled. "This is the outfit all right. I asked the driver before we left. He knew him right away, was talking to him only a couple of days ago. Geez, will I surprise him. He don't even know I'm over here yet, I don't think. Wait'll I write Mom."

The truck churned on and on, bouncing, jolting and swaying. The men no longer cursed, but righted themselves and tried unsuccessfully to doze. At last the truck came to a halt. The driver came to the back and dropped the tail gate. A young lieutenant appeared, lean and muddy.

"Pile out, men. Leave your equipment on the side of the road, bring your mess kits and follow me." The lieutenant's right eye twitched continuously and it seemed as though he were winking at them in some secret joke.

The men climbed out, cursing as they staggered in the slippery knee-deep mud. They followed him off the road to a tent hidden among the trees.

"It's a hot meal. Eat all you want." The lieutenant glanced at his watch. "We'll leave in half an hour, so don't go wandering off."

As they filed past the food, the cooks looked at them curiously as though they were some kind of freaks. The lieutenant stood to one side, holding a cup of coffee, still winking at them sadly.

At this time at the front a truck was starting back from the lines. Under the canvas were more soldiers, but these were dead. Piled like cord wood, the rigid bodies refused to yield even to the bouncing and swaying of the truck. The truck struck a rock submerged in the mire and as it heaved and slithered over it a silver identification bracelet slipped from under the canvas flap and fell at the side of the road. There were no curses from this load of passengers and the truck wallowed on.

The lieutenant winked at his watch. "At ease, men. I'm Lieutenant Case. You men will all be in my platoon, the second. Let's go."

As the men reached the road the truck with the closed flaps went past, headed for the rear. When the men had all shouldered their packs, the lieutenant said, "Follow me," and they followed him in single file along the side of the road.

The rain had stopped and the sun shone feebly. The walking was hard and occasionally a man slipped to his knees in the slime. No one laughed.

Barrett walked at the head of the column behind the lieutenant. The mud didn't bother him much. In a little while he'd slip up behind Bill and tap him on the shoulder. Imagine his surprise when he turned. His lips broke into an unconscious smile.

Fifteen minutes later, his thoughts still in the same pleasant channel, Barrett's eye caught a glitter in the mud to his right. He picked up the identification braclet almost unconsciously and rubbed it on his sleeve.

WILLIAM F. BARRETT

32312405

Barrett laughed aloud. What a coincidence. Wait till he saw Bill. He'd kid him plenty and tell him that he came over to Belgium just to pick up after him like Mom did at home. He smiled and carefully put the bracelet in his pocket.

"Wait'll I write Mom," he thought.

The mingled irony and pathos of James Shaw's "Merry Christmas" are based, simply, on watching the snow fall.

JAMES SHAW

"Merry Christmas"

"Shaw, Shaw!"

The call came from the dugout in which I lived. Anticipating my attempt to stall for another minute, the voice continued in a compelling whisper, "It's eleven fifty-five, scout."

I inhaled a deep breath and let it go with a sigh. I drew my legs out of the unzipped sack. Putting on my unlaced boots and jacket, I crawled out to relieve my impatient friend.

Before I could rise off all fours, the spectacled owner of the awakening voice gave me the story. "The Jerry machine gun behind Ridge 679 has been firing away for the past three hours. The azimuth on the traders was 215 degrees. Those Krauts are still firing mortars from the gully behind the Aid Station. The azimuth on the sparks was 355 degrees."

With a hard edge in his voice, he continued: "I phoned it all in, but they probably won't do anything about it. Command

Post Personnel don't have to duck when mortar shells come from an aid station." I listened while slipping into the warm parka.

"Well, here's the compass—and, oh yes, Merry Christmas!"

"You'll find four grenades by the radio.

"Merry Christmas," I added, wrapping the parka closer around me.

Then I took my position at the hole in the wall of the half-demolished house. The Observation Post consisted of three badly battered rooms of a once six-room house perched on the peak of a snow-covered mountain. There were two ground-floor rooms and one upstairs. Our dugouts were in the dirt floors, and were covered with small logs and sandbags. All of this would have come to nought had the Germans decided to shell the place. Why they didn't still remains a mystery to me. It was certainly in their full view and the forward slope received a generous plastering every day. Perhaps they thought that the place was so obvious that we would not be foolish enough to use it.

The night was dark and it was not as cold as usual. As I was trying to read the azimuth on a number of gun flashes, it began to snow. Visibility at any distance became impossible. Disheartened by the futility of trying to peer through the mist of falling snow, I began to observe nearer objects. After looking from right to left, and from left to right, I concentrated my gaze on a familiar object.

It was lying close to the wall of the house just below my lookout. I had glanced at this dead German often in the week since his permanent arrival. The first exchange of pleasantries was unnerving, but afterwards both he and his buddies lying further downhill became accepted company. We knew they would never get any closer.

I watched the steady snowfall slowly cover him over. He lay there—one arm under him, the other outstretched, his fist still clinched on a rock. The snow was gradually filling his upturned helmet that lay by his head. He was a kind of symbol, I thought. I had always tried to make him a symbol of what we were fighting against. I wanted them all to end that way.

Tonight I began to think differently. I tried to resist the idea in my mind by looking out into the distance. All of the black ugly spots were disappearing in the snow.

The snow covered everything—a white blanket. As the mist began to thin, the scene reminded me of my childhood religion classes. I remembered my teacher telling me how baptism washed the soul white like snow. Of course this wasn't much of a comparison because the black, sinful-looking spots on the earth weren't washed away, just temporarily covered up. In only a few minutes mortal sin would come again to this beautiful scene in the form of a loud crunching wham. Though it was a poor parallel, it served to lull me into the reflective mood that I had been struggling against.

It was five past twelve. Christmas day had come. Thoughts of home and the Christmases of my childhood thronged into my mind. I knew somewhere people were happy. Would I ever see another Christmas, or would I ever see tomorrow? I gazed again at the white form lying face downward with one arm outstretched. With a feeling of longing and reverence I said:

"Merry Christmas, Jerry! May God be merciful to your soul—and to mine, also."

THEMATIC CONTRAST

One of the most common and effective methods of the short story without plot is that of *thematic contrast,* in which two situations, two characters, or two moods are juxtaposed symbolically to give the effect of an intellectual criticism powerfully implicit but never directly stated. For example, we can achieve a complete story by presenting two characters viewing the same objective situation but, by reason of their respective dispositions and temperaments, seeing the situation completely differently. Very often, this contrast has the artistic unity of irony.

You may ask: "Why does irony produce unity?" Irony carries with it a complete intellectual commentary or social criticism on the aspects of life that the creative artist presents. It gives an underlying unity of mood and of mental evaluation.

A development of this method through thematic contrast

is to be found in the case where two or more speakers are reviewing the character and activities of an absent person. The sophisticated reader finds in such a story the ironic means of knowing the real characters of the speakers. The absent person is merely a touchstone—a device of revelation —of the speakers' own respective psychological conflicts.

One student wrote a story in which he represented two speakers, one of whom was criticizing a woman whom he considered very miserly. The speaker described this woman as stingy and antisocial. The other speaker, often interrupting, contrasted her with another woman who had anonymously given much of her wealth to local charities, churches, and libraries. In constructing his dialogue, the student skillfully contrived a climax in which he implicitly conveyed the suggestion that, unknown to the speakers themselves, these two women so presented were one and the same person.

In Sinclair Lewis' *Main Street* two women view the same town. One woman, Carol Kennicott, is a person of broad social experience, to whom Gopher Prairie appears to be a mean and shabby town, distinguished by pretentiousness but not by elegance. Bea Sorenson, on the contrary, has been a hard-working farm girl with very restricted social contacts. To her, Gopher Prairie has a stimulating, romantic charm. Notice how Sinclair Lewis contrasts the two characters by the different viewpoints they take of the same external object.

SINCLAIR LEWIS [5]

Two Views of Gopher Prairie

When Carol had walked for thirty-two minutes she had completely covered the town, east and west, north and south; and she stood at the corner of Main Street and Washington Avenue and despaired.

Main Street with its two-story brick shops, its story-and-a-half wooden residences, its muddy expanse from concrete walk to walk, its huddle of Fords and lumber-wagons, was too small to

[5] Sinclair Lewis, *Main Street*, New York, Harcourt, Brace and Co.

absorb her. The broad, straight, unenticing gashes of the streets let in the grasping prairie on every side. She realized the vastness and the emptiness of the land. The skeleton iron windmill on the farm a few blocks away, at the north end of Main Street, was like the ribs of a dead cow. She thought of the coming of the Northern winter, when the unprotected houses would crouch together in terror of storms galloping out of that wild waste. They were so small and weak, the little brown houses. They were shelters for sparrows, not homes for warm laughing people. . . .

She glanced through the fly-specked windows of the most pretentious building in sight, the one place which welcomed strangers and determined their opinion of the charm and luxury of Gopher Prairie—the Minniemashie House. It was a tall lean shabby structure, three stories of yellow streaked wood, the corners covered with sanded pine slabs purporting to symbolize stone. In the hotel office she could see a stretch of bare unclean floor, a line of rickety chairs with brass cuspidors between, a writing-desk with advertisements in mother-of-pearl letters upon the glass-covered back. The dining-room beyond was a jungle of stained table-cloths and catsup bottles. . . .

She looked no more at the Minniemashie House.

A man in cuffless shirt-sleeves with pink arm-garters, wearing a linen collar but no tie, yawned his way from Dyer's Drug Store across to the hotel. He leaned against the wall, scratched a while, sighed, and in a bored way gossiped with a man tilted back in a chair. A lumber-wagon, its long green box filled with large spools of barbed-wire fencing, creaked down the block. A Ford, in reverse, sounded as though it were shaking to pieces, then recovered and rattled away. In the Greek candy-store was the whine of a peanut-roaster, and the oily smell of nuts.

There was no other sound nor sign of life. . . .

She fought herself: "I must be wrong. People do live here. It *can't* be as ugly as—as I know it is. I must be wrong. But I can't do it. I can't go through with it."

She came home too seriously worried for hysteria; and when she found Kennicott waiting for her, and exulting, "Have a walk? Well, like the town? Great lawns and trees, eh?" She was able to say, with a self-protective maturity new to her, "It's very interesting.". . .

So it chanced that Carol Kennicott and Bea Sorenson were viewing Main Street at the same time.

Bea had never before been in a town larger than Scandia Crossing, which has sixty-seven inhabitants.

As she marched up the street she was meditating that it didn't hardly seem like it was possible there could be so many folks all in one place at the same time. My! It would take years to get acquainted with them all. And swell people, too! A fine big gentleman in a new pink shirt with a diamond, and not washed-out blue denim working shirt. A lovely lady in a longery dress (but it must be an awful hard dress to wash). And the stores!

Not just three of them, like there were at Scandia Crossing, but more than four whole blocks!

The Bon Ton Store—big as four barns—my! it would simply scare a person to go in there, with seven or eight clerks all look-ing at you. And the men's suits, on figures just like human. And Axel Egge's, like home, lots of Swedes and Norskes in there, and a card of dandy buttons, like rubies.

A drug store with a soda fountain that was just huge, awful long, and all lovely marble; and on it there was a great big lamp with the biggest shade you ever saw—all different kinds of colored glass stuck together; and the soda spouts, they were silver, and they came right out of the bottom of the lampstand! Behind the fountain there was glass shelves, and bottles of new kinds of soft drinks, that nobody ever heard of. Suppose a fella took you *there!*

A hotel, awful high, higher than Oscar Tollefson's new red barn; three stories, one right on top of another; you had to stick your head back to look clear up on the top. There was a swell traveling man in there—probably been to Chicago lots of times.

Oh, the dandiest people to know here! There was a lady going by, you wouldn't hardly say she was any older than Bea herself; she wore a dandy new gray suit and black pumps. She almost looked like she was looking over the town, too. But you couldn't tell what she thought. Bea would like to be that way—kind of quiet, so nobody would get fresh. Kind of—oh, elegant.

A Lutheran Church. Here in the city there'd be lovely sermons, and church twice on Sunday, *every* Sunday.

And a movie show!

A regular theater, just for movies. With the sign "Change of
bill every evening." Pictures every evening!

There were movies in Scandia Crossing, but only once every
two weeks, and it took the Sorensons an hour to drive in—papa
was such a tight-wad he wouldn't get a Ford. But here she could
put on her hat any evening, and in three minutes' walk be to
the movies and see lovely fellows in dress-suits and Bill Hart and
everything. . . .

What did she care if she got six dollars a week? Or two! It
was worth while working for nothing, to be allowed to stay here.
And think how it would be in the evening, all lighted up—and
not with no lamps, but with electrics! And maybe a gentleman-
friend taking you to the movies and buying you a strawberry ice
cream soda!

Bea trudged back.

"Vell? You lak it?" said Tina.

"Ya, Ay lak it. Ay t'nk maybe Ay stay here," said Bea.

PATHOS IN THE SHORT STORY

There is a method of using emotions in the short story
whereby there is no correlation between emotions the character experiences and the resolution of these emotions through
conflict. This situation may be correctly described as *pathos.*
Pathos is the result of a deliberate artistic method in which
we express tender sympathy for a character whose problems
do not have any solvent or conclusion. The emotional problem in the story is not solved. It is merely stated.

The death of the Fair Elaine in the "Morte d'Arthur" and
the death of Ophelia in *Hamlet* leave us with a feeling of
deep sympathy, but there are no adequate solutions such as
there would be in tragic conclusions. In other words, the
underlying explanation of pathos springs from the fact that
the emotions experienced by the character and vicariously

by the audience do not relate to circumstances that either *directly* defeat or can be defeated. The circumstances are insurmountable and paralyzing, but they cannot be challenged by *conflict,* whether the result be successful or not. It is for this reason that pathos is an emotional situation more suited to the short story without plot than to the short story with plot. In the short story with plot effects of pathos are sometimes used, but are generally and artificially resolved by the technique of the happy ending. We have a good example of pathos in Morley Callaghan's "Luke Baldwin's Vow," but the effects of pathos in the story are incidental rather than essential.

A Reuters dispatch appearing in The New York *Times* of November 26, 1949, is a good example of pathos, and, incidentally, is a demonstration of how fidelity to fact and creative art can closely meet. The reader deeply pities the padre who, earnestly seeking to fulfill the social responsibilities of his office, meets insurmountable difficulties which he has to accept. Because of his acquiescence to what he understands to be superior authority, conflict is ruled out. He must suffer, he cannot fight back. The consequent result is pathos. The pathos in the news report should be contrasted with a "resolved" conflict such as that in Benét's "The Bishop's Beggar."

In the dark hours before dawn this morning Father Francesco Parise called the roll of his men in the muddy village street. He got 180 answers. Then, hitching up his frayed black cassock, he led them off on the five-mile tramp across the muddy fields. Father Francesco carried a mattock. So did most of the others.

Two hours later, as dawn broke, they arrived at their destination. Silently the men began attacking the stubborn virgin soil. Now and again the padre rasped the back of his hand reflectively over a five-day growth of beard as he fondly watched his flock, but his eyes also scanned the landscape for other things—particularly the police.

Father Francesco and his 180 men are land grabbers. The

nine acres of land they are working belongs to the Baron Barocco, proprietor of 8,000 acres of the soil of Southern Calabria.

The padre and his flock are only a small part of the thousands
of Southern Italian peasants who in the last few weeks have
taken possession of land.

Most of them have now left after being ordered off by the
police, but in a few places they cling stubbornly to the soil they
have wrested from the landowners. The men of Punta d'Ella
Castella are among these.

Punta d'Ella Castella is a collection of miserable stone houses
overlooking the sea near Crotone in Calabria Province. The
road that links it to the nearest village of Isola Capolrizutto,
eight miles inland, is passable only by mules and jeeps.

Padre Francesco knows each of his flock of 500 souls intimately. He was born among them, grew up with them and in
the past forty-two years has shared all their sorrows and their
joys.

Only twenty of the village's 200 men have any regular work.
The others are landless people who live on an average of forty
days' work a year on seasonal land work. They earn an average
of 300 lire (50 cents) for a dawn-to-dusk day's work.

Around them, as far as the eye can see—and further—stretches
the estate of the the great Baron Barocco. Six thousand acres of
the 8,000 are uncultivated, a hunting reserve. Request after request by the people of Punta d'Ella Castella for some portion
of the land has been refused in the past years.

The people came to Padre Francesco to tell him their troubles
and ask for his advice.

For the padre the decision was difficult. "I am only a simple
man," he said in an interview. He ran his fingers through his
thinning black hair and went on: "I know the law. I also think
I know justice. Sometimes I find it difficult to know which of
the two is right. I only know that they are not always the same."

Sitting alone by a flickering candle—the village oil supply had
run out—in his draughty house, Padre Francesco made his choice.
To the men already agitating for seizure of land he said simply,
"I will come with you." Early one morning, as a low ground
mist swirled damply through the village, the men, the padre at
their head, set out. Before sunset their work was done. Their

nine acres had been picketed and apportioned. Tilling started the next morning.

The padre smiled wanly when told that he was regarded as a Communist. "I am a humanist. I can only try to serve God in my own humble way. I don't know what a Communist is. They tell me they are bad people. Surely what I have done is not bad. Would He not have done the same?"

One day last week Padre Francesco received a summons from the Bishop of Crotone. He tramped seventeen miles to the Bishop's house. Late that night, dusty and tired, he stood in the Bishop's study. It was more than an hour before he came out. His face was sad as he trudged back to his waiting people.

Today the men of Punta d'Ella Castella and their pastor are sowing their ground with wheat. The villagers are cheerful as they demonstrate to one another with exaggerated gesture how high the waving heads of grain will reach in the summer. Only Padre Francesco is silent.

"That will surely be a great day when you bless our first crop, won't it, Father?" a smiling peasant asked today.

The padre did not reply. He turned away, ashamed of the tears in his eyes.

He thought again of the Bishop's words and of his transfer to another parish, and his heart was heavy with the sorrow of the farewell he soon would have to make to the people.

THE SHORT STORY WITH PLOT

The short story with plot differs from the short story without plot in the sense that it depends primarily for its emotional effect not on irony or overtone but on the resolution of a specific problem which the hero or protagonist faces. The solving of the conflict of circumstances is no less necessary than the psychological or intellectual evaluation of the circumstances themselves. Such an evaluation will often suffice for the short story without plot, but not for the short story with plot. The circumstances of the plot, therefore, must of themselves be of interest, be coherent, and artistically acceptable.

A certain confusion has arisen about the question of the probability of the plot or action. It may be said that conditional probability is all that is necessary. There must be an internal consistency between the course of the action and the conditions under which the short story writer has chosen to carry it out. The original hypothesis of the story need not be within the realm of our experience at all. We are willing to "suspend disbelief" in order to enter the conditions of artistic illusion. All creative writing is in a certain sense illusion. In this sense we must realize that art is distinct from real experience. In most cases this realization is so habitual, that one is unconscious of the need for it. But within the conditions of illusion, we expect consistency. Stephen Vincent Benét's "By the Waters of Babylon" makes a number of assumptions that are outside the reader's experience, but because they are presented with internal consistency and the characterization is human, the reader is not impeded from experiencing a strong emotional response. Once the reader has accepted the terms of the artistic illusion of such a story, and the artistic illusion has developed an adequate emotional force, the action can easily assimilate incidents which taken separately might appear unreal.

If the idea in your story is particularly violent and removed from ordinary experience, if it deals with the preternatural, for example, it is more important than ever for you to make it appear reasonable. Stephen Leacock's burlesque parody of the ghost story pointed up these dangers. On the other hand, Hugh Walpole's "The Tarn" successfully avoids them. Walpole's underlying psychological motivation explains the success of his story. The preternatural occurrence in the story is made more acceptable by its identification with the hero's sense of guilt. Aristotle said that the more general and universal aspects of experience make the best narrative material. Such material succeeds best when it touches upon values, no matter how unusual its plot or incident may be, that are universally held and recognizable by all men.

Character in relation to situation spells conflict and change. Short stories of the highest literary merit most closely follow the principle that character makes action. Benét's "The Bishop's Beggar" is a story of the highest artistic quality because it pre-eminently presents character expressed through action. Benét's story has the high subtlety of showing an organic growth and change in character as it expresses itself through action and is in turn affected by action.

The greatest short stories, like the greatest works of art, do not present life as black and white. They penetrate the complexity of experience, including the complexity of moral character. Walpole's "The Tarn" does not present a one-dimensional murderer. Rather, it presents a *man,* whose humanity we can understand, who happened to commit a murder. We can sympathize with him in the same sense that we can sympathize with Shakespeare's Macbeth. We cannot condone what he did, but we can understand how he came to do it.

In so far as a storyteller emphasizes an unusual plot situation, he tends to make plot more important than character. But even here a minimum degree of correlation between character and plot is necessary. Nevertheless, novelty of interpretation—of "angle"—will often be sufficient to justify a story, though such a story will not be that of the highest artistic class. A recent story in a national magazine reinterpreted the dwarfs, the small creatures of folklore who live underground, as the survivors of a previous atomic era. In the previous historical cycle men went underground to protect themselves from atomic bombardment. Under the influence of atomic radiation, the survivors had "mutated" to their present size and appearance. This "angle" alone, because of its analogy to contemporary circumstances, is in itself sufficient for reader interest.

Every story, to be effective, must contain suspense. Suspense implies that you tell the reader in the course of the story enough to arouse his curiosity, but *not* enough to satisfy it. "Keep to the point of interest, but with a minimum of revelation." Always in the reader's mind must be the suggestion of possible alternatives—of plot solution as in the short story with plot, of contrasting evaluations as in the short story without plot.

An understanding of the divisions of the action is helpful in creating the steps that lead to suspense.

A basic rule governs alike the course of action in the short story and in the one-act play. Everything in the action should form a link in a single chain of cause and effect. By this we mean that no question which the artist has put to the audience should be left unanswered—in the air, so to speak. These forms of writing demand the tightest discipline in avoiding the immaterial and the irrelevant. The action must not only be one; it must also be complete in itself. Whatever the problem is that the storyteller or dramatist offers us, it must be answered. Nothing connected with the course of the action must be left unaccounted for.

The divisions of the action in a short story or a play are the same. They may be schematized as follows; the terminology is interchangeable:

Causes—Exposition,
Growth—Tying of the Knot;[6] rising action,
Height—Climax,
Consequences—Untying of the Knot; falling action,
Close—Denouement.

(1) *Exposition* is the process in the short story that identifies the characters and explains the basic elements in the situation with which they will have to deal. Directness of approach, immediate relevance, are important in the exposition, so that the reader will have the essentials of the story clearly in mind. In "The Tarn" the exposition and the growth of the action come very close together. In "The Bishop's Beggar," where psychological analysis is of particu-

---

[6] Knot: the traditional metaphor from Aristotle's *Poetics*.

lar importance, the exposition is long and leisurely. It is the function of exposition to bring out the details of character that are to have an important bearing on the plot. The beginning of "Luke Baldwin's Vow" is particularly effective in this respect.

(2) The *Growth of the Action* results from the interplay and crisscrossing of the acts and motivations of the principal characters. At this point the storyteller must establish a gathering and deepening tension. Various artistic methods come into play here that are described in other sections of the book: the successful use of connotation and the techniques of poetry to create atmosphere, as in Walpole's "The Tarn" and in Leacock's parody, "Buggam Grange"; the use of *motif* concentrating growing emotional tension, as in Callaghan's "Luke Baldwin's Vow."

(3) The *Climax* in any work of art is the point of highest tension—that is the point where the choice of alternatives open to the characters is most sharply in focus and where the attention and curiosity of the reader are keenest. The climax may be reached by physical act or mental decision. In Benét's "The Bishop's Beggar," the climax is indicated in the ironic comment of the beggar as he views the possibility of the bishop becoming a cardinal:

"Your Eminence does not understand. Luigi is difficult as a bishop's beggar. As a cardinal's beggar, he would be overweening. You have no idea how overweening he would be."

The climax of any story may, of course, cover considerable space—just as the third act of a Shakespearean drama (always the climax for Shakespeare) presents a large body of material. But you can roughly indicate the climactic situation very often by the repeated motif (as in the remarks of the beggar in Benét's story) in relation to a new and decisive situation.

In "Luke Baldwin's Vow," Uncle Henry makes a climactic

decision (for which, of course, there has been careful psychological preparation):

"The plain fact is that the old dog isn't worth his keep any more. It's time we got rid of him."

In Walpole's "The Tarn" the climax is an act:

"Do you see that little jetty there?" Fenwick led Foster by the arm. "Someone built that out into the water. He had a boat there, I suppose. Come and look down. From the end of the little jetty it looks so deep and the mountains seem to close around."

Sometimes, the climax of a story can be presented under conditions of the most rigid artistic restraint. In a story by Osbert Sitwell there is a scene in which a lady and a gentleman are having tea together. In the course of the tea the man comes to know by an unguarded remark of the woman that she has murdered her husband. The woman, in the course of the tea, knows that the man knows. But no outward sign of such knowledge is given by either of the participants. The ironic surface of urbane conversation is maintained throughout.

(4) The *Consequences* follow from the climax. If the conflict is interesting, a reader will have sufficient motivation and impetus to follow the steps to its solution—steps which belong to the "falling action" of a story. A traditional method of sustaining interest between the climax and the close of a story is to create a new problem to be solved before the hero's success or failure is assured. The attempt to drown the dog in "Luke Baldwin's Vow" illustrates a means of sustaining fresh interest:

As Luke cried out wildly, "Don't! Please don't!" Carter dropped the stone, for the cry came too late; it was blurred by the screech of the big saws at the mill.

Particularly in mystery stories, one technique for creating

suspense has been labeled that of "deceptive reassurance." This device is particularly useful as a fresh source of interest. When a character is facing danger, he may, for a moment, place confidence in some personality or act which reassures him temporarily, only to leave him, after the confidence has been misplaced, more isolated than before. The tempo of fear is actually increased by this type of reassurance. Thus, for example, in one of Bulwer-Lytton's stories, a man is reading a book in a haunted house. He notices a shadow forming on his book, to which he pays no attention. Then he suddenly realizes that there has been no object between the light and the book he has been reading that would normally cause a shadow. Because there is no *natural* cause for it, the shadow at once becomes dire and ominous—and the suspense along with it. Particularly effective as a follow-up to the climax and as an example of ironic reassurance is this passage in "The Tarn":

He had the strangest fancy, but his brain was throbbing so fiercely that he could not think, that it was the tarn that was following him, the tarn slipping, sliding along the road, being with him so that he should not be lonely. He could almost hear the tarn whisper in his ear: "We did that together, and so I do not wish you to bear all the responsibility yourself. I will stay with you, so that you are not lonely."

(5) The *Denouement* or close of a story does not present special difficulty if the other divisions have been adequately handled. It is the natural resolution of the chain of events that derive from the climax. A short story should not end with rhetoric or explanation. A certain abruptness, irony, or casualness is often effective. Walpole, for example, in "The Tarn" emphasizes the universal irony of life going on as usual no matter what has happened to a particular individual:

It was a lovely morning. A twig of ivy idly, in the little breeze, tapped the pane.

The close of "Luke Baldwin's Vow" makes a philosophical comment on the *motif* of the story:

Putting his head down on the dog's neck, he vowed to himself fervently that he would always have some money on hand, no matter what became of him, so that he would be able to protect all that was truly valuable from the practical people of the world.

In "The Bishop's Beggar," a restatement is made of Luigi's ironic character:

Of the tomb of Luigi, the beggar—that no man knows. They say it was beside the bishop's, but, in one war or another, it was destroyed and there is no trace of it now. Yet Luigi was an arrogant spirit; perhaps he would have liked that best.

Luigi did not have to achieve holy poverty; he had had it thrust upon him. But the bishop had had to learn such poverty under the critical and testing eyes of Luigi. Yet, in the end, Luigi had set the pace, for he has no grave, and who can be poorer than that?

DIALOGUE

The construction of dialogue is particularly important both in the short story and in the one-act play. In acquiring the art of writing good dialogue, an excellent practice is to read good models aloud and to learn from this experience, rather than to follow any system of formal regulations. Effective dialogue suggests the rhythms of real life. Such dialogue, however, is in actuality quite distinct from the speech of real people. What we call "naturalness" in writing actually results from artistic convention. A stenographic report of actual conversation would not seem "real" at all.

Experiment

(1) Dialogue in the short story should admit of nothing superfluous to the "line" of the story. A storyteller may put

in certain idioms or turns of phrase, however, that may indicate character. The character thus indicated further affects the plot. Locate such passages in Benét's "The Bishop's Beggar."

(2) Dialogue should be brisk and economical, unless a character is meant to be prolix and long-winded. Show how the dialogue in Callaghan's "Luke Baldwin's Vow" meets this requirement.

(3) Dialogue in the short story must subserve the purpose of the narrative. Narrative and dialogue must be so interspersed that they synthesize together. Show how Hugh Walpole has used dialogue in this respect in "The Tarn."

(4) Draw a list of possible alternatives for the word *said* in dialogue.

Benét's sensitive and psychologically sustained narrative is a story of character transformation, where both the bishop and the beggar undergo a changing and deepening of their sense of values through their relationship to one another and to circumstances.

STEPHEN VINCENT BENÉT [7]

The Bishop's Beggar

It seems that in the old days there was a bishop of Remo, and he was a heedless and proud young man, though of good intentions. Now, that was possible in those days, when the fire and light of the new learning had spread through Italy and men drank, as if intoxicated, at a new spring. There were bishops who cared less for the Word of God than for their own splendor, and cardinals who were rather men of the world—and of no good world—than sons of the Church. I do not say that our bishop was as idle and self-seeking as some of these; I do say that he was a child of his time. He would have liked to be a

[7] Reprinted by permission of Brandt and Brandt.

lord, but his eldest brother was the lord; he would have liked to be a soldier, but his second brother was the soldier. So he went into the Church, for there, too, a man who bore a great name could rise. He was clever, he was ambitious, he had great connections. Now and then, to be sure, he asked a disquieting question, but the Baldis had always been original. The path that is rugged for many was made smooth for him from the first. When he was made bishop of Remo, at an early age, the fact did not surprise him. Since he was to be neither lord nor soldier, he found that pleasant enough.

All went well for him, at first. They were glad to have a young and handsome bishop at Remo, for the bishop before him had been old and ill-favored. It was a pleasure to no one to kiss his ring, and he frightened the children with his peering eyes. With the coming of our bishop all this was changed. There was a great to-do and refurbishing of the bishop's palace; the smells of good cooking drifted again from the bishop's kitchens; when the bishop drove through the city, men threw their caps in the air. There were fine new frescoes in the cathedral—a new way of chanting in the choir. As for sin and suffering—well, they are always with us. The people of Remo liked to sin pleasantly and be reminded of it as little as possible.

Nevertheless, at times, a grayness would come over our bishop's spirit. He could not understand why it came. His life was both full and busy. He was a friend to art, a host to the gay and the learned, a ruler of men. He did not meddle in things which did not concern him; he felt in his heart that there was no prize in the Church which might not be within his grasp. And yet, at times, there was a grayness within him. It was singular.

He could not show that grayness before the world, he could not show it to his secretary or the witty company that gathered at his table. He could wrestle with it in prayer, and so he did. But he found it no easy task. Had the Devil appeared before him with horns and a tail, he would have known what to do. But a grayness of spirit—a cool little voice in the mind which said to him now and then, "What do you in these robes, at this place, Gianfrancesco Baldi?"—that was another matter.

He came to find by experience that motion in the open air

helped him as much as anything. When the grayness oppressed him too severely, he would summon his coach and drive about the countryside. So one day, as he drove through a small country village in the hills beyond Remo, it happened. It was nobody's fault; the bishop's least of all. He saw to it that he had a skillful coachman and good horses as he saw to all matters. But when a tall, gangling boy darts across the street right under the nose of the horses, the most skillful coachman cannot always save him. There was a cry and a scream and a soft jar. Then, where the coach had passed, the boy lay writhing in the street.

The bishop always showed at his best in emergency. When he got out of the coach the angry shouts of the crowd died away to a respectful murmur. He lifted the boy into the coach with his strong arms and drove back with him to Remo. On the way he talked to him soothingly, though the boy was in too much pain to pay much attention to this graciousness. When they got to Remo he had the boy carried to a servant's room in the palace and doctors summoned for him. Later on he gave instructions about cleaning the coach.

At dinner his secretary recounted the little incident and all men praised the kindliness of the bishop. The bishop passed it off pleasantly, but, at heart, he felt a trifle irritated. He had not felt particularly drawn toward the boy; on the other hand, he could not have left him lying in the road.

By the next day, as such things do, the story had gone all over Remo and there were unusual demonstrations of good will as the bishop passed to the cathedral. The bishop received them with dignity, but his irritation remained. He disliked ostentatious shows of virtue and distrusted the fickleness of crowds. Nevertheless, it was his duty to see the boy, and he did so.

Washed, combed and rid of his vermin, the boy looked ordinary enough, though somewhat older than the bishop had thought him. His body was slight and emaciated, but he had a well-shaped head and large liquid eyes. These stared at the bishop with some intensity; indeed with such intensity that the bishop wondered, at first, if the boy might not be an idiot. But a little conversation proved him sound of mind, though rustic in speech.

His name was Luigi and he was an orphan, living as best he

could. In the summer he tended goats; in the winter he lived with his uncle and aunt, the tavern keepers, who fed him and beat him. His age was about nineteen. He had made his Easter duty as a Christian. He would never walk again.

Such were the facts of the case, and the bishop thought them over clearheadedly. He wondered what to do with the boy.

"Luigi," he said, "would you like to go back to your village?"

"Oh, no," said the boy. "It is a very good village, but now that I can no longer herd goats, there is no place in it for me. Besides, one eats better in Remo—I have had white cheese twice already." And he smacked his lips. His voice was remarkably strong and cheerful, the bishop noticed with surprise.

"Very well," said the bishop patiently. "You need not go back if you do not choose. You are now, in some sense, a ward of the Church, and the wings of the Church are sheltering." He looked at the boy's legs, lying limp and motionless under the covers, and felt, though against his will, the natural distaste of the hale man for the maimed. "You might learn some useful trade," he said thoughtfully. "There are many trades where the hands do all—a cobbler's, a tailor's, a basket weaver's."

The boy shook his head joyfully. "Oh, no, your lordship," he said. "Trades take so long to learn and I am very stupid. It would not be worth the expense, your lordship would be embarrassed."

"My lordship, perhaps, is the best judge of that," said the bishop a trifle grimly. He kept thinking of the boy's remark about white cheese; it must be a spare life indeed where white cheese was such a treat. "But we are reasonable," he said. "Come, what would you be?"

"A beggar!" said the boy, and his dark eyes shone with delight.

"A beggar?" said the bishop, astonished and somewhat revolted.

"Why, yes," said the boy, as if it were the most natural thing in the world. "For ten years my father begged on the cathedral steps. That was before your lordship's time, but he was an excellent beggar and a master of his craft. True, he was subject to continual persecutions and jealousies from the honorable corporation of the beggars of Remo, coming, as he did, from outside the city. It was that which caused the ruin of our fortunes, for, in the end, when he had begun to fail, they threw him down a well, where he caught a bad cold and died of it. But in his good days he could outbeg any two of them. If your lordship would care to have me demonstrate his celebrated fainting fit, when his eyeballs rolled backward in his head—"

"I can think of nothing I should like less," said the bishop, shocked and disgusted, for it seemed to him an unworthy thing that a sturdy young man, though a cripple, should think of nothing better than beggary. "Besides," he said, "these other beggars you speak of—if they persecuted your father, no doubt they would persecute you."

"Me?" said the boy, and laughed. "Oh, once they understood, they would not dare touch me—not even Giuseppe, the Hook. I would be your lordship's beggar—the bishop's beggar!" And a light as of great peace and contentment spread over his countenance.

The bishop stared at him for a long time in silence. "That is what you wish?" he said, and his voice was dry.

"That is what I wish, your lordship," said the boy, nodding his head.

"So be it," said the bishop with a sigh, and left him. But when his coachman came to him the next morning for orders, it was all he could do to keep from reviling the man.

The bishop was not the sort of man who liked beggars. Indeed, were it not for custom and Christian charity, he would long since have cleared them from the steps of his cathedral. He could not very well do that; he knew what an impression such a move would make. Nevertheless, when he passed among them, as he must at times, he saw to it that his almoner made a suitable distribution of small coins, but he himself did his best to see and smell them as little as possible. Their whines and their supplications, their simulated sores and their noisome rags —these were a fret and a burden to him.

Now, it seemed, he was to have a beggar of his own. He would have taken it as a suitable humiliation for pride, but he did not feel himself to be a proud man. Nor could he think of the accident as anything but an accident. Had he deliberately trodden the lad beneath the hoofs of his horses—but he had not. He was well liked, able, decisive, a rising son of the Church. Nevertheless, he was to have a beggar—every day he must see his beggar on the steps of the cathedral, a living reproach, a living lesson in idleness and heedlessness. It was a small thing, to be sure, but it darkened his dinner and made him sore at heart.

Therefore, being the man he was, he put a mask upon his face. He meant to speak of the thing, so it should be known— at least that might ward off ridicule. He spoke of it to his secretary; the secretary agreed that it was a very seemly and Christian idea of his lordship's, while the bishop wondered if the man laughed at him in his sleeve. He spoke of it to others; there were compliments, of course. Each time he spoke of it, it turned a small knife in his breast. But that did not keep him from speaking of it, nor from seeing that every care was given Luigi.

Nevertheless, he dreaded the day when Luigi would take up his post on the steps of the cathedral. He dreaded and yearned for it, both. For then, at last, the thing would be done. After that, like many things, it would become a custom and in time Luigi himself would fade into the mass of whining beggary that haunted the steps of the cathedral. But things were not to be quite that way.

He admired, while he detested, the thoroughness with which Luigi prepared himself for his profession. He heard the whine ring out from the servants' quarters—"ten scudi for Luigi!"—he saw the little cart and the crutches Luigi had made for himself. Now and then he heard his own servants laugh at the beggar's stories. This was hard enough to bear. But at last the day of parting came.

To his disgust, the bishop found the boy neither clean nor well clad, as he had been since his accident, but dirty and dressed in tatters. He opened his mouth to reprove the boy, then he shut it again, for it seemed pitifully true that a beggar must dress his part. Nevertheless, the bishop did not like it. He asked Luigi, coolly, how he meant to live.

"Oh, your lordship's secretary has found me a very suitable chamber," said Luigi eagerly. "It is on the ground floor of a rookery by the river and it has room for my crutches, my gear and my cart. He will move me there tonight. Tomorrow I will be at my post on the steps of the cathedral." And he smiled gratefully at the bishop. "That will be a great day," he said.

"So," said the bishop, who could not trust himself to say anything further.

"Yet before I go," said Luigi, "I must thank your lordship for his kindness, and ask your lordship's blessing on my work. That is only suitable."

The bishop stiffened. "I may bless you, Luigi," he said, "but your work I cannot bless. I cannot give the blessing of the Church to the work of a man who lives by beggary when he might live otherwise."

"Well, then, I must go unblessed," said Luigi cheerfully. "After all, your lordship has already done so much for me! The bishop's beggar! How my uncle and aunt will stare!"

Now, of all the *vainglorious, self-seeking, worthless, rascally sons of iniquity*—and to think that I stand your sponsor, said the bishop, but, fortunately, he did not say it aloud. Silently he extended his ring and Luigi kissed it with such innocent reverence that the bishop was sorely moved to give him his blessing after all. But he summoned up his principles and departed in silence.

The bishop slept ill that night, tormented by dreams of Luigi. He dreamed that, for his sins, he must carry Luigi on his back all the way up the steps of the cathedral. And as he mounted each step the weight upon his back became more crushing, till at last he woke, unrefreshed.

The next day he went to the cathedral in great state, though it was an ordinary Sunday. Yet he felt the state to be, in some measure, a protection. When he passed by the steps of the cathedral, the beggars set up their usual supplications. He sent his almoner among them; it was over quicker than he thought. He did not look for Luigi and yet he felt Luigi's eyes upon him as he stood there for a moment, splendid in robe and miter. Then the thing was finished.

In the cathedral that same day, he preached passionately against the sins of idleness and heedlessness. Seldom had he been so moving—he could feel that from his congregation. When Mass was over he retired to his palace, exhausted. Yet it was pleasant for him to walk about the palace and know that Luigi was not there.

It was just after vespers when his secretary came to him and told him that a man called Giuseppe, self-styled provost of the company of the beggars of Remo, requested an audience. The bishop sighed wearily and ordered the man brought before him. He was a squat fellow of great strength and an evil cast of countenance, for one side of his face had been so burned in a fire that it was as if he had two faces, one of them inhuman. Also, his left arm terminated in an iron hook.

"This is Giuseppe, the beggar, your lordship," said the secretary, with repugnance.

"Giuseppe, called Double-Face, also called the Hook, provost of the honorable company of the beggars of Remo," said Giuseppe in a rusty voice, and plumped on his knees.

The bishop raised him and asked his business.

"Well, your lordship, it's this new fellow, Luigi Lame-legs," said Giuseppe. "I've got nothing against him personal—I wouldn't hurt a fly myself in a personal way," and he grinned horribly—"but there he is in a good place on the steps, and your lordship's servants put him there. Well, now, if he's your lordship's beggar, that's one thing—though, even so, there's fees and vails to be paid, for that's the custom. But if he isn't your lordship's beggar—and your lordship paid him no attention this morning—"

"Stop!" said the bishop with anger. "Do you mean to tell me that the very steps of the cathedral are bartered and sold among you? Why, this is simony—this is the sin of simony!"

"Your lordship can call it hard words," said Giuseppe stolidly, "but that's been the way it's been done ever since there were beggars in Remo. I paid twenty crowns for my own place, and fought old Marco too. But that's beside the point. Your lordship has a right to a beggar if your lordship wants one—we're all agreed on that. But the question is: Is this man your lordship's beggar or isn't he?"

"And supposing I said he was not my beggar?" said the bishop, trembling.

"Well, that's all we'd want to know," said Giuseppe. "And thank your lordship kindly. I had my own suspicions of the

man from the first. But we've got him down by the river now—
Carlo and Benito and old blind Marta; she's a tough one, old
blind Marta—and once we're through with him, he'll trouble
your lordship no more." And sketching a clumsy salute, the
man turned to go.

"Stop!" said the bishop again. "Would you have the guilt of
murder upon your conscience?"

"Oh, your lordship takes it too hard," said Giuseppe, shuffling his feet. "What's one beggar more or less? We're not rich
folk or learned folk to bother a mind like your lordship's. We
breed and we die, and there's an end. And even at the best, it's
no bed of roses on the steps of the cathedral."

The bishop wished to say many things, but he could think of
only one.

"I declare to you that this man is my beggar," he said. "I
stretch my hand over him."

"Well, that's very nicely spoken of your lordship," said Giuseppe, in a grumbling voice, "and I dare say we can make room
for him. But if the man's to keep a whole skin, your lordship
had best come with me—old Marta was talking of ear splitting
when I left her."

So they found Luigi, bound but cheerful, in his first floor
chamber by the river, guarded by the persons Giuseppe had
described—a hunchback, a dwarf and a blind woman. The
window which gave upon the river was open, and a large sack,
weighted with stones, lay in one corner of the room. The
bishop's arrival produced a certain consternation on the part of
all but Luigi, who seemed to take it as a matter of course. After
the boy had been unbound the bishop addressed the beggars
with some vivacity, declared that Luigi was his beggar, and gave
him a piece of silver before all of them, in token. This seemed
to satisfy the company, who then crept away in silence.

"And yet have I done right? Have I done right?" said the
bishop, striding up and down the chamber. "I greatly fear I
have condoned the sin of simony! I have spent Mother Church's
substance among the unworthy! And yet, even so, your blood
may be upon my head!" and he looked at Luigi doubtfully.

"Oh, your lordship need not take it so hard," said Luigi, rub-
bing his arms. "All is safe enough now. I arranged about the

dues and vails with Giuseppe, while your lordship was discussing her state of grace with Marta. He's an honest fellow enough and his point is reasonable. One should not take a good place without money to keep it up. Had your lordship given me alms with your own hand this morning, our little difficulty would never have arisen. That was my fault—I assumed that your lordship knew."

"Knew?" said the bishop. "What should I know of such things? And yet, God forgive me, I am a priest and I should have knowledge of evil."

"It is merely a difference in knowledge," said Luigi gently. "Now, your lordship, doubtless, has never been in a room quite like this before."

The bishop stared at the damp walls and the mean chamber. He smelled the smell that cannot be aired from a room, the smell of poverty itself. He had never doubted his own experience before—when he had been first made a priest, he had gone on certain works of charity. Now it seemed to him that those works must have been rather carefully selected.

"No," he said, "I have never been in a room just like this one."

"And yet there are many of us who live in such rooms—and not all beggars," said Luigi. He changed his tone. "That was a fine rousing sermon your lordship gave us on idleness and heedlessness this morning," he said. "Hey, it brought the scudi forth from the good folks' pockets! An admirable sermon!"

"I am grateful for your encomiums," said the bishop bitterly. He glanced around the room again. "Is there nought else I can do?" he said unwillingly.

"No, thank your lordship," said Luigi, and his eyes were smiling. "I have a woman to cook my dinner—it is true she is a thief, but she will not steal from a cripple—and soon, with your lordship's patronage, I shall be able to afford a charcoal brazier. Moreover, my friends seem to have left me a sack. So, after dinner I shall say my prayers and go to bed to refresh myself for tomorrow's labor."

I shall say mine, too, for I need them, said the bishop, though he did not say it to Luigi.

So that was how it began. Soon enough, the bishop's beggar

was a familiar figure on the steps of the cathedral—one of the admitted curiosities of the town. He was well liked in his trade, for he always had a merry word or a sharp one for his clients —and it passed around until "Luigi says" became a byword. The bishop became used to him as one becomes used to a touch of rheumatism. Other men had their difficulties; he had his beggar. Now and then it seemed odd to the bishop that he had ever thought of the beggars on the steps as a vague and indistinguishable heap of misery and rags. He knew them all by now —blind Marta and Carlo, the dwarf, Giuseppe Double-Face, and Benito, the hunchback. He knew their ways and their thoughts. He knew the hovels where they lived and the bread they ate. For every week or so he would slip from his palace to visit Luigi's chamber.

It was necessary for him to do, for, to him, Luigi represented the gravest problem of the soul that he had yet encountered. Was the man even a Christian? The bishop was not sure. He professed religion, he followed the rites of the Church. Yet sometimes when he confessed him, the bishop was appalled. Every sin that could ravage the human heart was there—if not in act, then in desire—and all told so gaily! Sometimes the bishop, angrily, would tax him with willful exaggeration, and Luigi, with a smile, would admit the charge and ask for still another penance. This left the bishop confused.

Yet through the years there grew up between the two men a singular bond. The bishop may have been heedless; he was not stupid. Very soon he began to realize that there was another Remo than the city he had come to first—a city not of lords and scholars and tradesmen and pious ladies, but a city of the poor and the ignorant, the maimed and the oppressed. For, as Luigi said, when one lay all day on the steps of the cathedral one heard stories, and anyone will talk to a beggar. Some of the stories struck the bishop to the heart. He could hardly believe them at first, yet, when he investigated them, they were true. When he was convinced they were true, he set himself stubbornly to remedy them. He was not always successful—pleasant sinners like the Church to keep its own place. Now and then he discussed his efforts with Luigi, who listened, it seemed to the bishop, with an air of perfect cynicism. His attitude seemed to be that it was all very well for a man like the bishop to concern himself about these things, but he was the bishop's beggar and, if other folk starved and died, it was none of his concern. This irritated the bishop inordinately and made him more determined than ever.

Gradually, he noticed, the composition of his table changed. There were fewer courtiers and scholars, there were more priests from the country, smelling of poverty and chestnut bread. They came in their tattered cassocks, with their big red wrists; at first they were strange and ill-at-ease at his table. But the bishop was able to talk to them. After all, were they not like the old parish priest that Luigi talked of so often? When the ceremony of his table disturbed them he saw to it that there was less ceremony. Luigi mocked him for this and told him bluntly what his richer clients were saying. The bishop rebuked him for impertinence to his spiritual director and persisted.

It is strange how time flies when the heart is occupied. In no time at all, it seemed to the bishop, he was a middle aged man with gray at his temples, and Luigi a man in his thirties. That seemed odd to the bishop, he did not know where the time had gone. He thought of it, one morning, with a sense of loss. He had meant to do many things—he was still ambitious. Now, when night came, he was often too tired to think. The trouble of many people weighed upon his heart—the troubles of the peasants in the hills, who lived from hand to mouth, the troubles of Domenico, the shoemaker, who had too pretty a daughter, the troubles of Tessa, the flower seller, whose son was a thief. When he had first come to Remo, he had not had all these troubles. He picked up a letter on his desk—a letter that had lain there for days—and, having read it, sat staring.

The dreams of his youth came back to him, doubly hot, doubly dear. While he idled his life away in Remo his brother and his friends had been busy. They had not forgotten him, after all. Cardinal Malaverni, the great sage statesman whose hand was ever upon the strings of policy, meant to pass by Remo on his way to Rome. The bishop knew the cardinal—once, long ago, he had been one of the cardinal's promising young men. There was a letter also from the bishop's brother, the lord—a letter that hinted of grave and important matters. The bishop almost sobbed when he thought how long both letters had lain unanswered. He summoned his secretary and set himself about an unaccustomed bustle of preparation.

It often occurred to him, sorrowfully, within the next few days, how foolish it was to leave one's letters unopened. The preparations went forward for the cardinal's visit, yet it seemed to him that they went forward ill, though he could not put his finger upon the cause. Somehow he had got out of the way of the world where such things go forward smoothly; he was more used to his country priests than to entertaining distinguished visitors. Nevertheless, he botched together a few Latin verses, saw to it that the hangings in the guest chambers were cleaned and mended, drove his choirmaster nearly frantic and got in the way of his servants. He noticed that these were no longer afraid of him, but treated him with tolerant patience, more like a friend than a master, and this irked him oddly. What irked him even more, perhaps, was Luigi's shameless and undisguised self-interest in the whole affair.

"Ah, your lordship, we've waited a long time for this," he said, "but it's come at last. And everyone knows that a great man like Cardinal Malaverni doesn't come to a place like Remo for nothing. So all we have to do is to play our cards well, and then, when we move on, as we doubtless shall—well, I, for one, won't be sorry."

"Move on?" said the bishop, astonished.

The beggar yawned.

"But how else?" he said. "I have been the bishop's beggar. When your lordship is made a cardinal I will be the cardinal's beggar. The post will entail new responsibilities, no doubt, but I have confidence in my abilities. Perhaps I shall even employ an assistant for my actual begging—after all, it is often drafty on the steps of the cathedral."

The bishop turned and left him without a word. Yet what Luigi had said caused trouble and disquiet in his heart, for he knew that Luigi often had news of things to come before even the count of Remo had an inkling of them.

At last the great day of the cardinal's visit came.

Like all such days, it passed as a dream passes, with heat and ceremony and worry about small things. The Latin verses of welcome were unexpectedly well read; on the other hand, the choristers were nervous and did not sing their best. Two gentlemen of the cardinal's suite had to be lodged over the stables, much to the bishop's distress, and the crayfish for dinner had been served without sauce.

The bishop hoped that all had gone well, but he did not know. As he sat, at last, alone with his old friend in his study that overlooked the garden, he felt at once wrought up and drowsy.

This should be the real pleasure of the day, to sit with his old friend in the cool of the evening and renew contact with the great world. But the bishop was used to country hours by now and the feast had broken up late. He should be listening to the cardinal with the greatest attention, and yet those accursed crayfish kept coming into his mind.

"Well, Gianfrancesco," said the cardinal, sipping delicately at his wine, "you have given your tutor a most charming welcome. Your wine, your people, your guests—it reminds me somehow of one of those fine Virgilian eclogues we used to parse together. 'Tityre, tu patulae recubans—' "

"The choir," said the bishop—"the choir usually is—"

"Why they sang very well!" said the cardinal. "And what good, honest, plain-spoken priests you have in your charge!" He shook his head sadly. "I fear that we do not always get their like in Rome. And yet, each man to his task."

"They have a hard charge in these hills," said the bishop wearily. "It was a great honor for them to see Your Eminence."

"Oh, honor!" said the cardinal. "To see an old man with the gout—yes, I have the gout these days, Gianfrancesco—I fear we both are not so young as we were." He leaned forward and regarded the bishop attentively. "You, too, have altered, my old friend," he said softly.

"Your Eminence means that I have rusticated," said the bishop a trifle bitterly. "Well, it is true."

"Oh, not rusticated," said the cardinal, with a charming gesture. "Not at all. But there has been a change—a perceptible one—from the Gianfrancesco I knew." He took a walnut and began to crack it. "That Gianfrancesco was a charming and able young man," he said. "Yet I doubt if he would have made the count of his city do penance in his shirt, for his sins, before the doors of his cathedral."

"I can explain about that," said the bishop hurriedly. "The shirt was a silk one and the weather by no means inclement. Moreover, the count's new tax would have ruined my poor. It is true we have not always seen eye to eye since then, yet I think he respects me more than he did before."

"That is just what I said to your brother, Piero," said the cardinal comfortably. "I said, 'You are wrong to be perturbed about this, Piero, it will have a good effect.' Yes, even as regards the beggar."

"My beggar?" said the bishop, and sighed.

"Oh, you know how small things get about," said the cardinal. "Some small thing is seized upon; it even travels to Rome. The bishop's beggar—the beggar's bishop—the bishop who humbles his soul to protect the poor."

"But it was not like that at all," said the bishop, "I—"

The cardinal waved him aside. "Do not hide your good works beneath a bushel, Gianfrancesco," he said. "The Church herself has need of them. These are troubled times we live in. The French king may march any day. There is heresy and dissension abroad. You have no idea what difficult days may lie ahead." He watched the bishop intently. "Our Holy Father leans much upon my unworthy shoulder," he said, "and our Holy Father is beginning to age."

"That is sore news for us all," said the bishop.

"Sore indeed," said the cardinal. "And yet, one must face realities. Should our Holy Father die, it will be necessary for those of us who truly love the Church to stand together—more especially in the college of cardinals." He paused and with a silver nutpick extracted the last meat from the walnut. "I believe that our Holy Father is disposed to reward your own labors with the see of Albano," he said.

"The see of Albano?" said the bishop as if in a dream, for, as all men knew, Albano was an old and famous diocese outside the walls of Rome and he who was bishop of Albano wore a cardinal's hat.

"It might have a most excellent effect," said the cardinal. "I myself think it might. We have clever and able men who are sons of the Church. Indeed. And yet, just at this moment with both the French and the German parties so active—well, there is perhaps need for another sort of man—at least as regards the people." He smiled delightfully. "You would be very close to me as cardinal bishop of Albano—very close to us all," he said. "I should lean upon you, Gianfrancesco."

"There is nought that would please me more!" cried the bishop, like a boy. He thought for a moment of the power and the glory, of the great, crowded streets of Rome and the Church that humbles kings. "I would have to leave Remo?" he said.

"Well, yes, naturally, it would mean your having to leave Remo," said the cardinal. "Your new duties would demand it."

"That would be hard," said the bishop. "I would have to leave Luigi and all my people." He thought of them suddenly —the lame, the halt, the oppressed.

"Your people, perhaps," said the cardinal, "but certainly not Luigi. He should come with you by all means, as a living example."

"Oh, no, no, that would never do," said the bishop. "Your Eminence does not understand, Luigi is difficult enough as a bishop's beggar. As a cardinal's beggar, he would be overweening. You have no idea how overweening he would be."

The cardinal regarded him with a puzzled stare.

"Am I dreaming, Gianfrancesco?" he said. "Or are you declining the see of Albano and a cardinal's hat for no more reason than that you are attached to a beggar?"

"Oh, no, no, no!" cried the bishop, in an agony, "I am not in the least attached to him—he is my cross and my thorn. But you see, it would be so bad for him if I were to be made a cardinal. I tremble to think what would happen to his soul. And then there are all his companions—Giuseppe, the Hook, is dead, but there is still blind Marta, and Benito, the hunchback, and the new ones. No, I must stay in Remo."

The cardinal smiled—a smile of exasperation, "I think you have forgotten something, Gianfrancesco," he said. "I think you have forgotten that obedience is the first law of the Church."

"I am five times obedient," said the bishop. "Let our Holy Father do with me as he wills. Let him send me as a missionary to savages; let him strip me of my bishopric and set me to work in the hills. I shall be content. But while I have been given Remo, I have work to do in Remo. I did not expect it to be so when I first came here," he said in a low voice, "and yet, somehow, I find that it is so."

The cardinal said nothing at all for a long time.

Then at last he rose, and, pressing the bishop's hand, he retired to his own quarters. The bishop hoped that he was comfortable in them, though it occurred to him, in the uneasy sleep before dawn, that the chimney smoked.

Next morning the cardinal departed on his journey toward Rome without speaking of these matters further. The bishop felt sorry to see him go, and yet relieved. He had been very glad to see his old friend again—he told himself that. Yet from the moment of the cardinal's arrival there had been an unfamiliar grayness upon his spirit, and now that grayness was gone. Nevertheless, he knew that he must face Luigi—and that thought was hard for him.

Yet it went well enough, on the whole.

The bishop explained to him, as one explains to a child, that it did not seem as if God had intended him to be a cardinal, only bishop of Remo, and with that Luigi had to be content. He grumbled about it frequently and remarked that if he had known all this in the first place, he might never have accepted the position of bishop's beggar. But he was not any more overweening than before, and with that the bishop had to be satisfied.

Then came the war with the French, and that was hard upon the bishop. He did not like wars, he did not like the thought of his people being killed. Yet, when the count of Remo fled with most of his soldiery, and the mayor locked himself in his house and stayed there, shaking, there was no one to take over the rule of the town but the bishop. The very beggars in the streets cried out for him, he could not escape the task.

He took it with a heavy heart, under the mocking eyes of Luigi. With Luigi in his cart, he inspected the walls and defenses.

"Well, your lordship has a very pretty problem," said Luigi. "Half a dozen good cannon shots and the city will be taken by storm."

"I thought so, I feared so," said the bishop, sighing. "And yet my people are my people."

"Your lordship might easily compromise with the enemy," said Luigi. "They are angry with the count, it is true—they thought they had him bought over. Yet it would mean but two score hangings or so, and a tribute, properly assessed."

"I cannot permit my flock to be harried and persecuted," said the bishop.

"Well, if your lordship must die, I will die with your lordship," said Luigi. "Meanwhile, we might set the townsfolk to work on the walls—at least it will give them something to do. And yet, there may be another way."

So it was done and the bishop worked day and night, enheartening and encouraging his people. For once, all Remo was one, and the spirit and will that burned within it were the bishop's. Yet it seemed no time at all before the French sat down before Remo.

They sent a trumpet and a flag to demand the surrender of the city. The bishop received the young officer who came with the trumpet—a dark-faced man he was, with a humorous twist to his mouth. The bishop even took him on a tour of the walls, which seemed to surprise him a little.

"You are well defended," said the Frenchman politely.

"Oh, no, we are very ill defended," said the bishop. "My good children have been trying to strengthen the wall with sandbags, but, as you perceive, it is rotten and needs rebuilding. Moreover, the count was badly cheated on his powder. I must speak to him of it some time, for hardly a gun we have is fit to fire."

The Frenchman's astonishment grew. "I do not wish to doubt your lordship's word," he said, "but if those things are so, how does your lordship propose to defend Remo?"

"By the will of God," said the bishop very simply. "I do not wish my poor people killed; neither do I wish them oppressed. If needs must, I shall die in their stead, but they shall go scatheless. Ere you hang one man of Remo, I shall take the noose from around his neck and put it around my own."

"Your lordship makes things very difficult," said the Frenchman thoughtfully. "My king has no desire to attack the Church

—and, indeed, the walls of Remo seem stronger than your lordship reckons."

Then he was conscious of a plucking at his sleeve. It was Luigi, the beggar, in his little cart, who, by signs and grimaces, seemed to wish the Frenchman to follow him.

"What is it, Luigi?" said the bishop wearily. "Ah, yes, you wish to show our friend the room where we store the powder. Very well. Then he may see how little we have."

When the Frenchman rejoined the bishop, he was wiping sweat from his forehead and his face was white. The bishop pressed him to stay for a glass of wine, but he said he must return to his camp, and departed, muttering something incoherent about it being indeed the will of God that defended Remo.

When he had gone, the bishop looked severely upon Luigi, "Luigi," he said sternly, "I fear you have been up to some of your tricks."

"How your lordship mistakes me," said the beggar. "It is true I showed him three of my fellow beggars—and they did not seem to him in the best of health. But I did not say they had plague; I let him draw his own conclusions. It took me four days to school them in their parts, but that I did not tell him either."

"That was hardly honest, Luigi," said the bishop. "We know there is no plague in the town."

"We know also that our walls are rotten," said Luigi, "but the French will not believe that, either. Men of war are extremely suspicious—it is their weakness. We shall wait and see."

They waited and saw, for that night a council of war was held in the French camp and the officer who had come with the trumpet reported (a) that Remo was held in great force and strongly defended; (b) that its bishop was resolved to die in the breach, and (c) that there was plague in the city. Taking all these factors into account, the French wisely decided, after some forty-eight hours' delay, to strike camp and fall back on their main army—which they did just in time to take part in the historic defeat of the whole French invasion a week later. This defeat sealed for all time the heroic defense of Remo, for, had the part of the French army occupied before Remo rejoined their main body before, the historic defeat might have been as historic a victory for the French. As it was, all Italy rang with the name of the bishop of Remo.

But of all this the bishop knew nothing, for his beggar, Luigi, was dying.

As the French moved away they had loosed off a few cannon shot, more in irritation than for any real military purpose. However, one of the cannon shot, heedlessly aimed, struck the steps of the cathedral, and you may still see the scars. It also struck the cart wherein Luigi lay, directing his beggars at one task of defense or another. When the bishop first heard that his beggar was hurt, he went to him at once. But there was little that man could do but wait, and the waiting was long. It was not until seven weeks later that Luigi passed from this earth. He endured, indeed, till the messengers came from Rome.

After they had talked with the bishop, the bishop went alone to this cathedral and prayed. Then he went to see Luigi.

"Well?" said the dying man eagerly, staring at him with limpid eyes.

"His Holiness has been graciously pleased to make of me the first archbishop of Remo, placing under my staff, as well, the dioceses of Ugri and Soneto," said the bishop slowly. "But I have the news from Cardinal Malaverni, and I may remain here till I die." He stared at Luigi. "I do not understand," he said.

"It is well done. You have stayed by the poor in their poverty and the wretched in their hour of trial," said Luigi, and for once there was no trace of mockery in his voice.

"I do not understand. I do not understand at all," said the bishop again. "And yet I think you deserve recompense rather than I, Luigi."

"No," said Luigi, "that I do not."

The bishop passed his hand across his brow. "I am not a fool," he said. "It was well done, to humble my spirit. And yet, why did you do so, Luigi?"

"Why, that was my great sin," said Luigi. "I have confessed many, vain and imaginary sins, but never the real one till now." He paused, as if the words hurt him. "When your lordship's coach rolled over my legs, I was very bitter," he said. "A poor man has little. To lose that little—to lose the air on the hills and the springing step, to lie like a log forever because a bishop's coachman was careless—that made me very bitter. I had rather your lordship had driven over me again than taken me back to your palace and treated me with kindness. I hated your lordship for your indifferent kindness—I hated you for everything."

"Did you so, Luigi?" said the bishop.

"Yes," said Luigi. "And I could see that your lordship hated me—or, if not hated, loathed, like a crippled dog that one must be kind to without liking. So I set myself out to tease and torment your lordship—at first by being your beggar, then in other ways, I could not believe in goodness; I could not believe there could not come a moment when your lordship would turn upon me and drive me forth."

He paused a moment and wiped his mouth with a cloth.

"Yes, I could not believe that at all," he said. "But you were not to be broken, Gianfrancesco, my brother. The evil I showed you daily was like a knife in your heart and a burden on your back, but you bore the knife and the burden. I took delight in showing you how ill things went in your city—how, below the fair surface, there was misery and pain. And had you once turned aside from that misery and pain, I would have been satisfied, for then, bishop or no bishop, you would have lost your soul. Was that evil of me, Gianfrancesco?"

"Very evil in intent," said the bishop steadily, "for, while it is permitted to be tempted, it is evil to tempt. And yet proceed."

"Well," said Luigi, with a sudden and childlike stare, "it did not work. The more I tried to make you a bad man, the better man you became. You would not do what was ill, you would not depart from your poor, once you had known them—not even for a red hat or a count's favor. You would not do ill at all. So now we have defended Remo, the two of us, and I am dying." He stirred uneasily in his bed. "It is just as well," he said, with a trace of his old mockery. "I told my uncle I would live to be a cardinal's beggar, but I am not sure that I would have liked it. I have been the bishop's beggar so long. And yet, from the first I have loved you also, Gianfrancesco. Will you give me your blessing now, on me and my work—the blessing you denied me once?"

The bishop's face was wrung. Yet he lifted his hand and absolved and blessed Luigi. He blessed Luigi and his work in the name of the Father and of the Son and of the Holy Ghost. When that had been done, a smile appeared on Luigi's face.

"A very fine blessing," he said. "I must tell that to the Hook when I see him; he will be envious. I wonder is it drafty on the steps of heaven? A very fine blessing, your lordship. . . .ten. . . . scudi. . . .for. . . .Luigi." And with that his jaw dropped and it was over. But the bishop knelt beside the bed with streaming eyes.

And all that, to be sure, was a long time ago. But they still tell the story in Remo when they show the bishop's tomb. He lies upon it, fairly carven in marble. But carved all around the tomb are a multitude of beggars, lame, halt and misshapen, yet all praising God. And there are words in Latin which say, "It is not enough to have knowledge—these also are my sheep." Of the tomb of Luigi, the beggar—that no man knows. They say it was beside the bishop's but, in one war or another, it was destroyed and there is no trace of it now. Yet Luigi was an arrogant spirit; perhaps he would have liked that best.

Experiment

(1) Define the psychological conflict present in this story.

(2) What changes in character do the principals of this story undergo?

(3) Identify the *motifs* that Benét uses in this story.

(4) How does the beggar make the bishop aware of a certain unconscious hypocrisy in the bishop's motives?

(5) Show how Luigi helps the bishop to gain a greater sense of reality.

(6) What aspects of Benét's craftsmanship lead us to accept without question the statement that "through the years there grew up between the two men a singular bond"?

(7) Show how Luigi has a positive character of his own—a character that, in its own way, has as much strength as that of the bishop.

(8) Locate specific examples of irony and humor in the story.

(9) Luigi was an "arrogant spirit" and he tested the bishop to the full. Show how the revelation of Luigi's true inner nature constitutes a psychological climax to the story as fully effective as any plot climax.

"The Tarn" is a story of a murderer whose crime can be understood in human terms. His sense of remorse wins our pity. "The Tarn" has some elements of the "mystery" or "ghost" story, but for those readers who do not have an appetite for the preternatural its conclusion can be interpreted as the hysteria and nervous exhaustion of a man who has suddenly and impulsively denied his conscience.

HUGH WALPOLE [8]

The Tarn

I

As Foster moved unconsciously across the room, bent towards the bookcase, and stood leaning forward a little, choosing now one book, now another, with his eyes, his host, seeing the muscles of the back of his thin, scraggy neck stand out above his low flannel collar, thought of the ease with which he could squeeze that throat, and the pleasure, the triumphant, lustful pleasure, that such an action would give him.

The low, white-walled, white-ceilinged room was flooded with the mellow, kindly Lakeland sun. October is a wonderful month in the English Lakes, golden, rich, and perfumed, slow suns moving through apricot-tinted skies to ruby evening glories; the shadows lie then thick about that beautiful country, in dark purple patches, in long web-like patterns of silver gauze, in thick splotches of amber and grey. The clouds pass in galleons across the mountains, now veiling, now revealing, now descend-

[8] Reprinted by permission from Hugh Walpole's *The Silver Thorn*.

ing with ghost-like armies to the very breast of the plains, suddenly rising to the softest of blue skies and lying thin in lazy languorous colour.

Fenwick's cottage looked across to Low Fells; on his right, seen through side windows, sprawled the hills above Ullswater.

Fenwick looked at Foster's back and felt suddenly sick, so that he sat down, veiling his eyes for a moment with his hand. Foster had come up there, come all the way from London, to explain. It was so like Foster to want to explain, to want to put things right. For how many years had he known Foster? Why, for twenty at least, and during all those years Foster had been for ever determined to put things right with everybody. He could never bear to be disliked; he hated that anyone should think ill of him; he wanted everyone to be his friend. That was one reason, perhaps, why Foster had got on so well, had prospered so in his career; one reason, too, why Fenwick had not.

For Fenwick was the opposite of Foster in this. He did not want friends, he certainly did not care that people should like him—that is people for whom, for one reason or another, he had contempt—and he had contempt for quite a number of people.

Fenwick looked at that long, thin, bending back and felt his knees tremble. Soon Foster would turn round and that high, reedy voice would pipe out something about the books. "What jolly books you have, Fenwick!" How many, many times in the long watches of the night, when Fenwick could not sleep, and he heard that pipe sounding close there—yes, in the very shadows of his bed! And how many times had Fenwick replied to it: "I hate you! You are the cause of my failure in life! You have been in my way always. Always, always, always! Patronizing and pretending, and in truth showing others what a poor thing you thought me, how great a failure, how conceited a fool! I know. You can hide nothing from me! I can hear you!"

For twenty years now Foster had been persistently in Fenwick's way. There had been that affair, so long ago now, when Robins had wanted a sub-editor for his wonderful review, the *Parthenon,* and Fenwick had gone to see him and they had had a splendid talk. How magnificently Fenwick had talked that day; with what enthusiasm he had shown Robins (who was blinded by his own conceit, anyway) the kind of paper the *Parthenon* might be; how Robins had caught his own enthusiasm, how he had pushed his fat body about the room crying: "Yes, yes, Fenwick—that's fine! That's fine indeed!"—and then how, after all, Foster had got that job.

The paper had only lived for a year or so, it is true, but the connection with it had brought Foster into prominence just as it might have brought Fenwick!

Then, five years later, there was Fenwick's novel, *The Bitter Aloe*—the novel upon which he had spent three years of blood-and-tears endeavour—and then, in the very same week of publication, Foster brings out *The Circus,* the novel that made his name; although, Heaven knows, the thing was poor enough sentimental trash. You may say that one novel cannot kill another—but can it not? Had not *The Circus* appeared would not that group of London know-alls—that conceited, limited, ignorant, self-satisfied crowd, who nevertheless can do, by their talk, so much to affect a book's good or evil fortunes—have talked about *The Bitter Aloe* and so forced it into prominence? As it was, the book was still-born and *The Circus* went on its prancing, triumphant way.

After that there had been many occasions—some small, some big—and always in one way or another that thin, scraggy body of Foster's was interfering with Fenwick's happiness.

The thing had become, of course, an obsession with Fenwick. Hiding up there in the heart of the Lakes, with no friends, almost no company, and very little money, he was given too much to brooding over his failure. He *was* a failure and it was not his own fault. How could it be his fault with his talents and his brilliance? It was the fault of modern life and its lack of culture, the fault of the stupid material mess that made up the intelligence of human beings—and the fault of Foster.

Always Fenwick hoped that Foster would keep away from him. He did not know what he would not do did he see the man. And then one day, to his amazement, he received a telegram:

Passing through this way. May I stop with you Monday and Tuesday?—Giles Foster.

Fenwick could scarcely believe his eyes, and then—from curiosity, from cynical contempt, from some deeper, more mysterious motive that he dared not analyse—he had telegraphed—*Come.*

And here the man was. And he had come—would you believe it?—to "put things right." He had heard from Hamlin Eddis that Fenwick was hurt with him, had some kind of grievance.

"I didn't like to feel that, old man, and so I thought I'd just stop by and have it out with you, see what the matter was, and put it right."

Last night after supper Foster had tried to put it right. Eagerly, his eyes like a good dog's who is asking for a bone that he knows he thoroughly deserves, he had held out his hand and asked Fenwick to "say what was up."

Fenwick simply had said that nothing was up; Hamlin Eddis was a damned fool.

"Oh, I'm glad to hear that!" Foster had cried, springing up out of his chair and putting his hand on Fenwick's shoulder. "I'm glad of that, old man. I couldn't bear for us not to be friends. We've been friends so long."

Lord, how Fenwick hated him at that moment.

II

"What a jolly lot of books you have!" Foster turned round and looked at Fenwick with eager, gratified eyes. "Every book here is interesting! I like your arrangement of them, too, and those open bookshelves—it always seems to me a shame to shut up books behind glass!"

Foster came forward and sat down quite close to his host. He even reached forward and laid his hand on his host's knee. "Look here! I'm mentioning it for the last time—positively! But I do want to make quite certain. There *is* nothing wrong between us, is there, old man? I know you assured me last night, but I just want . . ."

Fenwick looked at him and, surveying him, felt suddenly an exquisite pleasure of hatred. He disliked the touch of the man's hand on his knee; he himself bent forward a little and, thinking how agreeable it would be to push Foster's eyes in, deep, deep into his head, crunching them, smashing them to purple, leaving the empty, staring, bloody sockets, said:

"Why, no. Of course not. I told you last night. What could there be?"

The hand gripped the knee a little more tightly.

"I *am* so glad! That's splendid! Splendid! I hope you won't think me ridiculous, but I've always had an affection for you ever since I can remember. I've always wanted to know you better. I've admired your talent so greatly. That novel of yours —the—the—the one about the aloe—"

"*The Bitter Aloe?*"

"Ah, yes, that was it. That was a splendid book. Pessimistic, of course, but still fine. It ought to have done better. I remember thinking so at the time."

"Yes, it ought to have done better."

"Your time will come, though. What I say is that good work always tells in the end."

"Yes, my time will come."

The thin, piping voice went on:

"Now, I've had more success than I deserved. Oh yes, I have. You can't deny it. I'm not falsely modest. I mean it. I've got some talent, of course, but not so much as people say. And you! Why, you've got so *much* more than they acknowledge. You have, old man. You have indeed. Only—I do hope you'll forgive my saying this—perhaps up here, shut away here, closed in by all these mountains, in this wet climate—always raining— why, you're out of things! You don't see people, don't talk and discover what's really going on. Why, look at me!"

Fenwick turned round and looked at him.

"Now, I have half the year in London, where one gets the best of everything, best talk, best music, best plays; and then I'm three months abroad, Italy or Greece or somewhere, and then three months in the country. Now, that's an ideal arrangement. You have everything that way."

Italy or Greece or somewhere!

Something turned in Fenwick's breast, grinding, grinding, grinding. How he had longed, oh, how passionately, for just one week in Greece, two days in Sicily! Sometimes he had thought that he might run to it, but when it had come to the actual counting of the pennies . . . And how this fool, this fat-head, this self-satisfied, conceited, patronizing . . .

He got up, looking out at the golden sun.
"What do you say to a walk?" he suggested. "The sun will last for a good hour yet."

III

As soon as the words were out of his lips he felt as though someone else had said them for him. He even turned half round to see whether anyone else were there. Ever since Foster's arrival on the evening before he had been conscious of this sensation. A walk? Why should he take Foster for a walk, show him his beloved country, point out those curves and lines and hallows, the broad silver shield of Ullswater, the cloudy purple hills hunched like blankets about the knees of some recumbent giant? Why? It was as though he had turned round to someone behind him and had said: "You have some further design in this."

They started out. The road sank abruptly to the lake, then the path ran between trees at the water's edge. Across the lake tones of bright yellow light, crocus-hued, rode upon the blue. The hills were dark.

The very way that Foster walked bespoke the man. He was always a little ahead of you, pushing his long, thin body along with little eager jerks, as though, did he not hurry, he would miss something that would be immensely to his advantage. He talked, throwing words over his shoulder to Fenwick as you throw crumbs of bread to a robin.

"Of course I was pleased. Who would not be? After all, it's a new prize. They've only been awarding it for a year or two, but it's gratifying—really gratifying—to secure it. When I opened the envelope and found the cheque there—well, you could have knocked me down with a feather. You could, indeed. Of course, a hundred pounds isn't much. But it's the honour. . . ."

Whither were they going? Their destiny was as certain as though they had no free will. Free will? There is no free will. All is Fate. Fenwick suddenly laughed aloud.

Foster stopped.

"Why, what is it?"

"What's what?"

"You laughed."

"Something amused me."

Foster slipped his arm through Fenwick's.

"It *is* jolly to be walking along together like this, arm in arm, friends. I'm a sentimental man. I won't deny it. What I say is that life is short and one must love one's fellow-beings, or where is one? You live too much alone, old man." He squeezed Fenwick's arm. "That's the truth of it."

It was torture, exquisite, heavenly torture. It was wonderful to feel that thin, bony arm pressing against him. Almost you could hear the beating of that other heart. Wonderful to feel that arm and the temptation to take it in your hands and to bend it and twist it and then to hear the bones crack . . . crack . . . crack. . . . Wonderful to feel that temptation rise through one's body like boiling water and yet not to yield to it. For a moment Fenwick's hand touched Foster's. Then he drew himself apart.

"We're at the village. This is the hotel where they all come in the summer. We turn off at the right here. I'll show you my tarn."

IV

"Your tarn?" asked Foster. "Forgive my ignorance, but what *is* a tarn exactly?"

"A tarn is a miniature lake, a pool of water lying in the lap of the hill. Very quiet, lovely, silent. Some of them are immensely deep."

"I should like to see that."

"It is some little distance—up a rough road. Do you mind?"

"Not a bit. I have long legs."

"Some of them are immensely deep—unfathomable—nobody touched the bottom—but quiet, like glass, with shadows only—"

"Do you know, Fenwick, I have always been afraid of water —I've never learnt to swim. I'm afraid to go out of my depth. Isn't that ridiculous? But it is all because at my private school, years ago, when I was a small boy, some big fellows took me and held me with my head under the water and nearly drowned me. They did indeed. They went farther than they meant to. I can see their faces."

Fenwick considered this. The picture leapt to his mind. He could see the boys—large, strong fellows, probably—and this skinny thing like a frog, their thick hands about his throat, his legs like grey sticks kicking out of the water, their laughter, their sudden sense that something was wrong, the skinny body all flaccid and still. . . .

He drew a deep breath.

Foster was walking beside him now, not ahead of him, as though he were a little afraid and needed reassurance. Indeed, the scene had changed. Before and behind them stretched the uphill path, loose with shale and stones. On their right, on a ridge at the foot of the hill, were some quarries, almost deserted, but the more melancholy in the fading afternoon because a little work still continued there; faint sounds came from the gaunt listening chimneys, a stream of water ran and tumbled angrily into a pool below, once and again a black silhouette, like a question-mark, appeared against the darkening hill.

It was a little steep here, and Foster puffed and blew.

Fenwick hated him the more for that. So thin and spare and still he could not keep in condition! They stumbled, keeping below the quarry, on the edge of the running water, now green, now a dirty white-grey, pushing their way along the side of the hill.

Their faces were set now towards Helvellyn. It rounded the cup of hills, closing in the base and then sprawling to the right.

"There's the tarn!" Fenwick exclaimed; and then added, "The sun's not lasting as long as I had expected. It's growing dark already."

Foster stumbled and caught Fenwick's arm.

"This twilight makes the hills look strange—like living men. I can scarcely see my way."

"We're alone here," Fenwick answered. "Don't you feel the stillness? The men will have left the quarry now and gone home. There is no one in all this place but ourselves. If you watch you will see a strange green light steal down over the hills. It lasts for but a moment and then it is dark.

"Ah, here is my tarn. Do you know how I love this place, Foster? It seems to belong especially to me, just as much as all your work and your glory and fame and success seem to belong to you. I have this and you have that. Perhaps in the end we are even, after all. Yes. . . .

"But I feel as though that piece of water belonged to me and I to it, and as though we should never be separated—yes. . . . Isn't it black?

"It is one of the deep ones. No one has ever sounded it. Only Helvellyn knows, and one day I fancy that it will take me, too, into its confidence, will whisper its secrets—"

Foster sneezed.

"Very nice. Very beautiful, Fenwick. I like your tarn. Charming. And now let's turn back. That is a difficult walk beneath the quarry. It's chilly, too."

"Do you see that little jetty there?" Fenwick led Foster by the arm. "Someone built that out into the water. He had a boat there, I suppose. Come and look down. From the end of the little jetty it looks so deep and the mountains seem to close round."

Fenwick took Foster's arm and led him to the end of the jetty. Indeed, the water looked deep here. Deep and very black. Foster peered down, then he looked up at the hills that did indeed seem to have gathered close round him. He sneezed again.

"I've caught a cold, I am afraid. Let's turn homewards, Fenwick, or we shall never find our way."

"Home, then," said Fenwick, and his hands closed about the thin, scraggy neck. For the instant the head half turned, and two startled, strangely childish eyes stared; then, with a push that was ludicrously simple, the body was impelled forward, there was a sharp cry, a splash, a stir of something white against the swiftly gathering dusk, again and then again, then far-spreading ripples, then silence.

V

The silence extended. Having enwrapped the tarn, it spread as though with finger on lip to the already quiescent hills. Fenwick shared in the silence. He luxuriated in it. He did not move at all. He stood there looking upon the inky water of the tarn, his arms folded, a man lost in intensest thought. But he was not thinking. He was only conscious of a warm, luxurious relief, a sensuous feeling that was not thought at all.

Foster was gone—that tiresome, prating, conceited, self-satisfied fool! Gone, never to return. The tarn assured him of that. It stared back into Fenwick's face approvingly as though it said: "You have done well—clean and necessary job. We have done it together, you and I. I am proud of you."

He was proud of himself. At last he had done something definite with his life. Thought, eager, active thought, was beginning now to flood his brain. For all these years he had hung around in this place doing nothing but cherish grievances, weak, backboneless—now at last there was action. He drew himself up and looked at the hills. He was proud—and he was cold. He was shivering. He turned up the collar of his coat. Yes, there was that faint green light that always lingered in the shadows of the hills for a brief moment before darkness came. It was growing late. He had better return.

Shivering now so that his teeth chattered, he started off down the path, and then was aware that he did not wish to leave the tarn. The tarn was friendly—the only friend he had in all the world. As he stumbled along in the dark this sense of loneliness grew. He was going home to an empty house. There had been a guest in it last night. Who was it? Why, Foster, of course—Foster with his silly laugh and amiable, mediocre eyes. Well, Foster would not be there now. No, he never would be there again.

And suddenly Fenwick started to run. He did not know why, except that, now that he had left the tarn, he was lonely. He wished that he could have stayed there all night, but because it was cold he could not, and so now he was running so that he might be at home with the lights and the familiar furniture—and all the things that he knew to reassure him.

As he ran the shale and stones scattered beneath his feet. They made a tit-tattering noise under him, and someone else seemed to be running too. He stopped, and the other runner also stopped. He breathed in the silence. He was hot now. The perspiration was trickling down his cheeks. He could feel a dribble of it down his back inside his shirt. His knees were pounding. His heart was thumping. And all around him the hills were so amazingly silent, now like india-rubber clouds that you could push in or pull out as you do those india-rubber faces, grey against the night sky of a crystal purple, upon whose surface, like the twinkling eyes of boats at sea, stars were now appearing.

His knees steadied, his heart beat less fiercely, and he began to run again. Suddenly he turned the corner and was out at the hotel. Its lamps were kindly and reassuring. He walked then quietly along the lake-side path, and had it not been for the certainty that someone was treading behind him he would have been comfortable and at ease. He stopped once or twice and looked back, and once he stopped and called out, "Who's there?" Only the rustling trees answered.

He had the strangest fancy, but his brain was throbbing so fiercely that he could not think, that it was the tarn that was following him, the tarn slipping, sliding along the road, being with him so that he should not be lonely. He could almost hear the tarn whisper in his ear: "We did that together, and so I do not wish you to bear all the responsibility yourself. I will stay with you, so that you are not lonely."

He climbed down the road toward home, and there were the lights of his house. He heard the gate click behind him as though it were shutting him in. He went into the sitting-room, lighted and ready. There were the books that Foster had admired.

The old woman who looked after him appeared.

"Will you be having some tea, sir?"

"No, thank you, Annie."

"Will the other gentleman be wanting any?"

"No; the other gentleman is away for the night."

"Then there will be only one for supper?"

"Yes, only one for supper."

He sat in the corner of the sofa and fell instantly into a deep slumber.

VI

He woke when the old woman tapped him on the shoulder and told him that supper was served. The room was dark save for the jumping light of two uncertain candles. Those two red candlesticks—how he hated them up there on the mantelpiece! He had always hated them, and now they seemed to him to have something of the quality of Foster's voice—that thin, reedy, piping tone.

He was expecting at every moment that Foster would enter, and yet he knew that he would not. He continued to turn his head towards the door, but it was so dark there that you could not see. The whole room was dark except just there by the fireplace, where the two candlesticks went whining with their miserable twinking plaint.

He went into the dining-room and sat down to his meal. But he could not eat anything. It was odd—that place by the table where Foster's chair should be. Odd, naked, and made a man feel lonely.

He got up once from the table and went to the window, opened it and looked out. He listened for something. A trickle as of running water, stir, through the silence, as though some deep pool were filling to the brim. A rustle in the trees, perhaps. An owl hooted. Sharply, as though someone had spoken to him unexpectedly behind his shoulder, he closed the window and looked back, peering under his dark eyebrows into the room.

Later on he went up to bed.

VII

Had he been sleeping, or had he been lying lazily, as one does, half dozing, half luxuriously not thinking? He was wide awake now, utterly awake, and his heart was beating with apprehension. It was as though someone had called him by name. He slept always with his window a little open and the blind up. To-night the moonlight shadowed in sickly fashion the objects in his room. It was not a flood of light nor yet a sharp splash, silvering a square, a circle, throwing the rest into ebony darkness. The light was dim, a little green, perhaps, like the shadow that comes over the hills just before dark.

He stared at the window, and it seemed to him that something moved there. Within, or rather against the green-grey light, something silver-tinted glistened. Fenwick stared. It had the look, exactly, of slipping water.

Slipping water! He listened, his head up, and it seemed to

him that from beyond the window he caught the stir of water, not running, but rather welling up and up, gurgling with satisfaction as it filled and filled.

He sat up higher in bed, and then saw that down the wallpaper beneath the window water was undoubtedly trickling. He could see it lurch to the projecting wood of the sill, pause, and then slip, slither down the incline. The odd thing was that it fell so silently.

Beyond the window there was that odd gurgle, but in the room itself absolute silence. Whence could it come? He saw the line of silver rise and fall as the stream on the window-ledge ebbed and flowed.

He must get up and close the window. He drew his legs above the sheets and blankets and looked down.

He shrieked. The floor was covered with a shining film of water. It was rising. As he looked it had covered half the short stumpy legs of the bed. It rose without a wink, a bubble, a break! Over the sill it poured now in a steady flow, but soundless. Fenwick sat up in the bed, the clothes gathered up to his chin, his eyes blinking, the Adam's apple throbbing like a throttle in his throat.

But he must do something, he must stop this. The water was now level with the seats of the chairs, but still was soundless. Could he but reach the door!

He put down his naked foot, then cried again. The water was icy cold. Suddenly, leaning, staring at its dark, unbroken sheen, something seemed to push him forward. He fell. His head, his face was under the icy liquid; it seemed adhesive and, in the heart of its ice, hot like melting wax. He struggled to his feet. The water was breast-high. He screamed again and again. He could see the looking-glass, the row of books, the picture of Dürer's "Horse," aloof—impervious. He beat at the water, and flakes of it seemed to cling to him like scales of fish, clammy to his touch. He struggled, ploughing his way towards the door.

The water now was at his neck. Then something had caught him by the ankle. Something held him. He struggled, crying: "Let me go! Let me go! I tell you to let me go! I hate you! I hate you! I will not come down to you! I will not—"

The water covered his mouth. He felt that someone pushed

in his eyeballs with bare knuckles. A cold hand reached up and caught his naked thigh.

VIII

In the morning the little maid knocked and, receiving no answer, came in, as was her wont, with his shaving-water. What she saw made her scream. She ran for the gardener.

They took the body with its staring, protruding eyes, its tongue sticking out between the clenched teeth, and laid it on the bed.

The only sign of disorder was an overturned water-jug. A small pool of water stained the carpet.

It was a lovely morning. A twig of ivy idly, in the little breeze, tapped the pane.

Experiment

(1) Show how Hugh Walpole strikes the keynote of his story at once.

(2) Explain how the storyteller motivates Fenwick's hatred of Foster.

(3) According to Aristotle, a tragic hero must not be an entirely good man, because, if such a man meets disaster, our reaction is one of indignation instead of pity and fear. Pity and fear, Aristotle considers, are the emotions that should be felt in regard to tragedy. The hero should not be an entirely bad man, because then we would experience no emotion whatever—we would merely think that the man deserved what he got. Show how the storyteller causes us to feel pity for Fenwick in spite of his being a murderer.

(4) What unpleasant traits are emphasized in the character of Foster?

(5) Locate examples of (a) irony; (b) deceptive reassurance.

(6) Show how natural description and the pathetic fallacy are used to make the denouement convincing.

(7) Show how the emphasis on justice makes the preternatural aspect of the story credible.

(8) Explain the ambiguity of the death of Fenwick.

Morley Callaghan is a Canadian novelist and short story writer. "Luke Baldwin's Vow" appeared in *The Saturday Evening Post,* March 15, 1947. It is the type of high quality short story, occasionally to be found in popular magazines, which emphasizes character portrayal. As you read it, note the overtones of humor and of pathos.

Morley Callaghan [9]

Luke Baldwin's Vow

That summer when twelve-year-old Luke Baldwin came to live with his Uncle Henry in the house on the stream by the sawmill, he did not forget that he had promised his dying father he would try to learn things from his uncle; so he used to watch him very carefully.

Uncle Henry, who was the manager of the sawmill, was a big, burly man weighing more than two hundred and thirty pounds, and he had a rough-skinned, brick-colored face. He looked like a powerful man, but his health was not good. He had aches and pains in his back and shoulders which puzzled the doctor. The first thing Luke learned about Uncle Henry was that everybody had great respect for him. The four men he employed in the sawmill were always polite and attentive when he spoke to them. His wife, Luke's Aunt Helen, a kindly, plump, straightforward woman, never argued with him. "You should try and be like your Uncle Henry," she would say to Luke. "He's so wonderfully practical. He takes care of everything in a sensible, easy way."

Luke used to trail around the sawmill after Uncle Henry not only because he liked the fresh clean smell of the newly cut wood and the big piles of sawdust, but because he was impressed by his uncle's precise, firm tone when he spoke to the men.

Sometimes Uncle Henry would stop and explain to Luke something about a piece of timber. "Always try and learn the essential facts, son," he would say. "If you've got the facts, you know what's useful and what isn't useful, and no one can fool you."

He showed Luke that nothing of value was ever wasted around the mill. Luke used to listen, and wonder if there was another man in the world who knew so well what was needed and what ought to be thrown away. Uncle Henry had known at once that Luke needed a bicycle to ride to his school, which was two miles away in town, and he bought him a good one. He knew also that Luke needed good, serviceable clothes. He knew exactly how much Aunt Helen needed to run the house, the price of everything, and how much a woman should be paid for doing the family washing. In the evenings Luke used to sit in the living room watching his uncle making notations in a black notebook which he always carried in his vest pocket, and he knew that he was assessing the value of the smallest transaction that had taken place during the day.

Luke promised himself that when he grew up he, too, would be admired for his good, sound judgment. But, of course, he couldn't always be watching and learning from his Uncle Henry, for too often when he watched him he thought of his own father; then he was lonely. So he began to build up another secret life for himself around the sawmill, and his companion was the eleven-year-old collie, Dan, a dog blind in one eye and with a slight limp in his left hind leg. Dan was a fat slow-moving old dog. He was very affectionate and his eye was the color of amber. His fur was amber too. When Luke left for school in the morning, the old dog followed him for half a mile down the road, and when he returned in the evening, there was Dan waiting at the gate.

Sometimes they would play around the millpond or by the dam, or go down the stream to the lake. Luke was never lonely when the dog was with him. There was an old rowboat that they used as a pirate ship in the stream, and they would be pirates together, with Luke shouting instructions to Captain

Dan and with the dog seeming to understand and wagging his tail enthusiastically. Its amber eye was alert, intelligent and approving. Then they would plunge into the brush on the other side of the stream, pretending they were hunting tigers. Of course, the old dog was no longer much good for hunting; he was too slow and lazy. Uncle Henry no longer used him for hunting rabbits or anything else.

When they came out of the brush, they would lie together on the cool, grassy bank being affectionate with each other, with Luke talking earnestly, while the collie, as Luke believed, smiled with the good eye. Luke would say things to Dan he could not say to his uncle or his aunt. Not that what he said was important; it was just stuff about himself that he might have told to his own mother or father if they had been alive. Then they would go back to the house for dinner, and after dinner Dan would follow him down the road to Mr. Kemp's house, where they would ask old Mr. Kemp if they could go with him to round up his four cows. The old man was always glad to see them. He seemed to like watching Luke and the collie running around the cows, pretending they were riding on a vast range in the foothills of the Rockies.

Uncle Henry no longer paid much attention to the collie, though once when he tripped over him on the veranda, he shook his head and said thoughtfully, "Poor old fellow, he's through. Can't use him for anything. He just eats and sleeps and gets in the way."

One Sunday during Luke's summer holidays when they had returned from church and had had their lunch, they had all moved out to the veranda where the collie was sleeping. Luke sat down on the steps, his back against the veranda post, Uncle Henry took the rocking chair, and Aunt Helen stretched herself out in the hammock, sighing contentedly. Then Luke, eyeing the collie, tapped the step with the palm of his hand, giving three little taps like a signal and the old collie, lifting his head, got up stiffly with a slow wagging of the tail as an acknowledgment that the signal had been heard, and began to cross the veranda to Luke. But the dog was sleepy; his bad eye was turned to the rocking chair; in passing, his left front paw went under the rocker. With a frantic yelp, the dog went bounding down the

steps and hobbled around the corner of the house, where he
stopped, hearing Luke coming after him. All he needed was
the touch of Luke's hand. Then he began to lick the hand
methodically, as if apologizing.

"Luke," Uncle Henry called sharply, "bring that dog here."
When Luke led the collie back to the veranda, Uncle Henry
nodded and said, "Thanks, Luke." Then he took out a cigar, lit
it, put his big hands on his knees and began to rock in the chair
while he frowned and eyed the dog steadily. Obviously he was
making some kind of important decision about the collie.

"What's the matter, Uncle Henry?" Luke asked nervously.

"That dog can't see any more," Uncle Henry said.

"Oh, yes, he can," Luke said quickly. "His bad eye got turned
to the chair, that's all, Uncle Henry."

"And his teeth are gone, too," Uncle Henry went on, paying
no attention to what Luke had said. Turning to the hammock,
he called, "Helen, sit up a minute, will you?"

When she got up and stood beside him, he went on, "I was
just thinking about this old dog the other day, Helen. It's not
only that he's just about blind, but did you notice that when
we drove up after church he didn't even bark?"

"It's a fact he didn't, Henry."

"No, not much good even as a watchdog now."

"Poor old fellow. It's a pity, isn't it?"

"And no good for hunting either. And he eats a lot I suppose."

"About as much as he ever did, Henry."

"The plain fact is the old dog isn't worth his keep any more.
It's time we got rid of him."

"It's always so hard to know how to get rid of a dog, Henry."

"I was thinking about it the other day. Some people think
it's best to shoot a dog. I haven't had any shells for that shotgun
for over a year. Poisoning is a hard death for a dog. Maybe
drowning is the easiest and the quickest way. Well, I'll speak
to one of the mill hands and have him look after it."

Crouching on the ground, his arms around the old collie's
neck, Luke cried out, "Uncle Henry, Dan's a wonderful dog!
You don't know how wonderful he is!"

"He's just a very old dog, son," Uncle Henry said calmly.

"The time comes when you have to get rid of any old dog. We've got to be practical about it. I'll get you a pup, son. A smart little dog that'll be worth its keep. A pup that will grow up with you."

"I don't want a pup!" Luke cried, turning his face away. Circling around him, the dog began to bark, then flick his long pink tongue at the back of Luke's neck.

Aunt Helen, catching her husband's eye, put her finger on her lips, warning him not to go on talking in front of the boy. "An old dog like that often wanders off into the brush and sort of picks a place to die when the time comes. Isn't that so, Henry?"

"Oh, sure," he agreed quickly. "In fact, when Dan didn't show up yesterday, I was sure that was what had happened." Then he yawned and seemed to forget about the dog.

But Luke was frightened, for he knew what his Uncle was like. He knew that if his uncle had decided that the dog was useless and that it was sane and sensible to get rid of it, he would be ashamed of himself if he were diverted by any sentimental considerations. Luke knew in his heart that he couldn't move his uncle. All he could do, he thought, was keep the dog away from his uncle, keep him out of the house, feed him when Uncle Henry wasn't around.

Next day at noontime Luke saw his uncle walking from the mill toward the house with old Sam Carter, a mill hand. Sam Carter was a dull, stooped, slow-witted man of sixty with an iron-gray beard, who was wearing blue overalls and a blue shirt. He hardly ever spoke to anybody. Watching from the veranda, Luke noticed that his uncle suddenly gave Sam Carter a cigar, which Sam put in his pocket. Luke had never seen his uncle give Sam a cigar or pay much attention to him.

Then, after lunch, Uncle Henry said lazily that he would like Luke to take his bicycle and go into town and get him some cigars.

"I'll take Dan," Luke said.

"Better not, son," Uncle Henry said. "It'll take you all afternoon. I want those cigars. Get going, Luke."

His uncle's tone was so casual that Luke tried to believe they were not merely getting rid of him. Of course he had to do what he was told. He had never dared to refuse to obey an order from his uncle. But when he had taken his bicycle and had ridden down the path that followed the stream to the town road and had got about a quarter of a mile along the road, he found that all he could think of was his uncle handing old Sam Carter . the cigar.

Slowing down, sick with worry now, he got off the bike and stood uncertainly on the sunlit road. Sam Carter was a gruff, aloof old man who would have no feeling for a dog. Then suddenly Luke could go no farther without getting some assurance that the collie would not be harmed while he was away. Across the fields he could see the house.

Leaving the bike in the ditch, he started to cross the field, intending to get close enough to the house so Dan could hear him if he whistled softly. He got about fifty yards away from the house and whistled and waited, but there was no sign of the dog, which might be asleep at the front of the house, he knew, or over at the sawmill. With the saws whining, the dog couldn't hear the soft whistle. For a few minutes Luke couldn't make up his mind what to do, then he decided to go back on the road, get on his bike, and go back the way he had come until he got to the place where the river path joined the road. There he could leave his bike, go up the path, then into the tall grass and get close to the front of the house and the sawmill without being seen.

He had followed the river path for about a hundred yards, and when he came to the place where the river began to bend sharply toward the house his heart fluttered and his legs felt paralyzed, for he saw the old rowboat in the one place where the river was deep, and in the rowboat was Sam Carter with the collie.

The bearded man in the blue overalls was smoking the cigar; the dog, with a rope around its neck, sat contentedly beside him, its tongue going out in a friendly lick at the hand holding the rope. It was all like a crazy dream picture to Luke; all wrong because it looked so lazy and friendly, even the curling smoke from Sam Carter's cigar. But as Luke cried out, "Dan, Dan! Come on, boy!" and the dog jumped at the water, he saw that Sam Carter's left hand was hanging deep in the water, holding a foot of rope with a heavy stone at the end. As Luke cried out wildly, "Don't! Please don't!" Carter dropped the stone, for the cry came too late; it was blurred by the screech of the big saws at the mill. But Carter was startled, and he stared stupidly at the riverbank, then he ducked his head and began to row quickly to the bank.

But Luke was watching the collie take what looked like a long, shallow dive, except that the hind legs suddenly kicked up above the surface, then shot down, and while he watched, Luke sobbed and trembled, for it was as if the happy secret part of his life around the sawmill was being torn away from him. But even while he watched, he seemed to be following a plan without knowing it, for he was already fumbling in his pocket for his jackknife, jerking the blade open, pulling off his pants, kicking his shoes off while he muttered fiercely and prayed that Sam Carter would get out of sight.

It hardly took the mill hand a minute to reach the bank and go slinking furtively around the bend as if he felt that the boy was following him. But Luke hadn't taken his eyes off the exact spot in the water where Dan had disappeared. As soon as the mill hand was out of sight, Luke slid down the bank and took a leap at the water, the sun glistening on his slender body, his eyes wild with eagerness as he ran out to the deep place, then arched his back and dived, swimming under water, his open eyes getting used to the greenish-gray haze of the water, the sandy bottom and the imbedded rocks.

His lungs began to ache, then he saw the shadow of the collie floating at the end of the taut rope, rock-held in the sand. He slashed at the rope with his knife. He couldn't get much strength in his arm because of the resistance of the water. He grabbed the rope with his left hand, hacking with his knife. The collie suddenly drifted up slowly, like a water-soaked log. Then his own head shot above the surface, and while he was sucking in the air he was drawing in the rope, pulling the collie toward him and treading water. In a few strokes he was away from the deep place and his feet touched the bottom.

Hoisting the collie out of the water, he scrambled toward the bank, lurching and tumbling in fright because the collie felt like a dead weight.

He went on up the bank and across the path to the tall grass, where he fell flat, hugging the dog and trying to warm him with his own body. But the collie didn't stir, the good amber eye remained closed. Then suddenly Luke wanted to act like a resourceful, competent man. Getting up on his knees, he stretched the dog out on its belly, drew him between his knees, felt with trembling hands for the soft places on the flanks just above the hipbones, and rocked back and forth, pressing with all his weight, then relaxing the pressure as he straightened up. He hoped that he was working the dog's lungs like a bellows. He had read that men had been saved in this way.

"Come on, Dan. Come on, old boy," he pleaded softly. As a little water came from the collie's mouth, Luke's heart jumped, and he muttered over and over, "You can't be dead, Dan! You can't, you can't! I won't let you die, Dan!" He rocked back and forth tirelessly, applying the pressure to the flanks. More water dribbled from the mouth. In the collie's body he felt a faint tremor. "Oh, gee, Dan, you're alive," he whispered. "Come on, boy. Keep it up."

With a cough the collie suddenly jerked his head back, the amber eye opened, and there they were looking at each other. Then the collie, thrusting his legs out stiffly, tried to hoist himself up, staggered, tried again, then stood there in a stupor. Then he shook himself like any other wet dog, turned his head, eyed Luke, and the red tongue came out in a weak flick at Luke's cheek.

"Lie down, Dan," Luke said. As the dog lay down beside him, Luke closed his eyes, buried his head in the wet fur and wondered why all the muscles of his arms and legs began to jerk in a nervous reaction, now that it was all over. "Stay there, Dan," he said softly, and he went back to the path, got his clothes and came back beside Dan and put them on. "I think we'd better get away from this spot, Dan," he said. "Keep down, boy. Come on." And he crawled on through the tall grass till they were about seventy-five yards from the place where he had undressed. There they lay down together.

In a little while he heard his aunt's voice calling. "Luke. Oh, Luke! Come here, Luke!"

"Quiet, Dan," Luke whispered. A few minutes passed and

then Uncle Henry called, "Luke, Luke!" and he began to come down the path. They could see him standing there, massive and imposing, his hands on his hips as he looked down the path, then he turned and went back to the house.

As he watched the sunlight shine on the back of his uncle's neck, the exultation Luke had felt at knowing the collie was safe beside him turned to bewildered despair, for he knew that even if he should be forgiven for saving the dog when he saw it drowning, the fact was that his uncle was thwarted. His mind was made up to get rid of Dan, and in a few days' time, in another way, he would get rid of him, as he got rid of anything around the mill that he believed to be useless or a waste of money.

As he lay back and looked up at the hardly moving clouds, he began to grow frightened. He couldn't go back to the house, nor could he take the collie into the woods and hide him and feed him there unless he tied him up. If he didn't tie him up, Dan would wander back to the house.

"I guess there's just no place to go, Dan," he whispered sadly. "Even if we start off along the road, somebody is sure to see us."

But Dan was watching a butterfly that was circling crazily above them. Raising himself a little, Luke looked through the grass at the corner of the house, then he turned and looked the other way to the wide blue lake. With a sigh he lay down again, and for hours they lay there together until there was no sound from the saws in the mill and the sun moved low in the western sky.

"Well, we can't stay here any longer, Dan," he said at last. "We'll just have to get as far away as we can. Keep down, old boy," and he began to crawl through the grass, going farther away from the house. When he could no longer be seen, he got up and began to trot across the field toward the gravel road leading to town.

On the road, the collie would turn from time to time as if wondering why Luke shuffled along, dragging his feet wearily, his head down. "I'm stumped, that's all, Dan," Luke explained. "I can't seem to think of a place to take you."

When they were passing the Kemp place they saw the old man sitting on the veranda, and Luke stopped. All he could think of was that Mr. Kemp had liked them both and it had been a pleasure to help him get the cows in the evening. Dan had always been with them. Staring at the figure of the old man on the veranda, he said in a worried tone, "I wish I could be sure of him, Dan. I wish he was a dumb, stupid man who wouldn't know or care whether you were worth anything . . . Well, come on." He opened the gate bravely, but he felt shy and unimportant.

"Hello, son. What's on your mind?" Mr. Kemp called from the veranda. He was a thin, wiry man in a tan-colored shirt. He had a gray, untidy mustache, his skin was wrinkled and leathery, but his eyes were always friendly and amused.

"Could I speak to you, Mr. Kemp?" Luke asked when they were close to the veranda.

"Sure. Go ahead."

"It's about Dan. He's a great dog, but I guess you know that as well as I do. I was wondering if you could keep him here for me."

"Why should I keep Dan here, son?"

"Well, it's like this," Luke said, fumbling the words awkwardly: "My uncle won't let me keep him any more . . . says he's too old." His mouth began to tremble, then he blurted out the story.

"I see, I see," Mr. Kemp said slowly, and he got up and came over to the steps and sat down and began to stroke the collie's head. "Of course, Dan's an old dog, son," he said quietly. "And sooner or later you've got to get rid of an old dog. Your uncle knows that. Maybe it's true that Dan isn't worth his keep."

"He doesn't eat much, Mr. Kemp. Just one meal a day."

"I wouldn't want you to think your uncle was cruel and unfeeling, Luke," Mr. Kemp went on. "He's a fine man . . . maybe just a little bit too practical and straightforward."

"I guess that's right," Luke agreed, but he was really waiting and trusting the expression in the old man's eyes.

"Maybe you should make him a practical proposition."

"I—I don't know what you mean."

"Well, I sort of like the way you get the cows for me in the evenings," Mr. Kemp said, smiling to himself. "In fact, I don't think you need me to go along with you at all. Now, supposing

I gave you seventy-five cents a week. Would you get the cows for me every night?"

"Sure I would, Mr. Kemp. I like doing it, anyway."

"All right, son. It's a deal. Now I'll tell you what to do. You go back to your uncle, and before he has a chance to open up on you, you say that you've come to him with a business proposition. Say it like a man, just like that. Offer to pay him the seventy-five cents a week for the dog's keep."

"But my uncle doesn't need seventy-five cents, Mr. Kemp," Luke said uneasily.

"Of course not," Mr. Kemp agreed. "It's the principle of the thing. Be confident. Remember that he's got nothing against the dog. Go to it, son. Let me know how you do," he added, with an amused smile. "If I know your uncle at all, I think it'll work."

"I'll try it, Mr. Kemp," Luke said. "Thanks very much." But he didn't have any confidence, for even though he knew that Mr. Kemp was a wise old man who would not deceive him, he couldn't believe that seventy-five cents a week would stop his uncle, who was an important man. "Come on, Dan," he called, and he went slowly and apprehensively back to the house.

When they were going up the path, his aunt cried from the open window, "Henry, Henry, in heaven's name, it's Luke with the dog!"

Ten paces from the veranda, Luke stopped and waited nervously for his uncle to come out. Uncle Henry came out in a rush, but when he saw the collie and Luke standing there, he stopped stiffly, turned pale and his mouth hung open loosely.

"Luke," he whispered, "that dog had a stone around his neck."

"I fished him out of the stream," Luke said uneasily.

"Oh. Oh, I see," Uncle Henry said, and gradually the color came back to his face. "You fished him out, eh?" he asked, still looking at the dog uneasily. "Well, you shouldn't have done that. I told Sam Carter to get rid of the dog, you know."

"Just a minute, Uncle Henry," Luke said, trying not to falter. He gained confidence as Aunt Helen came out and stood beside her husband, for her eyes seemed to be gentle, and he went on bravely, "I want to make you a proposition, Uncle Henry."

"A what?" Uncle Henry asked, still feeling insecure, and wishing the boy and the dog weren't confronting him.

"A practical proposition," Luke blurted out quickly. "I know Dan isn't worth his keep to you. I guess he isn't worth anything to anybody but me. So I'll pay you seventy-five cents a week for his keep."

"What's this?" Uncle Henry asked, looking bewildered. "Where would you get seventy-five cents a week, Luke?"

"I'm going to get the cows every night for Mr. Kemp."

"Oh, for heaven's sake, Henry," Aunt Helen pleaded, looking distressed, "let him keep the dog!" and she fled into the house.

"None of that kind of talk!" Uncle Henry called after her. "We've got to be sensible about this!" But he was shaken himself, and overwhelmed with a distress that destroyed all his confidence. As he sat down slowly in the rocking chair and stroked the side of his big face, he wanted to say weakly, "All right, keep the dog," but he was ashamed of being so weak and sentimental. He stubbornly refused to yield to this emotion; he was trying desperately, trying to turn his emotion into a bit of good, useful common sense, so he could justify his distress. So he rocked and pondered. At last he smiled. "You're a smart little shaver, Luke," he said slowly. "Imagine you working it out like this. I'm tempted to accept your proposition."

"Gee, thanks, Uncle Henry."

"I'm accepting it because I think you'll learn something out of this," he went on ponderously.

"Yes, Uncle Henry."

"You'll learn that useless luxuries cost the smartest of men hard-earned money."

"I don't mind."

"Well, it's a thing you'll have to learn sometime. I think you'll learn, too, because you certainly seem to have a practical streak in you. It's a streak I like to see in a boy. O.K., son," he said, and he smiled with relief and went into the house.

Turning to Dan, Luke whispered softly. "Well, what do you know about that?"

As he sat down on the step with the collie beside him and listened to Uncle Henry talking to his wife, he began to glow with exultation. Then gradually his exultation began to change to a vast wonder that Mr. Kemp should have had a such a perfect understanding of Uncle Henry. He began to dream of someday being as wise as old Mr. Kemp and knowing exactly how to handle people. It was possible, too, that he had already learned some of the things about his uncle that his father had wanted him to learn.

Putting his head down on the dog's neck, he vowed to himself fervently that he would always have some money on hand, no matter what became of him, so that he would be able to protect all that was truly valuable from the practical people in the world.

Experiment

(1) Explain the importance of the *motif* of Uncle Henry's practicality in the development of the narrative:

"You should try and be like your Uncle Henry," she would say to Luke. "He's so wonderfully practical. He takes care of everything in a sensible, easy way."

(2) Show how the storyteller makes clear the values of Uncle Henry, at the same time that he suggests a certain inhuman exaggeration about them.

(3) Show how the storyteller convincingly motivates the secret life of Luke with Dan, his dog.

(4) Explain the storytelling value of the statement: "Luke would say things to Dan he could not say to his aunt or his uncle."

(5) Show how the storyteller leads up to the climax: "The plain fact is that the old dog isn't worth his keep any more. It's time we got rid of him."

(6) How does the storyteller manage to make the giving of artificial respiration to the dog seem natural and acceptable?

(7) Why is the story interesting and psychologically convincing in that Uncle Henry keeps to his original character pattern, "You'll learn that useless luxuries cost the smartest of men hard-earned money"?

(8) Show how the *motif* of the story establishes a universal symbolism in the concluding paragraph of the story.

Review Questions

(1) Define *humor* and analyze one example of your own choosing.

(2) How does *wit* differ from *humor?*

(3) What is the purpose of a classical satire?

(4) What is the function of parody?

(5) Distinguish between fancy and imagination.

(6) What attractions does fantasy possess for a reader?

(7) Explain the importance of characterization in the short story.

(8) What are the advantages of a short story without plot?

(9) Explain the techniques of thematic contrast and of pathos.

(10) Explain the divisions of the short story with plot.

REWORKING OLD IDEAS AND THEMES

All writers have absorbed ideas and suggestions both from the artists of antiquity and from their contemporaries. Such absorption of ideas is quite a different thing from plagiarism. The rich associative and connotative powers of art are such that you may be quite original and independent in what you have to say and yet wisely use the forms and suggestions of others. You may find it interesting to contrast Malory's account of "The Passing of Arthur" with that of Tennyson in his *Idylls of the King.* Tennyson treats the identical facts handled by Malory and, occasionally, actually repeats certain phrases of Malory that appeal to him on the poetic level.

Tennyson is heavily indebted to Malory, yet manages to work quite independently. If you are thinking of taking up creative writing as a career, you will find a storehouse of old material which you may rehandle and reshape in relation to modern problems and modern needs.

Scripture has repeatedly served as raw material for fresh creative work. Its stories have been constantly retold by novelists, playwrights, and poets. Contrast the original account of the fall of Babylon in the *Apocalypse* and the associated ideas derived from it in Benét's "By the Waters of Babylon." With these extracts is a free-verse poem emphasizing social criticism, written as an assignment by a student after he had heard the original extract from the *Apocalypse* read aloud.

St. John the Apostle wrote the *Apocalypse* on the Island of Patmos in 96. The *Apocalypse* has been interpreted in various ways, but its suggestive and symbolic power touches so many fields of truth and experience that it has served as an ignition point for the minds of many creative artists.

Can you make some suggestions as to where the great power of the following extract lies?

The Fall of Babylon [10]

And after this I saw another angel coming down from heaven, having great authority, and the earth was lighted up by his glory. And he cried out with a mighty voice, saying, "She has fallen, she has fallen, Babylon the great; and has become a habitation of demons, a stronghold of every unclean spirit, a stronghold of every unclean and hateful bird; because all the nations have drunk of the wrath of her immorality, and the kings of the earth have committed fornication with her, and by the power of her wantonness the merchants of the earth have grown rich."

And I heard another voice from heaven saying, "Go out from her, my people, that you may not share in her sins, and that you may not receive of her plagues. For her sins have reached even

---

[10] *Apocalypse* 18:1-24.

to heaven, and the Lord has remembered her iniquities. Render to her as she also has rendered, and give her the double according to her works; in the cup that she has mixed, mix for her double. As much as she glorified herself and gave herself wantonness, so much torment and mourning give to her. Because in her heart she says, 'I sit a queen, I am no widow, and I shall not see mourning.' Therefore in one day her plagues shall come, death and mourning and famine; and she shall be burnt up in fire; for strong is God who will judge her."

And the kings of the earth who with her committed fornication and lived wantonly will weep and mourn over her when they see the smoke of her burning, standing afar off for fear of her torments, saying,

"Woe, woe, that great city, Babylon,
　　that strong city,
For in one hour has thy judgment come!"

And the merchants of the earth will weep and mourn over her; for no one will buy their merchandise any more: merchandise of gold and silver, and precious stones and pearls, and fine linen and purple, and silk and scarlet, and all thyine wood, and all vessels of ivory, and all vessels of precious stone, and of brass, and of iron, and of marble, and cinnamon and amomum and spices, and ointment and frankincense, and wine and oil, and fine flour and wheat, and beasts of burden and sheep and horses, and chariots and slaves, and souls of men. And the fruit which was the desire of thy soul departed from thee; and all the fat and splendid things perished from thee, and men will find them nevermore. The merchants of these things, who grow rich by her, will stand afar off for fear of her torments, weeping and mourning, and saying,

"Woe, woe, that great city, which was clothed
　　in fine linen and purple and scarlet,
　　and gilded in gold, and precious stone, and pearls;
For in one hour riches so great were laid waste!"

And every shipmaster, and everyone who sails to a place, and mariners, and all who work upon the sea, stood afar off, and cried out as they saw the place of her burning, saying, "What city is like to this great city?" And they cast dust on their heads, and cried out weeping and mourning, saying,

"Woe, woe, the great city,
    wherein all were made rich who had their ships at sea,
    out of her wealth;
For in one hour she has been laid waste!"
Make merry over her, O heaven, and you the saints and the apostles and the prophets, for God has judged your cause upon her.

And a strong angel took up a stone, as it were a great millstone, and cast it into the sea, saying, "With this violence will Babylon, that great city, be overthrown, and will not be found any more. And the sound of harpers and musicians and fluteplayers and trumpet will not be heard in thee any more; and any craftsman of any craft will not be found in thee any more. And light of lamp will not shine in thee any more; and voice of bridegroom and of bride will not be heard in thee any more; because thy merchants were the great men of the earth; for by the sorcery all the nations have been led astray. And in her was found the blood of prophets and of saints, and of all who have been slain upon the earth."

Experiment

(1) To what extent is this piece of writing (a) allegory? (b) narrative? (c) drama?

(2) Illustrate the mounting effectiveness of the *motif*, "Woe, woe, that great city."

(3) Show why the symbolism and comprehensive suggestiveness of this passage make it particularly effective as a starting point for the work of other creative writers.

(4) Why does the phrase, "the souls of men," constitute a climax to the list of merchandise in which Babylon deals?

(5) Does St. John express pity over the destruction of the city, or does he rejoice over its disappearance as a manifestation of justice?

(6) Explain the use of pathos in this selection.

(7) Show how the intensive sense of desolation is technically created by the repetition at the end of succeeding sentences of the words, "any more."

(8) Would you classify this piece of writing as poetry or as creative prose? Justify your answer by concrete examples.

"By the Waters of Babylon" is another example of Stephen Vincent Benét's sensitive story technique. It is a story distinguished by the appropriateness of the language and imagery to the setting. As you read it, do you notice the way in which Benét creates unusual effects of atmosphere?

STEPHEN VINCENT BENÉT [11]

By the Waters of Babylon

The north and the west and the south are good hunting ground, but it is forbidden to go east. It is forbidden to go to any of the Dead Places except to search for metal and then he who touches the metal must be a priest or the son of a priest. Afterwards, both the man and the metal must be purified. These are the rules and the laws; they are well made. It is forbidden to cross the great river and look upon the place that was the Place of the Gods—this is most strictly forbidden. We do not even say its name though we know its name. It is there that spirits live, and demons—it is there that there are the ashes of the Great Burning. These things are forbidden—they have been forbidden since the beginning of time.

My father is a priest; I am the son of a priest. I have been in the Dead Places near us, with my father—at first, I was afraid. When my father went into the house to search for the metal, I stood by the door and my heart felt small and weak. It was a dead man's house, a spirit house. It did not have the smell of man, though there were old bones in a corner. But it is not fitting that a priest's son should show fear. I looked at the bones in the shadow and kept my voice still.

[11] Reprinted by permission of Brandt and Brandt.

Then my father came out with the metal—a good, strong piece. He looked at me with both eyes but I had not run away. He gave me the metal to hold—I took it and did not die. So he knew that I was truly his son and would be a priest in my time. That was when I was very young—nevertheless, my brothers would not have done it, though they are good hunters. After that, they gave me the good piece of meat and the warm corner by the fire. My father watched over me—he was glad that I should be a priest. But when I boasted or wept without a reason, he punished me more strictly than my brothers. That was right.

After a time, I myself was allowed to go into the dead houses and search for metal. So I learned the ways of those houses— and if I saw bones, I was no longer afraid. The bones are light and old—sometimes they will fall into dust if you touch them. But that is a great sin.

I was taught the chants and the spells—I was taught how to stop the running of blood from a wound and many secrets. A priest must know many secrets—that was what my father said.

If the hunters think we do all things by chants and spells, they may believe so—it does not hurt them. I was taught how to read in the old books and how to make the old writings—that was hard and took a long time. My knowledge made me happy—it was like a fire in my heart. Most of all, I liked to hear of the Old Days and the stories of the gods. I asked myself many questions that I could not answer, but it was good to ask them. At night, I would lie awake and listen to the wind—it seemed to me that it was the voice of the gods as they flew through the air.

We are not ignorant like the Forest People—our women spin wool on the wheel, our priests wear a white robe. We do not eat grubs from the tree, we have not forgotten the old writings, although they are hard to understand. Nevertheless, my knowledge and my lack of knowledge burned in me—I wished to know more. When I was a man at last, I came to my father and said, "It is time for me to go on my journey. Give me your leave."

He looked at me for a long time, stroking his beard, then he said at last, "Yes. It is time." That night, in the house of the priesthood, I asked for and received purification. My body hurt but my spirit was a cool stone. It was my father himself who questioned me about my dreams.

He bade me look into the smoke of the fire and see—I saw and told what I saw. It was what I have always seen—a river, and, beyond it, a great Dead Place and in it the gods walking. I have always thought about that. His eyes were stern when I told him— he was no longer my father but a priest. He said, "This is a strong dream."

"It is mine," I said, while the smoke waved and my head felt light. They were singing the Star song in the outer chamber and it was like the buzzing of bees in my head.

He asked me how the gods were dressed and I told him how they were dressed. We know how they were dressed from the book, but I saw them as if they were before me. When I had finished, he threw the sticks three times and studied them as they fell.

"This is a very strong dream," he said. "It may eat you up."

"I am not afraid," I said and looked at him with both eyes. My voice sounded thin in my ears but that was because of the smoke.

He touched me on the breast and the forehead. He gave me the bow and three arrows.

"Take them," he said. "It is forbidden to travel east. It is forbidden to cross the river. It is forbidden to go to the Place of the Gods. All these things are forbidden."

"All these things are forbidden," I said, but it was my voice that spoke and not my spirit. He looked at me again.

"My son," he said. "Once I had young dreams. If your dreams do not eat you up, you may be a great priest. If they eat you, you are still my son. Now go on your journey."

I went fasting, as is the law. My body hurt but not my heart. When the dawn came, I was out of sight of the village. I prayed and purified myself, waiting for a sign. The sign was an eagle. It flew east.

Sometimes signs are sent by bad spirits. I waited again on the flat rock, fasting, taking no food. I was very still—I could feel the sky above me and the earth beneath. I waited till the sun was beginning to sink. Then three deer passed in the valley going east—they did not mind me or see me. There was a white fawn with them—a very great sign.

I followed them, at a distance, waiting for what would happen. My heart was troubled about going east, yet I knew that

I must go. My head hummed with my fasting—I did not even see the panther spring upon the white fawn. But, before I knew it, the bow was in my hand. I shouted and the panther lifted his head from the fawn. It is not easy to kill a panther with one arrow but the arrow went through his eye and into his brain. He died as he tried to spring—he rolled over, tearing at the ground. Then I knew I was meant to go east—I knew that was my journey. When the night came, I made my fire and roasted meat.

It is eight suns' journey to the east and a man passes by many Dead Places. The Forest People are afraid of them but I am not. Once I made my fire on the edge of a Dead Place at night and, next morning, in the dead house, I found a good knife, little rusted. That was small to what came afterward but it made my heart feel big. Always when I looked for game, it was in front of my arrow, and twice I passed hunting parties of the Forest People without their knowing. So I knew my magic was strong and my journey clean, in spite of the law.

Toward the setting of the eighth sun, I came to the banks of the great river. It was half-a-day's journey after I had left the god-road—we do not use the god-roads now for they are falling apart into great blocks of stone, and the forest is safer going. A long way off, I had seen the water through trees but the trees were thick. At last, I came out upon an open place at the top of a cliff. There was the great river below, like a giant in the sun. It is very long, very wide. It could eat all the streams we know and still be thirsty. Its name is Ou-dis-sun, the Sacred, the Long. No man of my tribe had seen it, not even my father, the priest. It was magic and I prayed.

Then I raised my eyes and looked south. It was there, the Place of the Gods.

How can I tell what it was like—you do not know. It was there, in the red light, and they were too big to be houses. It was there with the red light upon it, mighty and ruined. I knew that in another moment the gods would see me. I covered my eyes with my hands and crept back into the forest.

Surely, that was enough to do, and live. Surely it was enough to spend the night upon the cliff. The Forest People themselves do not come near. Yet, all through the night, I knew that I should have to cross the river and walk in the places of the gods, although the gods ate me up. My magic did not help me at all and yet there was a fire in my bowels, a fire in my mind. When the sun rose, I thought, "My journey has been clean. Now I will go home from my journey." But even as I thought so, I knew I could not. If I went to the Place of the Gods, I would surely die, but, if I did not go, I could never be at peace with my spirit again. It is better to lose one's life than one's spirit, if one is a priest and the son of a priest.

Nevertheless, as I made the raft, the tears ran out of my eyes. The Forest People could have killed me without fight, if they had come upon me then, but they did not come. When the raft was made, I said the sayings for the dead and painted myself for death. My heart was cold as a frog and my knees like water, but the burning in my mind would not let me have peace. As I pushed the raft from the shore, I began my death song—I had the right. It was a fine song.

"I am John, son of John," I sang. "My people are the Hill People. They are the men.
I go into the Dead Places but I am not slain.
I take the metal from the Dead Places but I am not blasted.
I travel upon the god-roads and am not afraid. E-yah!
I have killed the panther, I have killed the fawn! E-yah! I have come to the great river. No man has come there before.
It is forbidden to go east, but I have gone, forbidden to go on the great river, but I am there.
Open your hearts, you spirits, and hear my song.
Now I go to the Place of the Gods, I shall not return.
My body is painted for death and my limbs weak, but my heart is big as I go to the Place of the Gods!"

All the same, when I came to the Place of the Gods, I was afraid, afraid. The current of the great river is very strong—it gripped my raft with its hands. That was magic, for the river itself is wide and calm. I could feel evil spirits about me, in the bright morning; I could feel their breath on my neck as I was swept down the stream. Never have I been so much alone—I tried to think of my knowledge, but it was a squirrel's heap of winter nuts. There was no strength in my knowledge any more and I felt small and naked as a new-hatched bird—alone upon the great river, the servant of the gods.

Yet, after a while, my eyes were opened and I saw. I saw both banks of the river—I saw that once there had been god-roads across it, though now they were broken and fallen like broken vines. Very great they were, and wonderful and broken—broken in the time of the Great Burning when the fire fell out of the sky. And always the current took me nearer to the Place of the Gods, and the huge ruins rose before my eyes.

I do not know the customs of rivers—we are the People of the Hills. I tried to guide my raft with the pole but it spun around. I thought the river meant to take me past the Place of the Gods and out into the Bitter Water of the legends. I grew angry then —my heart felt strong. I said aloud, "I am a priest and the son of a priest!" The gods heard me—they showed me how to paddle with the pole on one side of the raft. The current changed it-self—I drew near to the Place of the Gods.

When I was very near, my raft struck and turned over. I can swim in our lakes—I swam to the shore. There was a great spike of rusted metal sticking out into the river—I hauled myself up upon it and sat there, panting. I had saved my bow and two arrows and the knife I found in the Dead Place but that was all. My raft went whirling downstream toward the Bitter Water. I looked after it, and thought if it had trod me under, at least I would be safely dead. Nevertheless, when I had dried my bow-string and re-strung it, I walked forward to the Place of the Gods.

It felt like ground underfoot; it did not burn me. It is not what some of the tales say, that the ground there burns forever, for I have been there. Here and there were the marks and stains of the Great Burning, on the ruins, that is true. But they were old marks and old stains. It is not true either, what some of our priests say, that it is an island covered with fogs and enchant-ments. It is not. It is a great Dead Place—greater than any Dead Place we know. Everywhere in it there are god-roads, though most are cracked and broken. Everywhere there are the ruins of the high towers of the gods.

How shall I tell what I saw? I went carefully, my strung bow in my hand, my skin ready for danger. There should have been the wailings of spirits and the shrieks of demons, but there were not. It was very silent and sunny where I had landed—the wind and the rain and the birds that drop seeds had done their work—the grass grew in the cracks of the broken stone. It is a fair island—no wonder the gods built there. If I had come there, a god, I also would have built.

How shall I tell what I saw? The towers are not all broken—here and there one still stands, like a great tree in a forest, and the birds nest high. But the towers themselves look blind, for the gods are gone. I saw a fish-hawk, catching fish in the river. I saw a little dance of white butterflies over a great heap of broken stones and columns. I went there and looked about me—there was a carved stone with cut-letters, broken in half. I can read letters but I could not understand these. They said UBTREAS. There was also the shattered image of a man or a god. It had been made of white stone and he wore his hair tied back like a woman's. His name was ASHING, as I read on the cracked half of a stone. I thought it wise to pray to ASHING, though I do not know that god.

How shall I tell what I saw? There was no smell of man left, on stone or metal. Nor were there many trees in that wilderness of stone. There are many pigeons, nesting and dropping in the towers—the gods must have loved them, or, perhaps, they used them for sacrifices. There are wild cats that roam the god-roads, green-eyed, unafraid of man. At night they wail like demons but they are not demons. The wild dogs are more dangerous, for they hunt in a pack, but them I did not meet till later. Everywhere there are the carved stones, carved with magical numbers or words.

I went north—I did not try to hide myself. When a god or a demon saw me, then I would die, but meanwhile I was no longer afraid. My hunger for knowledge burned in me—there was so much that I could not understand. After a while, I knew that my belly was hungry. I could have hunted for my meat, but I did not hunt. It is known that the gods did not hunt as we do—they got their food from enchanted boxes and jars. Sometimes these are still found in the Dead Places—once, when I was a child and foolish, I opened such a jar and tasted it and found the food sweet. But my father found out and punished me for it strictly, for, often, that food is death. Now, though, I had long gone past what was forbidden, and I entered the likeliest towers, looking for the food of the gods.

I found it at last in the ruins of a great temple in the midcity. A mighty temple it must have been, for the roof was painted like the sky at night with its stars—that much I could see, though the colors were faint and dim. It went down into great caves and tunnels—perhaps they kept their slaves there. But when I started to climb down, I heard the squeaking of rats, so I did not go—rats are unclean, and there must have been many tribes of them, from the squeaking. But near there, I found food, in the heart of a ruin, behind a door that still opened. I ate only the fruits from the jars—they had a very sweet taste. There was drink, too, in bottles of glass—the drink of the gods was strong and made my head swim. After I had eaten and drunk, I slept on the top of a stone, my bow at my side.

When I woke, the sun was low. Looking down from where I lay, I saw a dog sitting on his haunches. His tongue was hanging out of his mouth; he looked as if he were laughing. He was a big dog, with a gray-brown coat, as big as a wolf. I sprang up and shouted at him but he did not move—he just sat there as if he were laughing. I did not like that. When I reached for a stone to throw, he moved swiftly out of the way of the stone. He was not afraid of me; he looked at me as if I were meat. No doubt I could have killed him with an arrow, but I did not know if there were others. Moreover, night was falling.

I looked about me—not far away there was a great, broken god-road, leading north. The towers were high enough, but not so high, and while many of the dead-houses were wrecked, there were some that stood. I went toward this god-road, keeping to the heights of the ruins, while the dog followed. When I had reached the god-road, I saw that there were others behind him. If I had slept later, they would have come upon me asleep and torn out my throat. As it was, they were sure enough of me; they did not hurry. When I went into the dead-house, they kept watch at the entrance—doubtless they thought they would have a fine hunt. But a dog cannot open a door and I knew, from the books, that the gods did not like to live on the ground but on high.

I had just found a door I could open when the dogs decided to rush. Ha! They were surprised when I shut the door in their faces—It was a good door, of strong metal. I could hear their foolish baying beyond it but I did not stop to answer them. I was in darkness—I found stairs and climbed. There were many stairs, turning around till my head was dizzy. At the top was another door—I found the knob and opened it. I was in a long small chamber—on one side of it was a bronze door that could not be opened, for it had no handle. Perhaps there was a magic word to open it but I did not have the word. I turned to the door in the opposite side of the wall. The lock of it was broken and I opened it and went in.

Within, there was a place of great riches. The god who lived there must have been a powerful god. The first room was a small ante-room—I waited there for some time, telling the spirits of the place that I came in peace and not as a robber. When it seemed to me that they had had time to hear me, I went on. Ah, what riches! Few, even, of the windows had been broken—it was all as it had been. The great windows that looked over the city had not been broken at all though they were dusty and streaked with many years. There were coverings on the floors, the colors not greatly faded, and the chairs were soft and deep. There were pictures upon the walls, very strange, very wonderful—I remember one of a bunch of flowers in a jar—if you came close to it, you could see nothing but bits of color, but if you stood away from it, the flowers might have been picked yesterday. It made my heart feel strange to look at this picture—and to look at the figure of a bird, in some hard clay, on a table and see it so like our birds. Everywhere there were books and writings, many in tongues that I could not read. The god who lived there must have been a wise god and full of knowledge. I felt I had right there, as I sought knowledge also.

Nevertheless, it was strange. There was a washing-place but no water—perhaps the gods washed in air. There was a cooking place but no wood, and though there was a machine to cook food, there was no place to put fire in it. Nor were there candles or lamps—there were things that looked like lamps but they had neither oil nor wick. All these things were magic, but I touched them and lived—the magic had gone out of them. Let me tell one thing to show. In the washing-place, a thing said "Hot" but it was not hot to the touch—another thing said "Cold" but it was not cold. This must have been a strong magic but the magic was gone. I do not understand—they had ways—I wish that I knew.

It was close and dry and dusty in their house of the gods. I have said the magic was gone but that is not true—it had gone from the magic things but it had not gone from the place. I felt the spirits about me, weighing upon me. Nor had I ever slept in a Dead Place before—and yet, tonight, I must sleep there. When I thought of it, my tongue felt dry in my throat, in spite of my wish for knowledge. Almost I would have gone down again and faced the dogs, but I did not.

I had not gone through all the rooms when the darkness fell. When it fell, I went back to the big room looking over the city and made fire. There was a place to make fire and a box with wood in it, though I do not think they cooked there. I wrapped myself in a floor-covering and slept in front of the fire—I was very tired.

Now I tell what is very strong magic. I woke in the midst of the night. When I woke, the fire had gone out and I was cold. It seemed to me that all around me there were whisperings and voices. I closed my eyes to shut them out. Some will say that I slept again, but I do not think that I slept. I could feel the spirits drawing my spirit out of my body as a fish is drawn on a line.

Why should I lie about it? I am a priest and the son of a priest. If there are spirits, as they say, in the small Dead Places near us, what spirits must there not be in that great Place of the Gods? And would not they wish to speak? After such long years? I know that I felt myself drawn as a fish is drawn on a line. I had stepped out of my body—I could see my body asleep in front of the cold fire, but it was not I. I was drawn to look out upon the city of the gods.

It should have been dark, for it was night, but it was not dark. Everywhere there were lights—lines of light—circles and blurs of light—ten thousand torches would not have been the same. The sky itself was alight—you could barely see the stars for the glow in the sky. I thought to myself, "This is strong magic," and trembled. There was a roaring in my ears like the rushing of rivers. Then my eyes grew used to the light and my ears to the sound. I knew that I was seeing the city as it had been when the gods were alive.

That was a sight indeed—yes, that was a sight: I could not have seen it in the body—my body would have died. Everywhere went the gods, on foot and in chariots—there were gods beyond number and counting and their chariots blocked the streets. They had turned night to day for their pleasure—they did not sleep with the sun. The noise of their coming and going was the noise of many waters. It was magic what they could do—it was magic what they did.

I looked out of another window—the great vines of their bridge were mended and the god-roads went east and west. Restless, restless, were the gods and always in motion! They burrowed tunnels under rivers—they flew in the air. With unbelievable tools they did giant works—no part of the earth was safe from them, for, if they wished for a thing, they summoned it from the other side of the world. And always, as they labored and rested, as they feasted and made love, there was a drum in their ears—the pulse of the giant city, beating and beating like a man's heart.

Were they happy? What is happiness to the gods? They were great, they were mighty, they were wonderful and terrible. As I looked upon them and their magic, I felt like a child—but a little more, it seemed to me, and they would pull down the moon from the sky. I saw them with wisdom beyond wisdom and knowledge beyond knowledge. And yet not all they did was well done—even I could see that—and yet their wisdom could not but grow until all was peace.

Then I saw their fate come upon them and that was terrible past speech. It came upon them as they walked the streets of their city. I have been in the fights with the Forest People—I have seen men die. But this was not like that. When gods war with gods, they use weapons we do not know. It was fire falling out of the sky and a mist that poisoned. It was the time of the Great Burning and the Destruction. They ran about like ants in the streets of their city—poor gods, poor gods! Then the towers began to fall. A few escaped—yes, a few. The legends tell it. But, even after the city had become a Dead Place, for many years the poison was still in the ground. I saw it happen, I saw

the last of them die. It was darkness over the broken city and
I wept.

All this, I saw. I saw it as I have told it, though not in the
body. When I woke in the morning, I was hungry, but I did
not think first of my hunger for my heart was perplexed and
confused. I knew the reason for the Dead Places but I did not
see why it had happened. It seemed to me it should not have
happened, with all the magic they had. I went through the
house looking for an answer. There was so much in the house
I could not understand—and yet I am a priest and the son of a
priest. It was like being on one side of the great river, at night,
with no light to show the way.

Then I saw the dead god. He was sitting in his chair, by
the window, in a room I had not entered before and, for the
first moment, I thought that he was alive. Then I saw the skin
on the back of his hand—it was like dry leather. The room was
shut, hot and dry—no doubt that had kept him as he was. At
first I was afraid to approach him—then the fear left me. He
was sitting looking out over the city—he was dressed in the
clothes of the gods. His age was neither young nor old—I could
not tell his age. But there was wisdom in his face and great
sadness. You could see that he would have not run away. He
had sat at his window, watching his city die—then he himself
had died. But it is better to lose one's life than one's spirit—
and you could see from the face that his spirit had not been
lost. I knew, that, if I touched him, he would fall into dust—
and yet, there was something unconquered in the face.

That is all of my story, for then I knew he was a man—I knew
then that they had been men, neither gods nor demons. It is a
great knowledge, hard to tell and believe. They were men—
they went a dark road, but they were men. I had no fear after
that—I had no fear going home, though twice I fought off the
dogs and once I was hunted for two days by the Forest People.
When I saw my father again, I prayed and was purified. He
touched my lips and my breast, he said, "You went away a boy.
You come back a man and a priest." I said, "Father, they were
men! I have been in the Place of the Gods and seen it! Now
slay me, if it is the law—but still I know they were men."

He looked at me out of both eyes. He said, "The law is not

always the same shape—you have done what you have done. I could not have done it in my time, but you come after me. Tell!"

I told and he listened. After that, I wished to tell all the people but he showed me otherwise. He said, "Truth is a hard deer to hunt. If you eat too much truth at once, you may die of the truth. It was not idly that our fathers forbade the Dead Places." He was right—it is better the truth should come little by little. I have learned that, being a priest. Perhaps, in the old days, they ate knowledge too fast.

Nevertheless, we make a beginning. It is not for the metal alone we go to the Dead Places now—there are the books and the writings. They are hard to learn. And the magic tools are broken—but we can look at them and wonder. At least, we make a beginning. And, when I am chief priest we shall go beyond the great river. We shall go to the Place of the Gods— the place newyork—not one man but a company. We shall look for the images of the gods and find the god Ashing and the others—the gods Lincoln and Biltmore and Moses. But they were men who built the city, not gods or demons. They were men. I remember the dead man's face. They were men who were here before us. We must build again.

Experiment

(1) Show how the symbolism of "Babylon" in the *Apocalypse* is sufficiently universal to apply by analogy to any great city.

(2) Show how Benét gives his story immediacy and "contact."

(3) Explain the kind of language Benét uses to express the reactions of a simpler people to a complex civilization.

(4) Illustrate Benét's descriptive skill in suggesting the magnitude of destruction that took place in Babylon.

(5) Illustrate Benét's skill in making the familiar knowledge that we have about New York City seem strange.

(6) The sacred song sung by the hero is cast in the manner of early heroic and religious poetry. What does it lend to the atmosphere of the story?

(7) Indicate the overtones of social criticism in the story.

(8) This story was written quite a few years before the evolution of atomic energy. Show how the symbolism of the story is sufficiently general to cover any type of technological destruction.

(9) Show how the story gains in strength and beauty, and avoids morbidity, by emphasizing the heroism of the dead gods—"But it is better to lose one's life than one's spirit—and you could see from the face that his spirit has not been lost."

"Cosmopolis" is a free-verse poem with a marked overtone of social theme. It is an exercise in elaboration written by a young college student after a reading of the "Fall of Babylon" in the *Apocalypse* and of "By the Waters of Babylon" by Stephen Vincent Benét. Would you say that this young writer has created his own sense of form and that his work has many mature qualities?

PETER GLICKERT
Cosmopolis

It was still far away.
In the ionosphere.

In the summit of the steel mountain a man paced.
"This is mine," he said.
And looking out on the grandeur below his window, he said,
"And all this, too. All of it is mine, to do what I like with.
From out of the rubble I dragged myself,
And all I have I owe to myself and none other.
I am the first to see the sun rise; the last to see it set.
I glory in what most deserves glory:
Myself."
Thus spoke the Giant.

A clarion rang, and a man hobbled in to meet the Giant,
"I am looking for a just man," the man said.
"A just man is just a man," said the Giant,
"You will not find him here."
It is easy for those at the bottom to talk of justice and the equal-
    ity of all men, for they but say it so that all may be like to
    them: stupid and powerless.
But this I say to you:
"Justice is a fallacy because I am not as the rest of men; I am
    better for I am keener and smarter than any man or beast
    in the universe. Just look at me. Isn't my position in the
    world a fitting proof of my innate superiority?"
"But are you more than just a creature of God as we all are?"
    said the man.
"God?"
The Giant's roar shook the steel mountain, and the earth around
    it.
It echoed many times thru the canyons of the city.
"There is no God. I am but a creature of chance.
And besides, my dealing in the stock market, in the banks of the
    world, and in every single major trading and gambling
    place on this globe prove beyond the shadow of a doubt
    that I am
The master of chance itself.
And the way I think must be correct;
Look who I am!"

The old man spoke again:
"I come from the people of a far-off land.
In these days the sun is hidden from them,
For they can find no market for the wares they make.
And the harder they work,
The more will be their sorrow in the future.
It is you who have erected the walls that bind us to our sorrow."
"And what is that to me?" asked the Giant.

It is nearer now.
In the upper stratosphere.

A woman sat admiring her own image.
"I am truly beautiful," she said.
"How many forms are prostrate at my feet?
There is no one in the universe who will not fall down in admiration of my beauty."

A herald called, and a man hobbled in to meet the Beauty.
"I am looking for a just woman," he said.
"I am not just a woman," said the Beauty.
"How dare you come to me as you would to anyone else.
None of my husbands every approached me as you do."
"But is your body not made of the same elements and organs as the rest of mankind?"
"I really have not given the matter much thought," replied the Beauty.

Then the old man said:
"I come from distant land.
In these days my people are shades of shades.
A thousand shadows haunt our souls,
And our future is a puff of smoke
To be blown, directed, and shaped by unseen winds.
Your nation helps to blow those winds,
And there is no law to guide it.
No real law."
"I really have not given the matter much thought," said the Beauty.

It was in the lower stratosphere.
Nearing the atmosphere.

A man was in a metal box
Rising and descending.
"I am a success," he said.
"I need only do the lightest of toils
And may shirk when no one sees me.
My hours are short
My comforts are many
I am well-paid for whatever efforts I make.

The fruits of a fertile land are mine
And I have every right to them."

A torch flared and a man hobbled in to meet the Success.
"I am looking for a just man," he said.
"I am a just man," said the Success.
"I am good and kind to all who deserve it."
"Ah, then,
It is you I have been seeking all this time."

The old man spoke in this way:
"I come from a far-off land
Where men and women sweat to scrape
A barren land
And receive nothing for their labors.
It is up to you,
The just,
To open up your lands and hearts to them."
The Success replied:
"I am just
But I am not a fool.
What God has given *me*, I need not share with anyone."
The old man turned and left.

It was poised over the city now.

The old man walked on.
Past the steel mountains and the wooden hills.
He left the City of the World,
Muttering as he went:
"I saw God's hand poised,
Ready to strike down this City.
And I said,
'Oh, Lord,
I will find ten men
In this City
Who are just.
And then will Your rage be abated.' "
But I have not found them.

Indeed, I have not found one
Who loves You
And who loves his fellow man even half as much as he loves
     himself.
Whose heart burns with sorrow
At his brother's plight.
Whose hands
Are ready to toil for love.

"And so
It is done."
He paused to watch
The guided missile.
Guided
By whom?
It came as silent as the snow,
As death is wont to come.
"My City," the man said,
"My beloved City."

He turned away
In sadness,
Never to look back.

Nearer it came.
Suddenly it grew.
A moon.
A sun.
A greater sun than man has ever seen.
A burning, blistering
Sun.
A death, a judgment, a heaven, a hell.
Quicker than lightning
Quicker than light.
And silent.

Experiment

(1) Explain why the lack of identification caused by the use of "it" adds suspense to this piece of writing. Give examples from other pieces you have met in literature.

(2) Analyze the symbolism in this piece of writing from the viewpoint of its intelligibility.

(3) Analyze the effectiveness of the social criticism in the writing.

(4) This piece was written in class after a reading of "The Fall of Babylon." Locate the explicit suggestions in the writing that were taken from the original model.

(5) What other Biblical theme is used for suggestions besides "The Fall of Babylon"?

(6) To what extent would you say that this writing is poetry? To what extent would you say that is is creative prose?

(7) What use of *motif* is made here?

(8) What use of *generic description* is made here?

(9) Trace the patterns repeated in the last two selections and the authors' indebtedness to their prototype (or first example).

ELABORATING LEADS

As soon as you have acquired a little practice in the uses of connotation and *motif,* irony, humor, and the short story without plot, you will find it profitable and very interesting to undertake an experiment in elaboration. In such experiments you must not feel afraid of appearing foolish in the final result. After a few initial efforts, you will develop a greater sense of certainty and an instinct for the right form and for the limitations within which you should work. You may be asked to develop a given statement or quotation. You may develop this straightforwardly, humorously, or satirically, in any form or pattern that appeals to you. Naturally, you must not expect that all your results will be of equal value. Some may turn out to be very successful, while others prove abortive.

Common material for exercises in elaboration are:

(1) Commonplace expressions such as "Good-by, darling," "I'm looking forward to seeing you," "Case dismissed," "Where's the fire, Mac?" "He's a grand guy but—" "A very co-operative employee."

(2) Street cries like "Whaddya read?" "Keep moving."

(3) Newspaper captions; imaginatively stimulating but incomplete items; quotations from poems and ballads.

Ballads are particularly productive, because the connecting links in the story material have been lost and only the climactic high points remain. In the ballad of "Sir Patrick Spens" we are told with what suddenness Sir Patrick Spens was ordered out to sea by the King who "sits in Dunfermline toune Drinking the blude-red wine." In mid-winter, during a deadly storm, in spite of warning omens, Sir Patrick sets forth. Accompanying him is a crowd of Scots nobles who were right loath to wet their "cork-heeled shoes," the latter a symbol of their exalted station in life:

> Bot lang owre a' the play wer playd,
> Thair hats they swam aboone.
> *(But long before the action was over,*
> *Their hats swam above them.)*

We are told that "O long, long may the ladies stand, with their gold combs in their hair, waiting for their own dear Lords for they'll see them no more."

> Haf owre, haf owre to Aberdour,
> It's fiftie fadom deip,
> And thair lies guid Sir Patrick Spens
> With the Scots lords at his feit.

Students, in handling this theme, were fascinated by various possibilities in it. One aspect of the story suggests an anti-aristocratic bias on the part of the storyteller. He does not seem to deplore the drowning of the Scots lords very much. Any story lead here?

One student wrote an account in the first person of what she imagined the reactions of one of the ladies would be on hearing of this catastrophe. Another student wrote of the motivations and machinations of the blood-red-wine-drinking king, of his sinister objectives in sending the ship out. Nearly all the old ballads offer possibilities of this kind in the way of story elaboration.

A favorite with classes is the macabre "The Twa Corbies." In this ballad two crows are discussing the problem of where they will dine. One of them knows that a newly-slain knight lies dead behind an old church wall. Nobody, he says, knows that he lies there "but his hawk, his hound, and lady fair."

> His hound is to the hunting gane,
> His hawk to fetch the wild-fowl hame,
> His lady's ta'en another mate,
> So we may mak' our dinner sweet.

One crow gently suggests that he'll pluck out his bonny blue eyes and, with a lock of his golden hair, they will thatch their nest. Nobody knows where the knight is gone, though many moan for him.

> O'er his white banes, when they are bare
> The wind sall blaw for evermair.

The possibilities here for some kind of mystery story are numerous. Why is the death of the knight so secretive? Why has the lady taken another mate before the body of her late husband is quite cold? One student, impressed by the ghoulish aspects of the narrative, attempted with considerable success a modernized version in which a sailor meets two peroxide corbies at a bar; he injected ghoulish overtones into their most commonplace remarks.

Sometimes, just one line of an old ballad creates rich overtones which can be explored in fiction. Such is the odd line uttered by Edgar in Shakespeare's *King Lear,* "Childe Rolande to the dark tower came," which Robert Browning expanded into a poem of the same title. It is curious to note how Browning was fascinated by the mental associations suggested by "the dark tower." This was merely a suggestion from a stray line from a ballad that has been lost. The words survived in literature only as uttered by Edgar, disguised as an insane beggar in the heath scene in *King Lear.* For Browning the line served as a basis of a subtle and macabre allegory, in which symbols are used to represent psychological and moral values.

A knight is presented at the opening of the poem, seeking directions to the dark tower from a cripple who "waylays with his lies." The cripple writes the poet's epitaph:

> For pastime in the dusty thoroughfare,
> If at his counsel I should turn aside
> Into that ominous tract which, all agree,
> Hides the Dark Tower.

A lengthy allegorical description of the ominous tract follows. The dry blades pricked the mud "which underneath looked kneaded up with blood." He sees a river and

> Low scrubby alders kneeled down over it;
> Drenched willows flung them headlong in a fit
> Of mute despair, a suicidal throng.

The tower itself seems to concentrate the miasmic evil of this tortured country:

> What in the midst lay but the Tower itself?
> The round squat turret, blind as the fool's heart,
> Built of brown stone, without a counterpart
> In the whole world. The tempest's mocking elf

Points to the shipman thus the unseen shelf
He strikes on, only when the timbers start.

In a final vision the storyteller learns that the "lost adventurers, my peers are lost, lost." The elaboration closes with a final repetition of Shakespeare's ambiguous line now interpreted in terms of dark courage.

In a sheet of flame
I saw them and I knew them all. And yet
Dauntless the slug-horn to my lips I set
And blew. *"Childe Roland to the Dark Tower came."*

Modern newspaper reports provide almost equally rich suggestions. In the following experiment you will have a fairly extensive selection—some of which will undoubtedly appeal to you.

A particularly fine story was written one day in class from an Associated Press report of a ship that was discovered floating off Ocracocke, North Carolina. When the Coast Guard cutter arrived on the scene, those who boarded the ship found only a black cat. There was no sign of a crew anywhere, and the ship appeared to be in good condition. Here is mystery and suspense, although it requires courage on the part of the beginning writer to plunge into so dark and devious a possibility. Keep your eyes open for such suggestions in the newspapers, in lines of verse, and in familiar expressions uttered with unfamiliar overtones.

Experiment

(1) Find an incident suggested by newspaper clipping, ballad, or quotation, and attempt to elaborate it to create both suspense and irony. Leave the motivation of the act uncertain. Write as if the surface explanation seemed to be the correct one. But at the end of the story make the suggestion that the very reverse may be the true explanation. This in itself will constitute a climax.

(2) Attempt an ironic theme in which you open the situation with words spoken by one character *(motif)* and conclude with a repetition of the same words in a different symbolic light.

(3) Open a piece of writing with an analysis of a decisive choice to be made. Indicate psychologically why a character chooses a particular course. Show that the results of this decision are drastic and far from what the character anticipated. If you wish, this result may be viewed retrospectively from the point of view of accomplished fact or history: *e.g.,* Blücher's decision to take the sunken road in the Battle of Waterloo; the decision of a subordinate commander at Bastogne in the "Battle of the Bulge" in World War II.

(4) Present a character's last words. These words should imply an attitude of mind and decision which, without the character's foreknowledge, ironically contribute to his demise.

(5) Locate in G. K. Chesterton's *Tremendous Trifles* the following quotation:

It was simply a quiet conversation which I had with another man. But that quiet conversation was by far the most terrible thing that ever happened to me in my life.

From your knowledge of Chesterton's *Autobiography,* attempt to throw light on the background of this remark, which you should use as a psychological motif.

(6) Elaborate the following statement after you have gathered information about the life of St. Thomas More:

He told her, "Daughter Margaret, we two have talked of this thing more than twice or thrice, and I have told you that if it were possible for me to do the thing that might content the King's Grace, and God not offended, no man had taken this oath more gladly than I would do."

(7) Write a "mood" piece suitable for a "ghost" or "mys-

tery" story as suggested by the following quotation from Tennyson:

A hand that can be clasped no more—
Behold me, for I cannot sleep.
And like a guilty thing I creep
At earliest morning to the door.

He is not here; but far away
The noise of life begins again,
And ghastly through the drizzling rain
On the bald street breaks the blank day.

(8) Make an exposition of an adventure story from the following two suggestions.

Ill met by moonlight (Shakespeare).

Watch for me by moonlight,
I'll come to thee by moonlight, though Hell
should bar the way (Alfred Noyes).

(9) The following elaboration of the line, *Childe Roland to the Dark Tower came,* entitled "Tiger Lilies," was written by Padraic Colum.[12]

Childe Roland to the Dark Tower came,
And saw beside the grated vaults
The Tiger Lilies
On long, much-leaved and weedy stalks,
And wondered then what crookback knaves
Had these, their favors, on their graves,
What mocking jades!
He saw them in a gleam that edged
Down from the grinning waterspout,
And knew their gage:
Perverters of the lily's name,
With curled lips and tongues stuck out,
The sooty spotted flowers of flame!

[12] *Atlantic Monthly,* May, 1948, reprinted by permission of the author.

Compare this piece with Robert Browning's elaboration of the same cryptic line. Write an elaboration of your own.

(10) The following are excerpts from newspapers that possess possibilities for elaboration and story treatment. Locate similar material for yourself. An interesting exercise consists in locating the material, then building the elaboration. In submitting material, attach the newspaper excerpt to your title page. The material you select should possess "suggestiveness" rather than complete treatment in itself. It is your objective to supply the treatment.

(a) *Elaborate:*

Detroit, Oct. 23, 1949 (AP)—Robin the Robot, a hunk of mechanical man valued at $100,000 by his owner, made his debut yesterday. He is slightly over five feet tall, weighs 95 pounds and has 833 wires and 53 switches in him.

Patrick S. Rizzo, his inventor, a tool and die worker in a Detroit auto factory, said Robin is the first robot constructed to walk without wires or cables trailing.

The new robot operates on electric current by remote control and Mr. Rizzo can make him walk or dance. He makes the robot's mouth work, but Mr. Rizzo talks for him via a loudspeaker.

Mr. Rizzo said construction of the mechanical man took eight years, with the spare time of three years being used up in carving the head and seasoning the wood.

Suggested Treatment: This extract has possibilities for humorous and satiric treatment if you think that the processes of mechanizing humanity may go too far.

(b) *Elaborate:*

Paris, Jan. 30, 1949 (UP)—The great terror of New York, the "thing" New Yorkers never dare mention, is boredom, Jean Cocteau, French playwright, poet and motion picture director, said today.

"They drink to escape it, they go to the movies, to their psy-

chiatrist, they sit in front of television, there is no conversation,"
Mr. Cocteau said. He has just returned to France after twenty
days in New York.

"When you walk into a bar in New York," he said, "you see
a man sitting there eating a meal and looking at television at
the same time. The result is, he neither thinks nor eats. I have
a great fear eventually such a man will hire some one else to eat
his meal for him."

Suggested Treatment: Humor, the social theme. Thematic
contrast could be secured by a conversation between a character who believes as Cocteau does and a man who really
loves New York and television.

(c) *Elaborate:*

Springfield, Mo., Feb. 15, 1951 (UP)—The search for wealth is
under way again in the southwest Missouri Ozarks. This time the
prospectors are looking for uranium ore.

The mirage of old legends, including a story of a fabulous
"radium" mine, is attracting prospectors like a magnet to the
remote hills and valleys.

They're searching through the old caves and abandoned mine
shafts and taking examples of ore.

A magazine story published in 1912 came to light recently to
detail how three men in 1897 found a fantastic silver mine at
the end of a mountain canyon in Barry County.

As they left the cave, one of them wrote, one was stricken with
paralysis, one fainted, and the third temporarily lost his mind.
One of the men died later in a hospital at Carthage, his body re-
portedly covered with sores like burns.

But the cave, which came to be known in the area as the
"radium cave," later was blocked up in an ownership dispute and
was forgotten, except as a legend of the hills, until recently.

Suggested Treatment: Adventure story, story with plot.
Possible irony lies in the fact that what men formerly
shunned they will now quarrel over and compete to attain.

(d) *Elaborate:*

London, Feb. 21, 1950 (UP)—American Navy officers tried to solve the mystery of a yacht found abandoned and drifting in the Mediterranean 30 miles north of Tripoli, North Africa.

The ghost ship was sighted yesterday by the American destroyer Mackenzie, which identified the yacht in a message to London as the Imperia, owned by a Greek citizen living in Athens.

(Lloyd's Register of Shipping for 1948–9 lists an Imperia as an oil-burning, twin-screw vessel owned by the Egyptian government. Presumably the craft might have been purchased later by the Athens owner.)

The destroyer, noting the yacht was drifting in a glassy sea, investigated and found the crew was missing. Officers put a boarding party on the yacht and towed her to Tripoli.

A message said the Imperia was last reported to have left Tripoli on a 200-mile voyage to Malta, the British naval base in the Mediterranean north of Tripoli.

The mysterious fate of those aboard the Imperia recalled the case of the American brig Marie Celeste, which was found abandoned in the Atlantic Ocean 300 miles west of Gibraltar with all sails set in 1872.

The fate of the captain and crew aboard the Marie Celeste never was learned. The Marie Celeste sailed from New York harbor Nov. 7, 1872, with a cargo of alcohol for Genoa, Italy. She was found abandoned five weeks later.

Naval officers in London said they were at a loss to explain the case of the Imperia. They said there had been no heavy storms in the Mediterranean recently which could have washed the crew overboard.

Suggested Treatment: This is obviously material for a mystery story—a story with plot.

(e) *Elaborate:*

Green Bay, Wis., Oct. 23, 1949 (UP)—Mike Kornish's 30-year dream of being with his wife was ended today.

Five years after Mr. Kornish came from Yugoslavia in 1913, his wife followed him. But her ship was quarantined, and she was forced to return.

When Mr. Kornish learned this week that she had started the voyage again, he bought a house for the reunion.

Officials wondered how they would tell Mrs. Kornish that Mike was found dead in the basement of the home yesterday after apparently falling down a flight of stairs.

Suggested Treatment: This is a story situation demanding warm emotional treatment, ending in pathos.

(f) *Elaborate:*

Boston, Nov. 11, 1939 (AP)—Robert Frost, who was allergic to colleges in his youth, is back at one of his part-time alma maters as a lecturer—all keyed up about helping to make colleges become "factories for turning out human self-starters." He has started at Harvard the closest to a formal class he has had in twelve years of lecturing.

At 64, white-haired and rugged, Mr. Frost has not thrown in the sponge on his ideas that education should be a take-it-or-leave-it business instead of a day-after-day quizzing of boys with questions to which he already knew the answers.

His belief is in an "education by presence"—the stimulation of students to enterprise by the mere presence in their midst of men who have done things and have wide intellectual horizons.

He will give marks, of a sort, but they will be secondary. Mr. Frost will do most of the talking, but if mere talking will not stir up some enterprise among his hearers, he will "just keep silent —or even lie down on the desk until it is realized that what I want is self-starters, not followers of a set routine."

Suggested Treatment: An amusing satire could be written on this level, particularly from the point of view of a writer acquainted with educational jargon.

THE INTERVIEW

Two processes for conducting and writing a successful interview must be considered here: (1) obtaining the actual interview; (2) the presentation of the interview in a finished literary form.

Some confusion about the conduct of an interview arises from too journalistic a concept of "news." An interview is not a simple matter of giving information; it is also a matter of revealing human personality, so that character interpretation and psychological insight are as important in an interviewer as a "nose for news." We are unfortunately inclined to imagine that the value of the interview largely depends on the dramatic flavor and social importance of the interviewee.

Actually, for the purposes of writing an interesting interview, you do not need to go beyond the field of your own immediate experience. Here, as in the short story without plot, the problem again is to create intensity and to develop human interest. It is not a matter of capturing the unusual, the remote, or the sensational. The quality of the interview depends not so much on the glamor and importance of the person interviewed as upon the insight of the interviewer and the particular *questions* or *leads* he has created for his readers.

The lead or question of your interview should be presented in broad human terms: the struggle for existence, economic or political; the search for happiness; the influence of emotions such as love; the education of children; the meaning of the life of the interviewee in regard to the problems of interest to readers of the finished piece (kind of work done, difficulties encountered, recreational facilities, amount of money earned, personal satisfaction, social prestige). Sometimes it is possible for you to relate the material of the interview to some major social or political problem. This procedure is in itself an excellent lead. Examples of such problems are: labor-management relations; military service; scientific possibilities for social improvement; economic cycles of inflation and deflation.

In undertaking the interview, you should always keep in mind certain basic methods of procedure. It is helpful to

form the habit of noting such facts as these about the person
you are interviewing:

(1) The habitat of the subject—his place of work, his home,
his typical setting, recreational or social.

(2) The physical appearance of the subject—whether he is
thin or fat, tall or short; his complexion; his tone of voice;
the appearance of his eyes; the type of clothes he wears.

(3) His characteristic mannerisms or gestures, with their
corresponding general characteristics—nervousness, excitabil-
ity, reserve, or frankness. Obviously, if some one has been
kind enough to give an interview, only those mannerisms
should actually be presented in the written interview that
shed real light on the person's character and are based on
a fair, unbiased appraisal.

(4) An assessment should be made of the total meaning of
these observations from the point of view of the interviewer's
expectations. You want the interview to have the effect of
fluidity and of action, and the actual contrast often to be
found between what your subject is really like and what you
expected him to be like forms a natural and interesting part
of your story.

It is to be kept in mind that the surface marks of a person's appearance and behavior are not always an accurate
indication of what that person really is. Psychologists have
explained this lack of relationship between a person's ex-
terior and interior personality in terms of various defense
mechanisms, sublimations, and so on. But whatever psychological explanations may be given for these facts, artistically
they can be of great value. A gentle and mild-mannered
person may be cruel and ruthless in action; a bad-tempered
and aggressive individual may be kindly and sympathetic.
It is not merely the correlation between what the subject is
and what he appears to be that you must establish. Remember, contrast and opposition also constitute important material for the writer of interviews.

From practice and experience you will gain the power of
observation required in covering these topics. The more

quick and inclusive the approach to these situations, the better.

At first, you may have some difficulties in getting your subject to talk. You yourself may suffer from reserve or nervousness. The only way you can effectively overcome this situation is to concentrate on the matter in hand. The more relaxed you are in your own manner and the more perfected your ability to ask questions without being obvious or irritating, the more productive will be your results.

As distinct from writing an interview for news copy, where explicit answers may be expected from officials at a news conference, the more purely human-interest interviewer should avoid categorical approaches and the use of pencil and paper. Not many people will speak freely if they are conscious that their remarks are being taken down literally. It has been well said that "a notebook closes a man's mouth, while it opens his eyes." In the case of a news interview, an "official" interview, the situation is somewhat different. The interviewee may himself distinguish between what is "on" and "off" the record. He may also ask the right to see what you have written, your final product. Under such conditions, you have no choice but to write down direct quotations, and even to read them back to the interviewee, particularly if they are controversial. The important thing to keep in mind at all times is the general area of subject matter and the main points in that area which you wish to cover. If you are interviewing a man in relation to his particular work, you might have one underlying idea such as the social importance of his work, its physical hazards, its economic security, or its labor-management relationships. Only after the interview is over should you put down in note form the principal ideas and views exchanged, the manner of the subject's reaction to the questions, his background, appearance, and other details.

One point that cannot bear too much stress is the fact that what we call *natural* dialogue is essentially *artificial*. The naturalness, the realism of a well-written interview, is an aesthetic creation, not a scientific one. Actually, if a stenographic report were made of an interview, it would not sound like an interview at all. In this connection, the beginning writer is warned not to present the interview as if it were an excerpt from a cross-examination at a trial or legal proceedings. You do not falsify the validity of your interview by presenting the exchange of view with conscious artistry rather than with bald, scientific accuracy.

In writing the interview, remember that you are free to employ nearly all the various writing forms—description, narration, dialogue, thematic contrast, and so on. Naturally, therefore, your skill in interviewing will develop according to the competence you acquire in these separate techniques. In one sense, the interview belongs most closely to the narrative form. Two characters are always present in the finished work—the interviewer and the interviewee. Both will appear in the writing, though the emphasis, of course, should be placed upon the interviewee.

The main technical problem in writing the interview is the maintenance of the thread of continuity. This, in turn, depends upon the securing of a good lead when you start your interview.

Ultimately, the artistic value of the interview depends upon the human interest you inject into your writing. Does the subject come alive? Have you explained him in terms that will make his life interesting to your reader?

Experiment

Present to the instructor, class chairman, or discussion leader, the name of a person in your neighborhood, indicating sex, age, occupation. Give a tentative list of human interest questions on which you think this person may shed some light. After your plan has been approved, obtain the interview, write it according to the principles set forth here (500 words).

APPENDIX

METRICAL PATTERNS [1]

A. Pronunciation

Words in poetry are no different in sound from words in prose. They may be arranged differently to create more striking effects, but the poet has the same material to draw from as any writer has. Some persons read poetry as though it were written in a foreign language, stumble over accent, stop when there is no punctuation, intone in an odd fashion, and create a result which the poet never intended. The poet relies on the standard rules of grammar, the standard dictionary pronunciations. In reading poetry, then, words should be pronounced as usual, and pauses should be observed where punctuation indicates.

B. Meter

Poets arrange their words so that the accent will fall at regular intervals in each line. These accents are interrupted by unaccented syllables. The regular recurrence of accent in a poetic line is called meter. It is the equivalent of the basic beat in musical compositions. For example, in the prose line which follows, the accent (indicated by ´) is irregular:

I saw the steamer as it was chugging up the river.

A similar picture, arranged with attention to more orderly sound by Tennyson, is regular in its meter:

The market boat is on the stream.

C. Basic Patterns

There are four fundamental metrical patterns in English poetry:

[1] Reprinted, with permission, from *English in Review*, New York, The Declan X. McMullen Co., 1947.

333

(1) The *iambic,* which consists of two syllables, one unaccented followed by one accented ($\smile$ $'$);

(2) The *anapestic,* which consists of three syllables, two unaccented followed by one accented ($\smile$ $\smile$ $'$);

(3) The *trochaic,* which consists of two syllables, one accented followed by one unaccented ($'$ $\smile$);

(4) The *dactylic,* which consists of three syllables, one accented followed by two unaccented ($'$ $\smile$ $\smile$).

Three other metrical patterns, used less often, are:

(5) The *spondree,* which consists of two accented syllables ($'$ $'$);

(6) The *amphibrach,* which consists of three syllables, the accented occurring between the two unaccented ($\smile$ $'$ $\smile$);

(7) The *amphimacer,* which consists of three syllables, the unaccented occurring between the two accented ($'$ $\smile$ $'$).

Each of these individual groups is known as a foot. Lines of poetry are named from the predominant accent *and* the number of feet in a line.

EXAMPLES:

Ĭ spráng (*iambic monometer,* one foot, an iamb)

Yŏu háste | ăwáy (*iambic dimeter,* two feet, both iambs)

Ĭ ám out | ŏf húman | ĭty's reach (*anapestic trimeter,* three anapests)

Wáitĭng, | wátchĭng, | lóvĭng, | práyĭng (*trochaic tetrameter,* four trochees)

Cánnŏn tŏ | ríght ŏf thĕm (*dactylic dimeter,* two dactyls)

Hŏw swéet | thĕ moón | lĭght sleéps | ŭpón | thĭs bánk (*iambic pentameter,* five iambs)

Whĭch líke | ă woúnd | ĕd snáke | drags ĭts | slów léngth | ălóng (*iambic hexameter,* six iambs, also called an *Alexandrine*)

A line with seven feet is called *heptameter;* one with eight feet, *octameter.*

When lines are marked off into feet, by adding accent marks and separating each unit by a vertical line, the process is called *scansion*.

D. *Variations*

All lines of verse do not follow the basic pattern rigidly. Many variations are allowed, provided that there is reason for them. In the last example above, the first foot (*which like*) may be read as a trochee (or as a spondee); the fourth foot (*drags its*) must be read as a trochee; the fifth foot (*slow length*) is a spondee. Trochees often appear in iambic lines, dactyls in anapestic lines, and *vice versa*. This is called *inversion*.

EXAMPLE:

Down to | a sun | less sea.

Trochees may be used for dactyls, anapests for iambs, and *vice versa*. This is called *substitution*.

EXAMPLES:

My thoughts | still cling | to the mould | ering past.
Solemnly | answered the | sea, and | mingled its | roar with the | dirges.

In some lines a *pause* may take the place of an unaccented syllable.

EXAMPLE:

Break,   break,   break!

An unstressed syllable (or syllables) may be omitted *from the beginning* of an iambic or anapestic line, or *from the end* of a trochaic or dactylic line. This is known as *catalexis* and the line is called *catalectic*.

EXAMPLES:

Who | would be
A mer | man bold

Táke hĕr ŭp | téndĕrlў
Líft hĕr wĭth | cáre.

An unstressed syllable may be added to the beginning of trochaic lines, or to the end of iambic lines. This is known as *hypermeter* and the line is called *hypermetric*. An extra unaccented foot at the end of a line is also called a *feminine ending*.

EXAMPLES:

Whĕn thĕ hoúnds | ŏf Spríng | ăre ŏn
Wín | tĕr's trác | ĕs

E. Purposes of Meter

The different metrical patterns are chosen deliberately by the poet, to express the mood he wishes to establish. Again, they are comparable to music, which uses one measure for stateliness, another for gaiety, another to suggest reflection. Anapests and dactyls flow faster and express rapidity or softness or emotion set to lilting sound. The iambic and trochaic meters are more serious, more deliberate. Much English speech is iambic and this pattern is the most frequently used in English poetry.

F. The Caesura

An additional effect is achieved within a line of poetry by the pauses which occur naturally or which are indicated by the writer. There are ordinary pauses when punctuation indicates a slight pause; others come when the sense demands a temporary stop in the reading. The caesura may fall anywhere within the line, or at the end of a line. (Strictly, the caesura is a break caused when the end of a word falls within the foot itself.)

EXAMPLES (the caesura is indicated by ||):

They glide, || like phantoms, || into the wide hall; ||
Like phantoms || to the iron porch they glide, ||
Where lay the porter in uneasy sprawl, ||
With a huge empty flaggon by his side, ||

The wakeful bloodhound rose, || and shook his hide, ||
But his sagacious eye || an inmate owns.

—Keats

When lines end in punctuation, they are called *end-stopped;* when the sense continues into a second line, without such interruption, they are called *run-on.*

G. Rhyme

The underlying melody of music is also aided by several other devices, the most important of which are *rhyme, alliteration, assonance, onomatopoeia,* and figures of speech.

(1) *Perfect rhyme* is the agreement of two words which end with an accented syllable having the same vowel and consonant sounds, but preceded by a different consonant. Rhymes may be of one or more syllables.

EXAMPLES: *sky—die, city—pity, bell—well, hush—crush, banter— canter, charity—clarity, laconic—Ionic, hearkened—darkened, roses —encloses.*

(2) *Imperfect rhymes* violate these requirements.

EXAMPLES:

dolorous—sonorous (the accented syllable does not rhyme)
love—Jove (spelling is the same, but pronunciation differs)
charity—rarify (accent is on two different syllables; *y* has different sounds; *f* and *t* do not rhyme)
cherishes—perisheth (final sounds are not the same)
sea—see (sounds are identical, but so is preceding consonant)

(3) *Internal rhyme.* Rhyme usually occurs at the end of a line, but it may be found, in addition, within the line.

EXAMPLE:

"Each day, all *day,*" these poor folks *say,*
"In the same old *year*-long, *drear*-long *way,*
We *weave* in the mills and *heave* in the kilns."—Lanier

(4) *Masculine rhymes* are those in which the last syllable is accented (*did—bid, astound—rebound*); *feminine rhymes,* those in which more syllables than one are rhymed, but where the ac-

cent is not on the last syllable (*regretfully—forgetfully, leather—weather*).

H. Sound Devices

(1) *Assonance* is the repetition of the same vowel sounds in a line (or lines), without regard to surrounding consonants.

EXAMPLES:

"R*o*ll on, thou deep and dark blue *o*cean, r*o*ll!"—Byron
"The army of un*a*lterable l*a*w."—Meredith
" 'Mid hushed, c*oo*l-r*oo*ted flowers fragrant-eyed."—Keats
"At the s*ea*-down's edge betw*ee*n windward and l*ea*."—Swinburne

(2) *Alliteration* is the repetition of the same consonant sounds in one or more verses.

EXAMPLES:

"Roll on, thou *d*eep and *d*ark blue ocean, roll!"
"In *S*ummer *s*eason when *s*oft was the *s*un."—Langland
"*C*onvulse and *c*onsume us day by day."—Shelley
"Five *m*iles *m*eandering with a *m*azy *m*otion."—Coleridge

(3) *Onomatopoeia* is another device which appeals to the ear, by making words suggest the sound indicated in their meaning. Particularly effective are such words as: *bang, bubble, buzz, cackle, chatter, clang, clatter, clash, drone, drowsy, grate, gurgle, hiss, hoot, howl, jingle, murmur, plunge, roar, rumble, snarl, snort, splash, surge, tap, thud, whisper, whistle, whiz.*

EXAMPLES:

"The moan of doves in immemorial elms,
    And murmuring of innumerable bees."
                                        —Tennyson

"While I nodded, nearly napping, suddenly there came a tapping,
As of some one gently rapping, rapping at my chamber door."
                                        —Poe

"Loud sounds the axe, redoubling strokes on strokes;
    On all sides round the forest hurls her oaks
    Headlong. Deep-echoing groan the thickets brown;
    Then rustling, crackling, crashing, thunder down."
                                        —Pope

(4) *Repetition* is the use of the same word, for emphasis, in the one or more lines.

EXAMPLES:

"*Roll* on, thou deep and dark blue ocean, *roll!*"
"Tomorrow and tomorrow and tomorrow."
—Shakespeare
"To the throbbing of the bells,
Of the bells, bells, bells,
To the sobbing of the bells;
Keeping time, time, time."—Poe

I. The Stanza

Lines of poetry are gathered together into large patterns, known as *stanzas*. Each stanza usually develops a single thought; stanzas are, roughly, the equivalents of paragraphs in prose.

A frequent error is to call a stanza a verse; a verse is a single line. The most common stanza patterns in English poetry are the following:

(1) The *rhymed couplet* is composed of two lines which have identical rhymes.

EXAMPLE:

"Oft, on a plot of rising ground,
I hear the far-off curfew sound."—Milton

(2) The *heroic couplet* rhymes in the same way, but the lines must be iambic pentameters.

EXAMPLE:

"Be not the first by whom the new is tried,
Nor yet the last to lay the old aside."—Pope

(3) The *tercet* is a short stanza of three lines, with any rhyme scheme (sometimes identical; sometimes rhyming the first and third lines), and in any meter (generally iambic tetrameter).

EXAMPLE:

"I said, 'I toil beneath the curse,
But, knowing not the universe,
I fear to slide from bad to worse.' "—Tennyson

(4) The *quatrain* is a stanza of four lines, in which the rhyme scheme may be quite varied. In some quatrains the first and third lines rhyme, and the second and fourth; in others the first and fourth and the second and third; in still others the second and fourth rhyme and the others do not. Such patterns are usually indicated by letters; the first rhyme by *a;* the second by *b*

EXAMPLES:

"Full many a gem of purest ray serene (*a*)
    The dark unfathomed caves of ocean bear; (*b*)
Full many a flower is born to blush unseen, (*a*)
    And waste its sweetness on the desert air." (*b*)
                                    —Gray

"Ring out the grief that saps the mind, (*a*)
    For those that here we see no more; (*b*)
    Ring out the feud of rich and poor, (*b*)
    Ring in redress to all mankind." (*a*)
                                    —Tennyson

"There lived a wife at Usher's Well, (*a*)
    And a wealthy wife was she; (*b*)
    She had three stout and stalwart sons, (*c*)
    And sent them o'er the sea."(*b*)

The ballad stanza, the last illustrated, is also indicated as *abcb*.

The lines may be of any length, and many use any meter. The typical *ballad quatrain* is the last, with the first and third lines in iambic tetrameter and the second and fourth in iambic trimeter.

(5) The *quintet* is a five-lined stanza. It is not used very often by poets.

EXAMPLE:

"All the earth and air
    With thy voice is loud,
As, when night is bare,
    From one lonely cloud
The moon rains out her beams, and heaven is overflowed."
                                    —Shelley

(6) The *sestet* is a six-lined stanza, often composed of three sets of couplets. The second half of many sonnets employ the sestet form.

EXAMPLE:

> "She walks in beauty, like the night
> Of cloudless climes and starry skies;
> And all that's best of dark or bright
> Meet in her aspect and her eyes;
> Thus mellowed to that tender light
> Which heaven to gaudy day denies."
>
> —Byron

(7) The most popular seven-line stanza is the *rime royal*, used as early as Chaucer and as late as John Masefield. It consists of seven iambic pentameter lines, rhyming *ababbcc*.

(8) The *octave* is an eight-lined stanza, in which the rhyme scheme may be twice as varied as in the quatrain. Many of Burns's songs are written in octaves.

(9) The *ottava rima* is an eight-line stanza of iambic pentameter lines, rhyming *abababcc*. *Isabella* by Keats is in *ottava rima*.

(10) The *Spenserian stanza,* named after Edmund Spenser, who it in his *Faerie Queene,* is a stanza of eight verses of iambic pentameter, followed by a ninth line of iambic hexameter, rhyming *ababbcbcc*.

(11) The *sonnet* is a complete poem of fourteen lines of iambic pentameter. There are at least two forms. In one the poem consists of three quatrains, followed by a couplet. The rhyme scheme is often different from quatrain to quatrain, thus, *abab cdcd efef gg*. In another form the sonnet is composed of two parts, one of eight lines (an octave) and one of six (a sestet). The octet may rhyme *abbaabba;* the sestet may rhyme *cdecde* or may end in a couplet (*cdcdee*). Many variations are possible.

(12) *Blank verse* is iambic pentameter which does not employ rhyme. Shakespeare's plays, Milton's *Paradise Lost,* Arnold's *Sohrab and Rustum,* Wordsworth's *Tintern Abbey* and parts of Tennyson's *Idylls of the King* are written in blank verse.

(13) *Free verse,* as distinct from blank verse, avoids both a regular rhythmical pattern and the use of rhyme.

EXAMPLE:

"I, that was a child, my tongue's use sleeping,
Now I have heard you,
Now in a moment I know what I am for—I awake,
And already a thousand singers, a thousand songs, clearer,
    louder, and more sorrowful than yours,
A thousand warbling echoes have started to life within me,
Never to die."

—Whitman

INDEX

343